ROUTLEDGE LIBRARY EDITIONS: POLITICS OF THE MIDDLE EAST

Volume 9

CONTEMPORARY YEMEN

CONTEMPORARY YEMEN
Politics and Historical Background

Edited by
B.R. PRIDHAM

LONDON AND NEW YORK

First published in 1984 by Croom Helm Ltd

This edition first published in 2016
by Routledge
4 Park Square, Milton Park, Abingdon, Oxon OX14 4RN
605 Third Avenue, New York, NY 10017

Routledge is an imprint of the Taylor & Francis Group, an informa business

© 1984 B. R. Pridham

All rights reserved. No part of this book may be reprinted or reproduced or utilised in any form or by any electronic, mechanical, or other means, now known or hereafter invented, including photocopying and recording, or in any information storage or retrieval system, without permission in writing from the publishers.

Trademark notice: Product or corporate names may be trademarks or registered trademarks, and are used only for identification and explanation without intent to infringe.

British Library Cataloguing in Publication Data
A catalogue record for this book is available from the British Library

ISBN: 978-1-138-83939-7 (Set)
ISBN: 978-1-315-68049-1 (Set) (ebk)
ISBN: 978-1-138-92232-7 (Volume 9) (hbk)
ISBN: 978-1-138-92234-1 (Volume 9) (pbk)

Publisher's Note
The publisher has gone to great lengths to ensure the quality of this reprint but points out that some imperfections in the original copies may be apparent.

Disclaimer
The publisher has made every effort to trace copyright holders and would welcome correspondence from those they have been unable to trace.

CONTEMPORARY YEMEN:
POLITICS AND HISTORICAL BACKGROUND

EDITED BY B.R. PRIDHAM

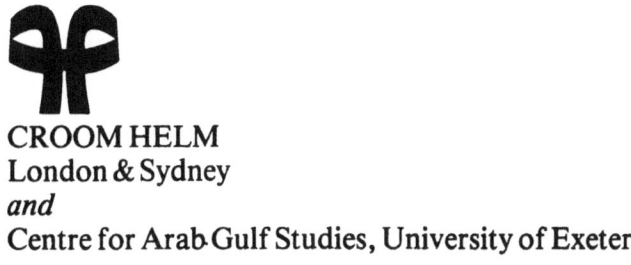

CROOM HELM
London & Sydney
and
Centre for Arab-Gulf Studies, University of Exeter

© 1984 B. R. Pridham
Croom Helm Ltd, Provident House, Burrell Row,
Beckenham, Kent BR3 1AT

Croom Helm Australia Pty Ltd, First Floor, 139 King Street,
Sydney, NSW 2001, Australia

British Library Cataloguing in Publication Data

Contemporary Yemen.
   1. Yemen — Politics and government
   2. Yemen (People's Democratic Republic) — Politics and government
   I. Pridham, B. R.
   320.953'3   JQ1825.Y4A4

ISBN 0-7099-2084-9

Printed and bound in Great Britain
by Billing & Sons Limited, Worcester.

CONTENTS

List of Tables and Figures		vii
Preface		ix
Note on Transliteration		xi
1.	Towards a Sociology of the Islamisation of Yemen *D. Thomas Gochenour*	1
2.	Memduh Pasha and Aziz Bey: Ottoman Experience in Yemen *Jon Mandaville*	20
3.	The Free Yemeni Movement: 1935–62 *Leigh Douglas*	34
4.	The Rise of the National Liberation Front as a Political Organisation *Helen Lackner*	46
5.	The PDRY: Three Designs for Independence *Salem Omar Bukair*	63
6.	The Yemeni Revolution of 1962 Seen as a Social Revolution *Mohammed A. Zabarah*	76
7.	Nation-building and Political Development in the Two Yemens *John Peterson*	85
8.	Education for Nation-building — the Experience of the People's Democratic Republic of Yemen *Saeed Abdul Khair Al-Noban*	102
9.	South Yemen since Independence: an Arab Political Maverick *Manfred Wenner*	125
10.	Modernisation of Government Institutions 1962–9 *Ahmed Al-Abiadh*	147
11.	Tribal Relations and Political History in Upper Yemen *Paul Dresch*	154

12. The Judicial System in Democratic Yemen 175
    Naguib A. R. Shamiry
13. Aspects of North Yemen's Relations with Saudi Arabia 195
    M. S. El Azhary
14. Soviet Relations with South Yemen 208
    Fred Halliday
15. The Communist Party of the People's Democratic Republic of Yemen: an Analysis of its Strengths and Weaknesses 232
    John Duke Anthony
16. The Genesis of the Call for Yemeni Unity 240
    Sultan Nagi
17. Prospects for Yemeni Unity 261
    Ursula Braun

Glossary of Arabic and Turkish Words Not Explained on First Appearance 270

Index 274

TABLES AND FIGURES

Tables

8.1	PDRY: Comparison of Education Expenditure in 1972 and 1980	113
8.2	PDRY: Comparison of Enrolment in Education in 1972 and 1980	114
8.3	PDRY: Percentage of Participation in Education by Governorate, Sex and Age Group	121

Figures

Frontispiece: Map of Contemporary Yemen		xii
1.1	Yemen's Ecological Zones	3
1.2	Medieval Yemen	4
1.3	Central Highlands Plains: a Detail	13
8.1	PDRY: New Education Structure, 1980	118
8.2	PDRY: Education Pyramid, 1979/80	124
11.1	Tribes of Upper Yemen	155

PREFACE

The chapters in this book are a selection of the papers presented to a symposium on contemporary Yemen held in July 1983 by Exeter University's Centre for Arab Gulf Studies, in collaboration with the Universities of Aden and San'a'. A second volume containing a further selection, *Economy, Society and Culture in Contemporary Yemen*, is planned to follow.

Yemen, for the purposes of the symposium, was held to be what some contributors to this book describe as 'Greater' or 'natural' Yemen, that is the area now constituting the states of the Yemen Arab Republic (YAR) and the People's Democratic Republic of Yemen (PDRY).

The specific question of Yemeni unity is examined in two chapters, but this whole book rests on the belief that the two states can usefully be studied together on two grounds. Not only do the people inhabiting them explicitly share a sense of common identity as Yemenis, but each of the two states achieved its present conformation during the crucial period of the 1960s, exerting in the process an intimate influence on each other. The 1962 revolution which set up the YAR and the withdrawal in 1967 of the British colonial authorities from what became the PDRY are rightly treated throughout this book as having an importance beyond mere national boundaries. We are reminded more than once that the build-up of nationalism in the colonial South was contemporary with the search for a national republican system in the North.

It was in the consideration of shared Yemeni experience that the participation of the two Yemeni universities and of other Yemeni scholars and administrators was particularly valuable. Until very recent years publications outside the Middle East on the Yemen have been scarce, and for helping to fill that gap credit was already due to some of the distinguished participants in the symposium. But the Yemeni point of view has been even less heard in the English-speaking world, and the symposium was the first of its kind in having official participation from North and South. The opportunity was not lost; there are in this book accounts and analyses of events which are radically different from the customary treatment in Western (especially British) publications and they illustrate the great value of first-hand experience and involvement. At its international symposia, of which this was the sixth, the Centre for Arab Gulf Studies welcomes differing and indeed controversial interpretations of the themes under discussion. Neither the editor nor of course the Centre itself is in any way responsible for the opinions expressed.

The chapters in this volume deal with history, internal and international politics, and administrative subjects. The second volume to follow will comprise contributions on social, economic and cultural aspects. In the nature of things the two volumes cannot claim to provide a systematic coverage of all aspects of contemporary Yemen. Each chapter, however, represents an expert's insight into his particular field, and no field of importance is overlooked. The editor's role has therefore been minimal; the contributions are basically in the form in which they were presented and no attempt has been made to modify one in the light of another.

For successfully gathering together from many countries so much expertise on the Yemen and harnessing it to a well-conceived spread of subjects my thanks go to Professor M. A. Shaban, the Director of the Centre for Arab Gulf Studies, who chaired the symposium, and to Mr H. G. Balfour-Paul, who organised it from first to last.

NOTE ON TRANSLITERATION

A simplified and uniform system of Arabic transliteration has been used throughout this book. Diacritical marks are not used but, as is usual nowadays, the *hamza* is represented by ' and the *'ain* by '. Both are omitted from initial capital letters. The very few ambiguities which result from the simplification will present no problems to an Arabic speaker. Proper names which are familiar in the English-speaking world, e.g. Gamal Abdul Nasser, have been left in their familiar, not transliterated, forms.

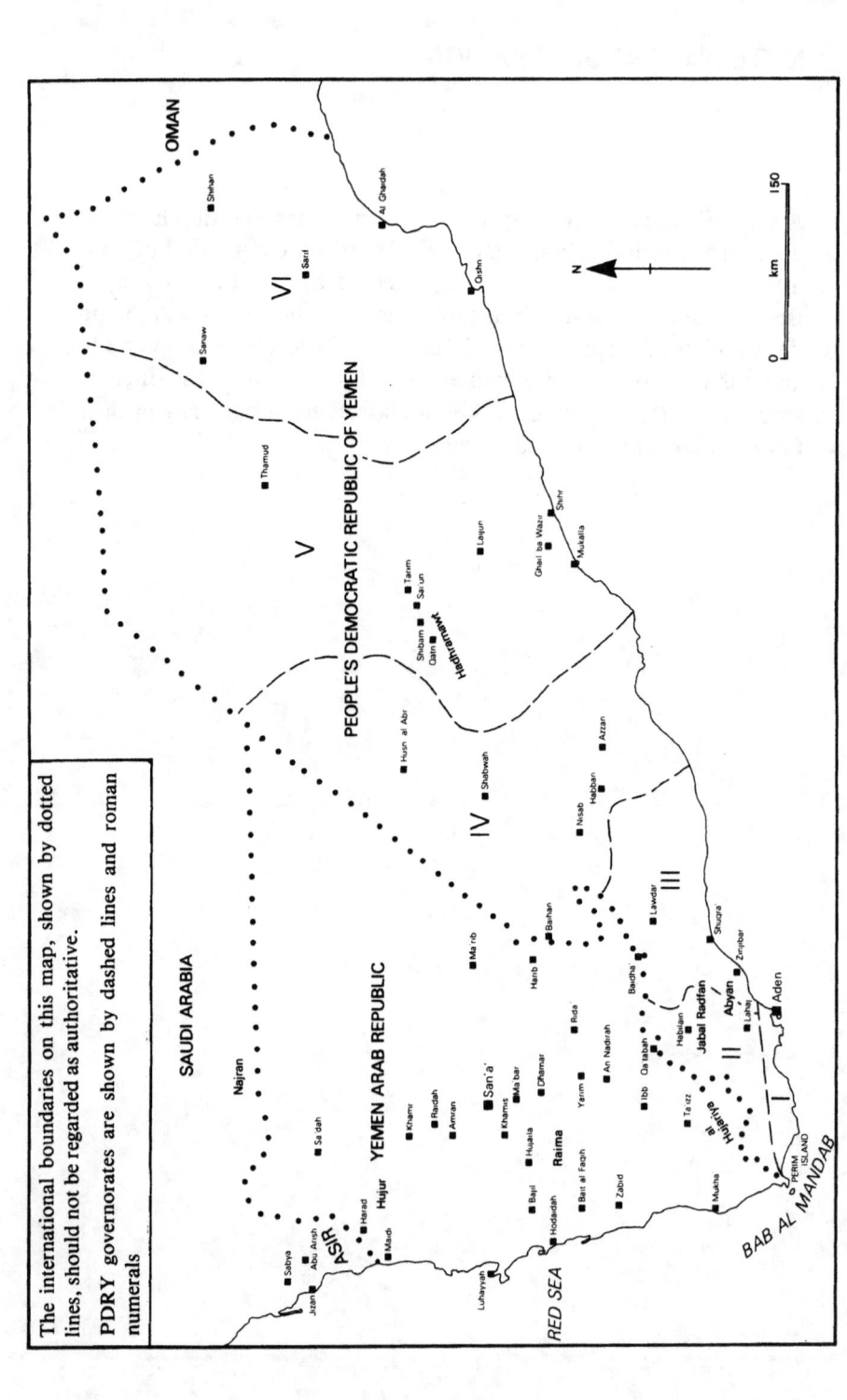

1 TOWARDS A SOCIOLOGY OF THE ISLAMISATION OF YEMEN

D. Thomas Gochenour

> Une doctrine, quelle qu'elle soit, n'existe pas seulement par son contenu, mais aussi par les hommes qui la professent, et il y a interaction, bien évidemment, entre les caractères de ce contenu et ceux de ces hommes.
>
> ... il ne reste pas moins que la doctrine elle-même apparait sous un éclairage tout à fait différent selon l'importance numérique et les caractéristiques sociales des hommes qu'elle soutient. (Claude Cahen, 'La changeante portée sociale de quelques doctrines religieuses'[1])

In the past the study of Islamic sects and the history of Islamic diversity have dwelt almost exclusively on dogmatic and doctrinal developments and on the subtleties of theology. Muslim heresiographers — those who documented the sects of Islam — initially set the limits and aims of this study by their laborious efforts to fabricate in a neat schematic package the doctrinal differences of a sufficient number of sects to demonstrate the God-given wisdom of Muhammad's prophecy: that in Islam, unlike the 71 sects of Christianity or the 72 of Judaism, there would be 73 sects, all but one of them bound for eternal perdition.

Far too little attention has been given to the historical study of real sects possessing a substantial number of followers, and to the necessary relationship that exists between doctrines and the character of a sect and the type of society that finds it persuasive and attractive. We are fortunate that Yemen offers us such a wealth of textual materials from both its pre-Islamic and Islamic periods; materials that permit us to construct fairly accurately throughout its history a detailed and well-documented sociology of Islam, and especially the Islamic sects that settled in Yemen.

It has been frequently pointed out that the dominant social character of Islam was most favourably predisposed to an urban, mercantile, Arabic-speaking society. Allied with this society was that of the traditional Northern Arab nomadic tribes. Neither of these two societies was well established in any part of Yemen in the early seventh century AD. The evidence is overwhelming, in fact, that Yemen's initial allegiance to Islam was at best only superficial. In the first three centuries of Islam, after the Arab conquests and after the great caliphates moved the centre of Islamic activity far from Yemen, it can be fairly said that Yemen became a backwater and that Islam and Islamic instruction were restricted to a handful of key towns and cities, such as San'a', Janad, Aden and Zabid. Our sources for this period, while scanty, are sufficient for us to see that much of the rest of the Yemen, Asir, Najran, large parts of the Tihama, the eastern basin or Sayhad and many of the small Himyaritic 'baronies' were not in the least ruled by Islamic law, ritual or taxation. We have to look to the concurrent arrivals of the Zaidi and the Isma'ili-Fatimid *da'was* in the late ninth century AD (third century *hijra*) to find the true beginnings of the thorough Islamisation of Yemeni society.

But we first must understand the nature of that society before we can assume the processes by which Islam became the dominant social determinant of all or most of Yemen. In pre-modern societies, such as Yemen's until just a few years ago, geographical determinants often play the greatest part in shaping the character, organisation and potentiality of a society. They also appear to the actors of history as the most immutable forces. It is my assumption that the last major change in the geographical features that imprinted a distinct shape on Yemeni society was the collapse of the irrigation systems around Ma'rib with the subsequent demise of a large, sedentary, agricultural society on the Eastern Slope of Yemen some 1,500 years ago.

When we examine Yemen in its Islamic period, more than thirteen centuries, it can indeed be said that the severe geographical constraints of Yemen's physical geography are for all intents and purposes immutable. They are as easily perceptible today as they are from recent historical commentary or from our oldest historical descriptions of the country. In general, in the medieval period, Yemen consisted of five distinct ecological zones; regions defined as much by landscape and topography as they are by factors such as soil fertility, average annual rainfall and its distribution, or the length of growing seasons. These zones are: the Eastern Slope and Desert, the Northern Highlands, the Southern Highlands and wadi bottoms, the Western Mountains and wadis, and the Tihama.

Towards a Sociology of the Islamisation of Yemen 3

Figure 1.1: Yemen's Ecological Zones

4 *Towards a Sociology of the Islamisation of Yemen*

Figure 1.2: Medieval Yemen

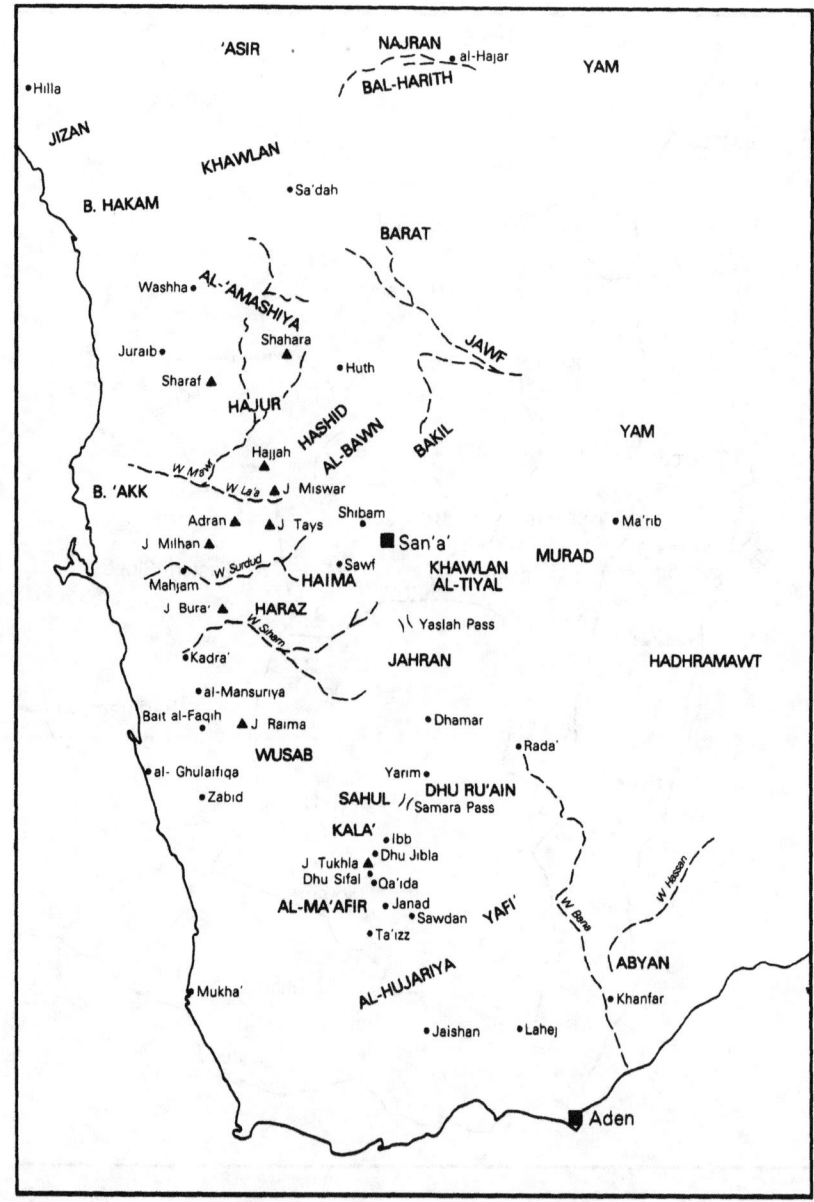

The Tihama or coastal plain running from Asir to Abyan is familiar to everyone for its torrid climate, humid yet nearly rainless weather, its fertile soils and its drab topography. Agriculture has always held great potential in this region where the periodic floods from the mountain streams had sufficient flow to allow for irrigation or to furnish a reliable sub-surface water-table. The ease of transport due to the flat terrain and the two chief entrepôts of Aden and Zabid — the latter with its port of al-Ghulaifiqa — ensured the area a secure and lucrative income from the transit trade. But these same factors meant that the Tihama has been throughout history a defenceless land, subjected repeatedly to conquerors and marauders. As a result its society has always been fragmented, relatively poor and politically unorganised. Nomadic tribes entered the Tihama, pillaging and disrupting its trade routes, from at least the year AD 500,[2] and they remained an important, albeit unstable, part of the population until Imam Ahmad was finally able to crush the nomadic tribes called the Zaraniq in the 1950s.[3] Slaves were also systematically brought into the Tihama from at least the early ninth century[4] under the Ziyadid regime, and the Rasulids' large-scale agricultural development programmes relied on large numbers of African slave labourers (*'abid*). The settled peoples were derived from tribal peoples who had immigrated from the highlands.[5] The resultant picture of the Tihama is that of a society that has long been docile, subjected and politically weak.

The Eastern Slope conforms to what in antiquity has been called the Sayhad basin,[6] that is those areas lying east and north of a line that is equivalent to the 1,700-metre line, including the eastern Jawf. This is also a virtually rainless area where agriculture was solely possible where the waters of the tremendous but unpredictable floods could be harnessed, as they were at Ma'rib. After the collapse of the antique states which had organised the irrigation systems needed for agriculture, the entire economy of the Eastern Slope collapsed too and the area was usurped by nomadic tribes coming from the north and east, foremost amongst them the tribes of Madhhij, Kinda and Yam. Throughout the Islamic period this ecological zone has been characterised by this nomadic tribal society, sparsely populated by unsubdued pastoralists. The Madhhij tribes, in particular the tribes of Murad, the Janb confederation and Zubaid, had some percentage of sedentary members and they have been consistently the most important historical actors of the Eastern Slope because of their great interaction with the inhabitants of the central highlands.

The Northern Highlands is an area of high, rocky plateaus and basins that is interrupted by many peaks and occasional volcanism. It extends from Asir to the Yaslah pass in the south, and is bounded on the west by a precipitous natural barrier, the Western Escarpment, and on the east by a less abrupt dropping off at approximately the 1,700-metre mark. The entire area is on average more than 2,000 metres above sea level. Five major basins or plains are included within this zone: the Najran valley, the *haql* Sa'da, the upper Jawf, the *qa'* San'a' and the *qa'* al-Bawn. There is sufficient predictable rainfall throughout this region to permit dry-crop cultivation, although rainfall levels decrease in general from west to east, and also from south to north.

Since high antiquity the Northern Highlands have been the home of Yemen's proud, sedentary tribesmen. This tribal society is unusual for the stability that has characterised the tribes' territories which have throughout the Islamic period given definition and identity to the tribes. The tribes of the Northern Highlands have apparently always had a stratified society composed of tribesmen, a class of protected people and slaves, the latter two strata at no point in the Islamic period comprising more than a very small minority. A tribesman, *qabili*, usually was understood to be a free landowner and warrior, who farmed his own land and defended his honour jealously. Rarely did any one tribesman own a disproportionately greater share of land than his fellow tribesmen, *qaba'il*.[7] Even amongst the tribesmen there was an aristocracy, however, of notable warriors and leaders called *ashraf* from whose ranks the tribe elected its shaikhs, called variously *'aqil*, *naqib*, *sayyid* or *shaikh*. The ashraf throughout Yemen's history often became hereditary aristocrats who remained influential leaders in their tribes even when they were no longer the actual tribal shaikh; family dynasties like the al-Du'am family of Arhab Jawf, the Abu Barakat family of Khawlan al-Tiyal, the Al al-Dahhak of Hashid, or the Banu Malik of Ukail in Khawlan Quda'a. The protected people were also properly of two sorts: a resident intelligentsia for the tribes usually protected by *hijra* arrangements, and the 'weak' classes of artisans, small merchants, tradesmen and those who performed what the tribesman refused to do, all of whom lived as *jiran* (neighbours) of the tribes.[8]

The Southern Highlands embrace the plains of Jahran, Dhu Ru'ain, the province of al-Ma'afir (present day al-Hujariya) and the mountains of al-Yafi'; an area that roughly corresponds to the classical territory of the Himyarites. On the whole it is an area of lower elevation than the Northern Highlands (average elevation 1,500 to 1,900 metres) that receives more rainfall and possesses more fertile soils than the plateaus and basins of the Northern Highlands. Because it has historically been an agriculturally productive region it has long been more populous too.

The social organisation of the Southern Highlands was formulated by the Himyarite state in far antiquity. It was composed of many small fiefs ruled over by an aristocratic Himyaritic family with a central seat. Many of these families were the principal landowners in their district and held the bulk of the population in thrall. Many emigrated to Muhammad at Medina and were rewarded with yet more grants of land. The majority of the population was little more than docile, farming serfs who owned only a small proportion of the lands they inhabited. From our historical sources there does not appear to have been the same social distinction made between farmers and artisans and merchants as in the tribal societies of the Northern Highlands and the Eastern Slope. This feudalistic organisation persisted well into the late medieval period when the Ayyubids and Rasulids replaced it with their own feudal organisation. In the ninth and tenth centuries AD the Al Dhu Manakh and the Hiwaliyin (Yu'firids) were the last of the Himyarite baronial families to attempt to reconstruct an independent Himyarite confederal state.

The Western Mountains comprise a distinct ecological and social zone that is an area possessing a mixture of features found in the Highlands and the Tihama. Its chief physical feature is the presence of high, isolated mountain massifs separated one from another by deep, narrow wadi valleys. These mountain massifs are big enough to be considered ecological units in themselves. At the upper elevations, often above 2,000 metres, they receive ample rainfall which permits varied and extensive terrace agriculture. In contrast the wadi bottoms are hot and relatively rainless, but the cultivation of tropical crops is possible because of perennially flowing streams. The Western Mountains form the smallest ecological zone in Yemen, lying as they do between the Tihama in the west and the Western Escarpment in the east. The zone extents from the upper Mawr basin in the north, a region called al-Amashiya, includes all of Hajur and Haima, and continues to Wusab in the south. This zone includes the important massifs of Shahara, Sharaf, Hajja, Miswar, Haraz, Milhan, Bura' and Raima.

The society of the Western Mountains has been mixed from antiquity. The mountain tops have been occupied in the Islamic period by both tribal and Himyaritic peoples who often set up societies patterned after the tribal societies as they were organised and practised on the Northern Highlands. However, because of the small size of the mountain-top populations and the relative isolation of one mountain massif from another, the network and mechanisms of tribal alliances (*tahaluf* or *hilf*) did not operate as effectively as they did amongst the tribes of the Northern Highlands, where this institution was crucial for the tribes' ability to defend themselves against most enemies. As a result, these mountain-top societies had only their isolation and the mountain's natural defensive features to protect them from the ravages of tribal marauders and conquerors. On the other hand the peoples of the wadi bottoms were entirely defenceless. This second society was subjected repeatedly to incursions from nomads of the Tihama, especially from the Akk, and to the raids of the highland tribesmen who wrested ownership of the arable lands of the wadi bottoms to supplement their incomes. These wadi dwellers were often enthralled to the inhabitants of the mountain tops, who descended into the wadis only to collect tribute and to use the weekly markets which were located there. Because of this insecurity throughout history the wadis of the Western Mountains, unlike the wadi bottoms of the Southern Highlands, have been relatively underpopulated.

It is necessary to hold this thumbnail sketch of the ecological and social zones of Yemen in mind when we begin our examination of the process of the Islamisation of Yemeni society. Concerted efforts to teach Islamic doctrine and proper ritual, to exact the taxes and require the obligations commanded by the law and to imbue the comprehensive cultural baggage that accompanies Islam did not truly begin until the late ninth century AD. At that time a 300-year-old feud within the Khawlan Quda'a led to an invitation to a *shi'ite* claimant in the Hijaz who held to the Zaidi school, a man named Yahya bin al-Husain. He was invited to act in the traditional role as arbiter and mediator amongst the disputing tribes, but it was also an opportunity for him to introduce Zaidi teachings and to fulfil his personal ambitions to lead a Zaidi state as its *Imam*.

Yahya bin al-Husain, who later took the regnal name of Imam al-Hadi ilal-Haqq, brought in his entourage at least thirty Alids with their families. This group of shi'ites from the Hijaz, all scions of the *ahl al-bait*, became the nucleus of a religious aristocracy that was the primary impetus of the Zaidi da'wa. It grew slowly amongst the tribal populations of the Northern Highlands by the natural processes of generation and, in the first two centuries of the Zaidi da'wa in Yemen, by periodic infusions of new Alid immigrants from the Hijaz, Iran and Iraq. It was from the ranks of this nucleus that the Zaidi Imams were drawn, most of them direct descendants of Imam al-Hadi. This group of Alids — the majority of them called sayyids to indicate their descent from al-Hasan bin Ali bin Abi Talib, the rest called *sharifs* (pl. ashraf) to indicate both descendants of al-Husain bin Ali and all other Talibids — entered first into the tribal society of the Northern Highlands through the traditional tribal institution of hijra.[9] That is to say they settled in tribal lands, by invitation from the tribes, as a class of the protected peoples of the tribes. In return for performing 'high-culture' duties for the tribesmen — namely scribal work, calibrating calendars and star charts, reading and drafting documents — and acting in the same way as Imam al-Hadi had — namely as mediators, arbiters and negotiators — the sayyids and ashraf were honoured by the tribesmen and given lands sufficient to guarantee them an income. These lands, the buildings, chattels, and property on them, and the person of the sayyid, his family and any visitors, became considered an enclave called a hijra and were protected by the tribesmen's formal pledges and strong sense of honour. Generally the Zaidi sayyids exacted only two conditions: that within the hijra enclave the sayyid would rule all matters under the Islamic *shari'a*, and that should the tribesman appeal to the sayyid's judgements he should expect to be governed by that shari'a. In practice, however, over the years this latter condition was often allowed to lapse.

These Zaidi sayyids, of course, were the most important teachers of Zaidism and by exploiting the tribal institution of hijra they were enabled to infiltrate into the very heart of tribal social life in the Northern Highlands. They of course tried to settle in places other than the tribal hijras outside the Northern Highlands, most notably in San'a', but outside of the tribal lands they were never able to live in as much security and freedom from persecution. At the time of Imam al-Hadi's death the sayyids had established three hijra enclaves;[10] two and a half centuries later when the first of the foreign dynasties, the Ayyubids, conquered Yemen, the Zaidis had established sixteen additional such enclaves.[11] I was informed by the foremost sayyid of the Sa'da region that in 1960, shortly before the end of the Zaidi Imams' rule of Yemen, the hijras of the Zaidi sayyids numbered 47, most of them located in the Northern Highlands.

In addition, Imam al-Hadi and other Imams after him had the assistance of other groups of immigrants who were adherents of the Zaidi cause: Tabaristanis, Dailamites, shi'ites seeking refuge from the persecution of the Abbasid regime and scholars who had studied Mu'tazilite thought in Kufa or Basra and wanted to continue their studies with Zaidi scholars in Yemen. This group was more numerous than the sayyids and it continually received fresh infusions until the Persian Zaidi state was completely stamped out. From their ranks came the Zaidis' most loyal soldiers and as a group these people played a crucial role in teaching Islam and Zaidi doctrine. Amongst their greatest teachers were Abu Husain Ahmad bin Musa al-Tabari (d. c. AD 930), and Qadi Ja'far bin Ahmad bin Abd al-Salam al-Tamimi (d. AD 1177). But unlike the sayyids, the Zaidis from this group of immigrants had to assimilate into Yemeni society however they could. Often they remained in the towns such as Sa'da, San'a' or Dhamar, but when they entered tribal territory in the Northern Highlands most often they became part of the class of protected people called the jiran.

It was amongst the jiran, the non-tribal people living within a tribe's territory and under the tribe's protection, that these Zaidis first found the greatest number of converts. Musallim al-Lahji, writing in the mid-twelfth century, describes for us just what kind of people were Zaidis; they were shoemakers, bloodletters, polishers, chamberlains, poets and the landless. In other words, the conversion to Zaidism of the tribes of the Northern Highlands began amongst the lowest strata of tribal society. Throughout the early and middle medieval period (i.e. the tenth to early sixteenth centuries) the tribesmen themselves resisted accepting Zaidism, choosing instead to continue to deal with the sayyids and Imams through tradition-honoured political mechanisms. Tribes, through their shaikhs, contracted alliances with the Imams and felt obliged to maintain good relations with the Zaidis only in accordance with how the Imams dealt with their enemies. Their warriors assisted the Zaidi da'wa most frequently only when there was some immediate advantage or profit for them. The tribes accommodated the Zaidi sayyids because they desperately needed their services, and because the presence of a sayyid in their territory lent the entire tribe greater prestige and *baraka*. Not surprisingly, in return the sayyids of the hijra often became greater advocates of the interests of their hosts than they were of the Zaidi da'wa as represented by a reigning Imam. It was only later when the tribes were pressed by the greater threat of the Ottoman Turks that the qaba'il in great numbers began to abide by Zaidi law and rule and to acknowledge more sincerely their Islam. In other words Zaidism converted tribal society from the bottom up.

Shortly before the Zaidi Yahya bin al-Husain was invited to Yemen in the late ninth century, the Isma'ili-Fatimid da'wa in Iraq, a secret organisation proselytising for the imamate of a descendant of Isma'il bin Ja'far al-Sadiq, recruited, trained and despatched to Yemen two highly talented and inspiring missionaries, *da'is*; one, Abu al-Qasim Hasan bin Faraj bin Hawshab, an Iranian from Kufa, later often known as Mansur al-Yaman; and the other, Ali bin Fadl, a Yemeni shi'ite originally from Jaisan in Ma'afir of the Southern Highlands. These two men spent nearly twenty years, about which we know virtually nothing, teaching and setting up their secret propaganda network from their respective seats of Adan La'a in the Western Mountains and Yafi' in the Southern Highlands. It was only at the turn of the tenth century that the two openly announced their mission, and simultaneously they launched a vigorous campaign of conquest that shattered the two chief Himyarite baronies of the time, the Yu'firid and Manakhi states. Ali bin Fadl, supported as he was by tribesmen from Yafi' and Madhhij, won spectacular successes throughout Yemen, but his influence and success in spreading the Fatimid mission and attracting converts and adherents were vitiated by the radicalism of his personal regime. There is good reason to believe the reports that in fact Ibn Fadl was a supporter of a secessionist movement within the Fatimid organisation which was called the Qarmatian movement, and that as a consequence the Fatimid Imam sent an agent to Yemen to murder him.

Mansur al-Yaman Ibn Hawshab won a more perdurable achievement. His proselytisation and training of missionaries reached the social groups that were to be the nucleus of the Isma'ili-Fatimid movement in Yemen for the next millennium. He appealed to the traditional elites, both Himyarite and Hamdanid, who lived in the mixed societies of the mountain tops in the Western Mountains region. His initial supporters came from the baronial families who were leaders within their own small communities — such as the Himyarities Al Zawahi of Hababa, J. Dila' and J. Masani', or the Banu Siba' of J. Miswar, or the Hamdanid Banu Shawir on J. Maytak — but who had been disenfranchised and enthralled to the Yu'firid state by the Yu'firid clients who ruled those districts.[12] When Ibn Hawshab's conquests began to challenge the tribal domains of the Northern Highlands the Zaidis joined their natural allies in the tribes to conduct a holy war, *jihad*, that succeeded in containing the Fatimid da'wa in the Western Mountains. But Imam al-Hadi's persistent difficulties in Najran were adroitly exploited by Ibn Hawshab, and his agents, da'is, found eager and sympathetic adherents amongst the nomadic tribesmen of Yam who lived in the eastern reaches of Najran, the fringes of Yemen, and who felt that al-Hadi and the Zaidis had dealt with them far too harshly. Even after Ibn Hawshab died (AD 913) and the Fatimid armies suffered a crushing defeat at the hands of the Zaidi and tribal army at Nughash (AD 920), this coalition of Fatimid supporters — disenfranchised elites of the Western Mountains, and the Yam tribes in the far north-eastern parts of Yemen — sustained the Fatimid da'wa ever afterwards.

It was from this core that Ali bin Muhammad al-Sulaihi came. His father was a devout Muslim *qadi* who was sympathetic to the Fatimids although in legal matters he was a *sunni*. He was a man of considerable wealth and power descended from a family of Hashid origin that had emigrated from Qudam to Haraz, both in the Western Mountains. Haraz in the early eleventh century was a mixed society of seven small tribes from both Himyarite and Hamdanid origins, a place that had long remained outside the mainstream of Yemeni politics, whether of the Highlands or the Tihama. Ali was sent as a youth to Kawkaban to study with the chief Fatimid da'i of the day, Sulaiman bin Abdallah al-Zawahi, who recognised in the young man the right materials for reviving the the Fatimid movement in Yemen. Al-Zawahi was proved to be right: after winning widespread respect throughout the Western Mountains for his piety, leadership skills and prowess at arms, Ali bin Muhammad al-Sulaihi invited all of the faithful Fatimid supporters and da'is to J. Masar on Haraz to proclaim his mission to proselytise openly for the Fatimid caliph in Cairo.

There can be little doubt that al-Sulaihi received financial help from the Fatimid caliph. Large amounts of money were always needed to attract the troops needed to sustain an army or campaign anywhere in Yemen, and especially to prevent the enemy from bribing away one's own troops. One of al-Sulaihi's first acts in fact was raising funds from the devout Fatimid supporters who rallied to his appeal. Al-Sulaihi's initial successes in Haraz attracted sufficient support from Himyarite barons from other mountain-top societies of the region, such as J. Tays, Adran, Haima, J. Raima, and as far away as Hajur, to enable him to begin campaigning in the Tihama. Fatimid successes there were the source of the huge amount of funds needed to raise large armies and mount a campaign against the Highlands. When he met and defeated the combined armies of the Hamdan tribes at Sawf led by the Hashid sultan of San'a', Abu Hashid bin Yahya

Figure 1.3: Central Highlands Plains: a Detail

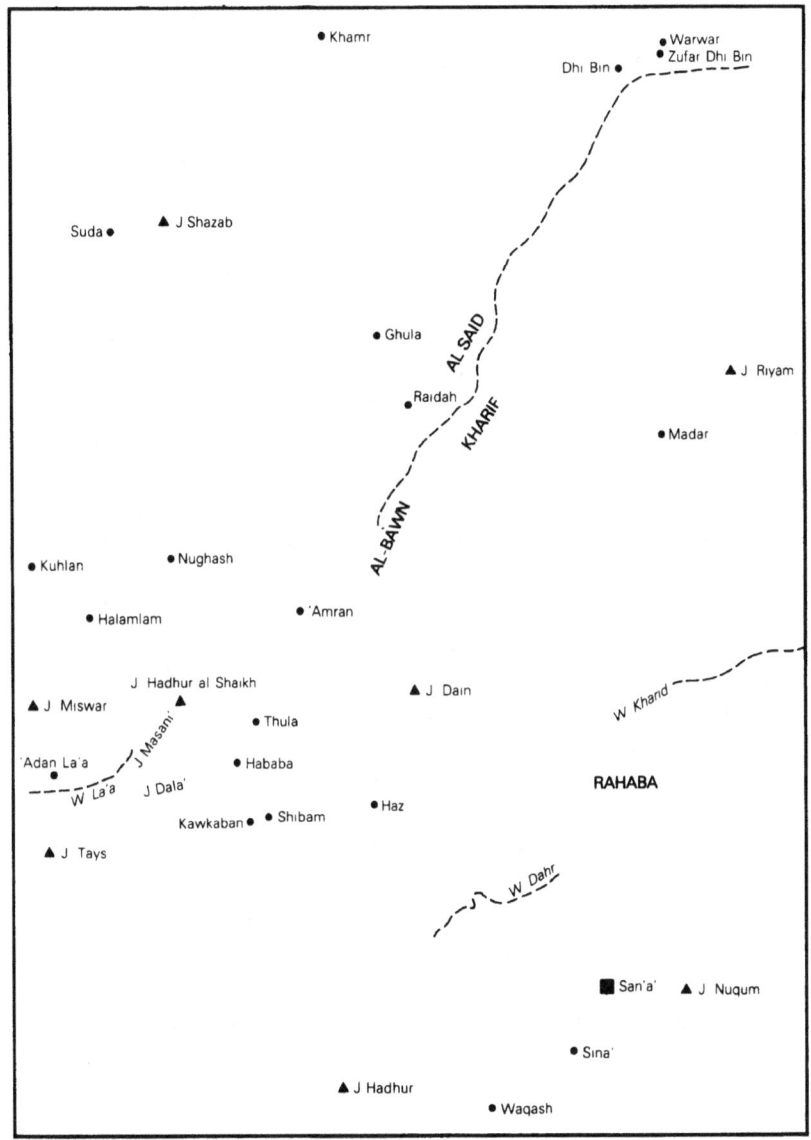

bin al-Dahhak, the Sulaihid state was born. His armies became swollen with success-seekers, and the Himyarite barons of the Southern Highlands, the Banu Karandi of Kala' and Ma'afir, the Al Tuba'i of Sahul and the Banu Dhu Kala' of J. Hubaish, as well as the Banu Shihab of the San'a' basin, were quick to rally to al-Sulaihi's cause.[13]

The Sulaihid state was founded above all on the vestiges of the Himyarite feudalistic social system. The traditional Himyarite barons with their clients and vassals quickly became the elites within the Sulaihid state, some even becoming members of the Fatimid religious hierarchy.[14] They were the providers of the troops for the Sulaihid armies and it was through them that the taxes and tribute for the state were collected. By contrast, al-Sulaihi and his successors were constantly harassed by the tribesmen of the Northern Highlands who were led in their resistance by the Zaidi sayyids. Ali al-Sulaihi won several great victories in the Bawn that subdued the tribes of Hamdan until his death in 1066, and other armies defeated and killed two Zaidi claimants to the imamate, but neither he nor his successors were ever able to incorporate the tribes into the mechanism of his state or to interest them in the Fatimid da'wa. The Fatimid favouritism for the Yam, a major tribe which installed itself in the plains of al-Rahaba at Dhu Marmar and later came to be the sultans of San'a', almost ensured the hostility of the Hamdan tribes, both Hashid and Bakil. This meant that the Fatimids and the Sulaihid state existed forever with an implacable foe in their backyard.

The Sulaihid-Fatimid state possessed the seeds of its own destruction and failure within its own organisation from the very start. First, the Fatimids, who were also called the Batiniya, held a religious doctrine that maintained a sharp distinction between the outward rituals, creeds and meaning of Islam and the inner, esoteric meanings that were divulged only to initiates. For this reason there was always a huge gap between supporters, the subjects and the true elite of Fatimid believers. The Fatimids never took any conscientious steps to win widespread conversion of the masses.[15] Furthermore, the structure of the Fatimid da'wa, while well elaborated in theory, in practice never operated very effectively, particularly after the Fatimid da'wa was transformed from a small, clandestine, revolutionary cadre into a large empire with far-flung autonomous satellites such as the Sulaihid state. Throughout the later history of the Sulaihid state there were constant tensions between the caliph's agents and central da'wa machine and the native, Yemeni da'is and the Sulaihid clients.[16] The fissiparous nature of Fatimid doctrine and organisation was translated further into several very damaging schisms at the heart of the Fatimid movement; first the Nizari schism in the late eleventh century, and then, more serious for Yemen, the Hafizi-Tayyibi schism in 1130. These schisms had devastating consequences for the Sulaihid state. Worse still was the ineffectiveness of Sulaihid leadership when the disorder of these schisms raised doubts. Ali bin Muhammad was a dynamic, vigorous leader; qualities that were woefully lacking in his successors: his son, al-Mukarram, was crippled by polio after his campaign in the Tihama only two years after his father's death. His successor, Saba' bin Ahmad bin al-Muzaffar, was laughably short in stature. After him rule passed to a woman, Queen Arwa, who was politically shrewd but never led an army nor won a single military adventure throughout her long reign. But in the final analysis the Fatimid movement was doomed to become an insignificant, isolated minority community, because it never won extensive popular support. If it had not been for the loyal service of two client families of Yam, the Hamdanids ruling in San'a' and the Zurai'ids in Aden, the Sulaihids would have been swept away sooner than they actually were. The Sulaihids never won popular support because they built their political structure, and thus their fortunes, on the despotic and outmoded Himyaritic social order. Well before the Ayyubids entered Yemen in 1174, when they began systematically to hunt down and persecute Fatimid adherents, the Fatimid-Isma'ili da'wa had ceased to operate with either a political or communal identity.

The rapid demise of the Fatimids, especially in the Southern Highlands around their capital of Dhu Jibla and their citadel atop J. Ta'kar, was primarily the result of the proselytisation of a then newly introduced sect, the Shafi'i school of sunni Islam. Introduced first into Yemen in Janad and its immediate environs in the early eleventh century, the Shafi'i school came quickly to win the religious inclinations and loyalties of the peasants who had long been oppressed by their traditional Himyarite lords. The Shafi'i school — without the centralised hierarchical organisation of the Isma'ilis and without the charismatic leadership and divinely endowed aristocracy of the Zaidi sayyids — spread very rapidly through the Southern Highlands, establishing new urban centres of learning and commerce that attracted hundreds and then thousands who were alienated by the Sulaihids' rule. These new centres included at first Dhu Sifal, Sahfana, Qa'ida, Ibb, Ta'izz and Sawdan, and then later in the Tihama, Bait al-Faqih and al-Mansuriya. Our chief source for this early conversion process is Ibn Samura's work, *Tabaqat fuqaha' al-Yaman*[17] which clearly demonstrates not only how the Shafi'i school spread its teachings but also how Islam in general had radiated outwards in successive generations like spokes from the hub around Janad.

By the opening of the twelfth century, the Shafi'is were confident enough, albeit still politically disenfranchised, to preach active resistance against what they viewed as the heresies of the Fatimid Sulaihid state, then loosely ruled over by Queen Arwa. Their widespread appeal and support were dramatically demonstrated in AD 1110 when seven brave Shafi'i *faqihs* took the premier Sulaihid fortress atop Jabal Ta'kar. When word got out of this *coup* 10,000 peasants rose in support of the faqihs. Furthermore, when the Sulaihid warlord al-Mufaddal tried to recapture the fortress the Khawlan al-Tiyal came to the assistance of the rebels. The Sulaihid forces were beaten and forced to ransom their fortress and sue for peace. The Shafi'i '*ulama*' also considered the Zaidis to be heretical but in these early centuries rarely did they have any contacts or disputes with them or their tribal supporters.

Shafi'i teaching spread into the Tihama in the twelfth century and its stress on the piety of the common man and resistance to oppression was to influence Ali bin Mahdi, although the Shafi'i faqihs of the Tihama were later to oppose his fanaticism and that of his sons as well.[18] The greatest boost to the Shafi'i school however was the arrival of the sunni Ayyubids who officially adopted it as the state school of law and doctrine while they were in Yemen. This official sponsorship, a policy maintained by the Rasulids afterwards, gave the Shafi'is a commanding political position in nearly all of the Southern Highlands, the Tihama and many parts of the Western Mountains; in short, the Ayyubids and Rasulids were quite willing to apply the force of the state's administrative and military organs to forbid the preaching of other sects and to foster instead Shafi'i teaching.[19]

This brings us to the dawn of the thirteenth century AD. Already by this time the great ferment of Islamic sectarianism outside Yemen had grown cold; a more rigid consensus of what Islam properly should be had set in. The aspirations of a great shi'ite revolution had been dissipated by the fissiparous squabbles of the Fatimids and the relentless persecution of the fanatically sunni Seljuks. With them shi'ite messianism had waned — the issues had become outdated and wearisome — and therefore the flow from the Hijaz and Iraq of ambitious Alids looking either for a haven or a state of their own had stopped. All of the Southern Highlands and most of the Tihama and the Western Mountains had been thoroughly Islamised. Al-Khazraji, writing at the beginning of the fifteenth century,[20] documents the continued spread of Shafi'i teachings into the northern Tihama and the societies of the Western Mountains. From the thirteenth century onwards the Zaidis expanded fitfully and cautiously, making their biggest gains in the areas around San'a', Dhamar and Rada', but Zaidi influence and control of these latter two areas were not fully asserted until after the first Ottoman evacuation of Yemen. One of the strongest attractions to Zaidism for the tribesmen was the centrality of the Zaidi concept of the imamate which favoured strong charismatic leadership. The Zaidi movement has always been fortunate that from the ranks of its sayyids it has managed to produce so frequently charismatic, dynamic and inspiring Imams, and whenever such an Imam arose the Zaidi movement enjoyed enormous and widespread support from the tribes. Of course when the opposite situation occurred, as it frequently did, it was as if the Zaidi movement had expired everywhere but in Sa'da. After the first Ottoman evacuation Zaidi proselytisation in the seventeenth and eighteenth centuries began to win supporters in the Eastern Slope as well, primarily amongst the Murad and Harib.

In conclusion we can see that the sectarian character of Yemen was finally set firmly from the beginning of the thirteenth century. At that time the Ayyubid and then Rasulid states joined with the forces of a Shafi'i mission to begin to restructure radically the society of the Southern Highlands and Tihama. Their political control effectively left only the most tribal areas (i.e. the Northern Highlands) open to Zaidi penetration and preaching. The border areas between the Zaidis in the north and the Shafi'is remained the last areas of sectarian competition. These areas were: first, the northern third of the Southern Highlands from the plains of Jahran to just south of Dhamar and from Ilhan to Rada'; and, second, the Western Mountains. This first area has had throughout history an equivocal social character and make-up that appear to have been the result of imposed Himyarite control and social patterns, giving way from the late tenth century to the more dominant and attractive social norms of tribalism as it was practised in the Northern Highlands. In the Western Mountains, especially the half of this zone lying to the north of Wadi La'a, just the opposite process seems to have occurred; the norms of tribalism and tribal identity have weakened and the people of this region have become less and less loyal and committed to the Zaidis or their tribal partners from Hamdan.

Notes

1. From Claude Cahen, *Les Peuples Musulmans dans l'Histoire Médiévale* (French Institute of Damascus, Damascus, 1977), p. 189.
2. We know this through the *ayyam* literature since at that time there began to be a series of feuds, raiding and battles in the northern Tihama such as Yawm A'yar and al-Naqi'a, Yawm Kulab II and Yawm al-Sara'im. See Egbert Meyer, *Der Historische Gehalt der Aiyam al-Arab* (Harrassowitz, Wiesbaden, 1970), pp. 12-19.
3. The nomads remained a large portion of the Tihama population in spite of the massive emigration of tribesmen from B. Akk and B. A'shara at the time of the Islamic *futuhat* in the 630s-670s.
4. Primarily *mamluks* intended for military service.
5. A large number of fractions from Khawlan Quda'a and Hajur migrated as documented in Hasan al-Hamdani, *Al-Iklil*, ed. Muhammad al-Akwa' (Matba'at al-Sunna al-Muhammadiya, Cairo, 1963), vol. I.
6. This term was first standandised by A. F. L. Beeston.
7. This was especially true as the qailite (petty princeling) families were swept away in the late ninth and tenth centuries.
8. For more details on tribal society the reader is recommended to consult the unpublished PhD thesis by Paul Dresch, 'The Northern Tribes of Yemen', Oxford University, 1982. For the historical structures of tribalism and their relations with Zaidism see my forthcoming book, *The Penetration of Zaydi Islam into Medieval Yemen* (Bonn).
9. While the terms 'sayyid' and 'sharif' had always held their standard and most general meanings, i.e. lord and noble respectively, the descendants of the ahl al-bait adopted these terms for themselves and made them into more specific, technical terms with a more specifically Islamic sense. Thus a descendant of the family of Muhammad was naturally called a lord among men, and noble. In the medieval period the use of these two terms, however, was not at all standardised. At times a descendant of Hasan bin Ali bin Abi Talib could be both a sayyid and a sharif. In Yemen's history it was only in the late medieval period that a sayyid came to mean a Hasanid, and a sharif meant a Husainid.
10. They were Sa'da, Khaywan and Athafit.
11. They were located at Warwar, Iyan, Madhab, Dhamar, Wadi'a, Raida, Huth, Marashi, Na'it, Madar, Washha, Hajar, Zufar, Barat, Shahara, Haidan. Some of these ceased to be hijras later.
12. The qailite family Al Tarif supported the Yu'firids and had been given much of Miswar, Dila', Masani' and Hadur al-Shaikh, and Bilad B. Qudam as their fief. All the sources censure them for their rapacity.
13. My information on the Sulaihids is drawn from the Delhi manuscript of volume VII of the *Uyun al-akhbar* by Imad al-Din Idris bin Ali bin Abdallah al-Qurashi, the Isma'ili ruler of the fifteenth century. I am greatly indebted to Nizar Ahmad Faruqi, formerly of Delhi, for his invaluable assistance in procuring this manuscript for me.
14. People such as Lamak bin Malik al-Hammadi, who was a leader of one of the seven tribes of Haraz. He became a da'i and was al-Sulaihi's personal emissary to the Fatimid court in Cairo from 1062 to 1066. He died in 1098, over ninety years old. For a list of the chief da'is of the Fatimids in Yemen see Ismail Poonawala, *Bio-bibliography of Isma'ili Literature* (Undena Publications, Malibu, California, 1977). Note especially that many of them were of Hajuri or Yami origins.
15. See Abbas Hamdani, 'Evolution of the Organisational Structure of the Fatimi Da'wah: The Yemeni and Persian Contribution' in *Arabian Studies* (Cambridge University Press, Cambridge, 1976), vol. III, p. 97.
16. The most famous case was the tragedy of Ibn Najib al-Dawla, sent from Cairo

to help the Sulaihids, but betrayed and murdered by them.

17. Edited by Fu'ad Sayyid (Dar al-Kutub al-Ilmiya, Beirut, 1957).

18. Our first references to Sufism in the Yemen come from this period, i.e. the twelfth century AD. Sufi mystics were active proselytisers in the Tihama especially but they also helped spread both the Hanafi and Shafi'i schools of Sunni Islam in the Southern Highlands and the Tihama. The Zaidis actively persecuted the Sufis who do not appear to have contributed anything to the religious life of the Northern Highlands or the Eastern Slope.

19. Zaidis were chased out of Dhu Jibla and Juraib in the Tihama in the late twelfth century.

20. In his work, *Tiraz a'lam al-zaman fi tabaqat a'yan al-Yaman*, MS Ta'rikh no. 130 in Western Library, Great Mosque, San'a'.

2 MEMDUH PASHA AND AZIZ BEY: OTTOMAN EXPERIENCE IN YEMEN

Jon Mandaville

The weather stays cloudless
  — But why, then, this smoke?
Nobody dies there
  — But what, then, this scream?
These Yemeni hands — ah, they are capable.

This, then is Yemen; its flower sharp cummin.
Those who go out there do not return from there.
I wonder why.
This, then, a fist; its roads precipitous.
Those who go out there do not return from there;
What's going on? (Ruhi Su, *Yemen Türküsü*)

Yemen today is no stranger to the Turks, nor the Turks to Yemen. One hundred years of Ottoman occupation in the sixteenth and seventeenth centuries marked the Yemeni countryside with buildings, cisterns, roads and gravestones in the Ottoman manner; it left the Turks with the beginnings of a tradition of melancholy folk songs about military service in Yemen. Ottoman government returned to Yemen in the nineteenth century, first at the hands of Muhammad Ali's troops and then in 1849 with troops directed by Constantinople. Only the Tihama was held initially. Then, in 1871, the decision was taken to undertake a full-scale occupation. This decision, made possible in large part by the opening of the Suez Canal in 1869, reflected a desire to pre-empt renewed Egyptian expansion into the Red Sea and Arabia.[1] It was also a challenge to expanding British influence along the Gulf and Red Sea coastlines of Arabia; a similar extension of Ottoman commitment took place that same year in al-Hasa on the opposite coast of Arabia. Behind both these factors of regional strategy lay a broader determination of the Ottoman government to reintegrate the old provinces of the empire into the new modernising Ottoman state.

Yemen was to be as much a part of that state as the provinces of Syria, Bursa, Adrianople or Tuna. All the reform legislation of the *tanzimat* was to be applied there — and from 1871 until the withdrawal of Ottoman government in 1918 it was — to the best of the Ottoman administrators' abilities and provincial budget. There was no better symbol of the determination behind this integration than the election of delegates from Yemen to the first Ottoman constitutional assembly in Constantinople in 1875-6.[2]

But how much, in fact, did the reforms mean to Yemen? G. Wyman Bury, well-known observer of Yemen at the turn of this century, noted in 1914, 'The proper development of Yemen, with its difficult terrain, is a task of magnitude . . . well worth attempting.'[3] And he was close to the mark when he commented on Ottoman public works there, 'many schemes of theoretical excellence have been inaugurated in Yemen only to die of inanition for lack of sustenance and support'.[4] Yet he was only close. Schemes and projects and new institutions there were aplenty, but not all of them died; many, in fact, lived on into Yemeni independence after the First World War. Though not measuring up to the attractive goals proposed by policy makers in Constantinople — and certainly not to the image of modernity held by a British officer — even their more limited realities were important enough. Taken together with the reformed Ottoman provincial system which administered them and the economic assumptions implicit in that system, they began that complex of change we call modernisation in Yemen. True enough, the initiation of this process was littered with setbacks. And no small part of the difficulty lay in the disagreements and misunderstandings on priorities which quickly developed between Ottoman officials in Yemen and their home ministries in Constantinople.

From the point of view of Ottoman officialdom in Constantinople, a broad spectrum of reform programmes and economic projects were needed to bring Yemen up to the level of development already reached in other provinces of the empire. The deadly and expensive cycle of revolt led by the Hamid al-Dins, however, forced most of the early reports and proposals for development into a focus on pacification measures.

The recommendations of the Reform Committee of 1898 reflect this short-term military approach, although their charge was a far broader one. Military forces were to be concentrated on the Zaidi tribes and regions influenced by the Imam. The Hujur and Hashid territories, then Maidi, Jizan and al-Wasim coastal territories should be occupied and put under tight administration. Then the occupation should be extended from Jizan up to Sa'da and neighbouring territories. To carry this out it was recommended that more troops should be sent, more barracks and hospitals built, pharmaceuticals and clothing sent, more transport animals — mules — sent. To support this military activity the telegraph lines should be extended from Luhayya up through Hujur, Hajja and Amran to San'a', and also north from Luhayya along the coast to Asir. Finally, leading supporters of the Zaidi Imam were to be exiled from Yemen.[5] This emphasis on military action continued in the numerous reports which followed.

The Memduh Commission of 1904 represents the beginning of a shift of policy. Hastily put together under the chairmanship of Memduh Pasha, Minister of the Interior, in response to the young Imam Yahya's revolt, it was charged with the task of finding alternatives to the simple use of force in dealing with the rebellion. It was, in the words of Memduh Pasha, to develop a programme which would allow Yemen to benefit from 'progress and civilisation [*terakki ve temeddün*] . . . just as other provinces had'; a programme which would win the people away from the rebels.[6]

Because of the extensiveness of the Memduh Commission's report, it is worth discussing in some detail as an example of the official view of Yemen from Constantinople more than thirty years after the reoccupation. The sources reviewed by the Commission in compiling its report offer a useful survey of the main points of concern raised over the period 1898 to 1904.

(1) Documents presented to the Council of State by the Reform Commission of 1898 detailing the need to build a railroad between Hodaida and San'a', the Yemeni perceptions of criminal law procedure and how the present-day shari'a courts ought to be organised, and steps needed to establish peace and law and order.
(2) A telegraphed report of 1898 received from the Governor of Yemen discussing a proposal for the restructuring of Yemen into four provinces.
(3) A report from the Governor of Yemen dated 1898 concerning agriculture and the development of local wealth and state income.
(4) A report from the Civil Service Office of the Council of State

based on intelligence reports concerning progress on administrative reform in Yemen.
(5) Despatches to the Palace from Yemen in response to queries from Sultan Abd al-Hamid concerning delays in settling Yemen's problems.
(6) Despatches from Yemen concerning implementation of orders to separate the Gendarme Service from the army.
(7) A collection of general status reports on Yemen from the Ministry of Interior dated 1902 to 1904.[7]

Two members of the Commission had previously visited Yemen as members of the earlier Reform Commission of 1898. To supplement their experience, testimony was obtained from two Yemeni leaders who had been exiled to Cyprus some months earlier: the Shaikh of Bani Dhi Husain, Naqib Salih bin Yahya, and al-Sayyid Yahya bin Ahmad al-Qibsi.[8]

The Memduh Commission was quick to recognise that most of the problems of government arose from the general poverty of the population, and therefore that the primary need was for economic development. Poverty drove many of the people to become soldiers in the army of the Imam; as such they received at least daily food rations. Poverty also meant a weak tax base, which in turn led to a drain on the central treasury. The sources of this poverty, the Commission reported, were ignorance of better methods of production, a poor road system for marketing produce and very complex land laws.[9]

For the marketing system, the Commission recommended at minimum the further development of the Hodaida-San'a' highway. At the same time, it was recognised that this road was too difficult an ascent to function adequately as a regular transport route. Consequently, the 1899 proposal for a 300-kilometre Hodaida-San'a' railroad by way of Hujaila was revived and strongly recommended:

> The agriculture of San'a' and Hodaida, and the trade and commerce between these two points, would easily pay for the capital investment and make a profit for the State . . . This matter is key to the foundations for reform in Yemen; the faster it is carried out, the sooner will its beneficial results be seen.[10]

To increase agricultural production, a team of agriculture-training experts was proposed. It would include an agriculture researcher to study land conditions, the current land-tenure system and current agricultural practices, and to propose reforms based on this study. There should be a specialist in tobacco cultivation and a number of farmers knowledgeable in fruit-tree cultivation and grafting. Model farms should be established, and the team should carry out training programmes. Selected seeds and young plants should be imported and distributed free to the people. On the Tihama, special efforts were to be made to develop the cultivation of cotton. An expert in its cultivation was to be appointed and seeds imported from Egypt, America, Izmir and Adana for free distribution. Indigo, the Tihama variety of which should have been competitive with the Indian variety, was not; an indigo expert was to be appointed to teach the people better cultivation and refining methods. He, as well as all of the other trainers, was to be on long-term appointment.

Without the development of water supplies little increase in agricultural productivity was possible. For this, old water courses in the mountains were to be cleared and wells drilled in the high valleys and plains. Engineers for this, as well as for surveying and building roads to water supplies, were to be appointed and drilling machinery and supplies sent with them. It was felt that a minimum of manpower support would be needed since the local population had a good deal of experience in such work.[11]

Education to combat ignorance drew the Commission's attention, although its recommendations amounted to no more than an expansion of existing programmes. Already by 1900 the Ottoman Public Education Law had been applied in Yemen. According to it, all education, from primary schools up to the secondary level, was to be provided free to all children. In 1899, in recognition of the inadequacy of the education budget to provide this in Yemen, a decree had been issued which dedicated 30 per cent of the coffee tax (*simsariye*) to the upkeep of early primary schools and the vocational schools in Hodaida and San'a'. The education budget, derived from 5 per cent of the *zakat*, paid the school maintenance and teachers' salaries (including those of teachers of religion) for the rest of the primary and secondary schools and teachers' institutes.[12] The Public Education Law also called for the appointment of a Director of Education to each provincial district (*sancak*). The administration of education of the province as a whole was to be carried out by a Chief Director, advised by an Educational Council made up of appropriate citizenry and presided over by the Deputy Governor.

The Memduh Commission found after reviewing all relevant documents that the system as a whole worked well. Suggestions that a separate Education Inspectorate Office be set up in San'a' were rejected as unnecessary and expensive. It was noted that in 1901 two night-schools for vocational studies, two night middle-schools, two teachers' institutes, six early primary and three later primary schools were open, serving 1,600 'enthusiastic and supportive' students. In short, progress was being made. It was noted, however, that special care should be taken by the Ministry of Education to design the curriculum for these schools to conform to local requirements and in co-operation with provincial officials.[13]

While the Commission expressed general contentment with the education system, offering no major plans for revision, it offered no pretence of satisfaction with the reformed Ottoman judicial system as applied in Yemen. This system had taken its procedural form in 1869 at the same time that the Provincial Administration Law of 1871 was taking shape.[14] Like that law, it also introduced an element of elected local participation, decreeing that courts at every level would have three elected members to assist the judge. Further, it set up three separate courts, civil, penal and commercial, and paralleled each with an appeals system. This procedure represented a significant departure from that of the traditional shari'a court in Yemen.

But a still more radical departure was the Ottoman reformed law itself. Already by 1871 commercial codes drawn almost entirely from French codes and thoroughly secular in nature had been instituted. Penal codes as well had been secularised. Only civil law remained of the shari'a proper; and after the government's de facto authorisation of Cevdet Pasha's *Mecelle* as a sole source of opinion for judicial reference in civil matters it appeared that civil law as well had become Europeanised.[15]

Both the electoral procedures of the judicial councils, as modest as they were, and the secularisation of law were intended by the Ottoman reformers to create an impartial administration of justice for the multi-religious population of their state. Both, however, by the same token directly undermined the basis of the legitimacy of the Zaidi imamate. The application of Ottoman reform law became, therefore, the central point of contention of Ottoman-Zaidi relations. The Memduh Commission went through report after report dealing with the courts. The first major document utilised, issued in 1882, dealt with modifications of the system to accommodate the lack of judges in Yemen trained in the new laws and procedure, and with the necessity of establishing an Inspectorate of Courts to reinforce the application of the system.[16] Another emerged from the Reform Committee of 1898,[17] and yet another in 1901.[18] There was no lack of documents on the perennial difficulties of applying a secularised judicial system for the first time in Yemen — nor on the use of the issue by the Imam to justify revolt — but neither was the Commission willing to suggest even minor modifications to ease the problem. There was no room for grand schemes there.

The Commission's approach to provincial administration was the same. While noting the usual problems of corruption and mismanagement, it offered no specific recommendations. It did, however, largely agree with the recommendation of the Reform Committee of 1898 to divide the province of Yemen into four: the province of San'a', with the districts of Dhamar and Hajja; of Ta'izz, with the districts of Hujariya and Qa'taba; of Hodaida, with the districts of Zabid and Abu Arish (including Sabya); and of Asir, with the districts of Makha'il and Ghamid.[19]

This recommendation had been passed on favourably by the Civil Service Office of the Council of State in 1900, with the proviso that the Governor of San'a' be paid twice the salary and hold veto power over any of the other three governors.[20]

The redivision of Yemen probably would have improved the responsiveness of government to the local needs. Yet the basic sources of discontent with administrative procedure would certainly have remained, and with this the Commission refused to tamper. No thought was given to devising a code of administration specific to Yemen, only to creating the conditions needed for the successful implementation of the administrative system already in effect. The key to that work was seen as economic development, which in turn would produce on the one hand sufficient taxes to run the government effectively, and on the other sufficient prosperity to eliminate most of the basis of support for rebellion. The final paragraph of the Commission's report focuses upon this rebellion; written as it was in the fall of 1904 it could scarcely do otherwise.

In that paragraph it was argued that there were three groups of people in Yemen in a state of rebellion. One received monthly salaries from the rebel chief; the second profited from the unrest by raiding and looting; the third group was loyal to Ottoman goverment but was overwhelmed by the threats and force of the rebels due to the lack of troops to defend them. If the Ottoman government were to offer the first two groups one or two riyals a month more than they received from the rebels, they would join the Ottoman Army. If they were sure of a steady income through trade and agriculture, they would immediately turn all thought to that:

> Yemen under local shaikhs and leaders offered no security and justice; thus, the people are prepared to accept firm and just rule. Once the rebellion is put down, institutional measures for useful reform should be pursued . . . but . . . Unless money is appropriated for these long-term measures, the suppression of the revolt will have only a temporary effect; revolt will break out again.[21]

In the last line of the report a last recommendation was made: a permanent commission to review Yemen affairs should be established in the Ministry of Interior.[22] It was not. Memduh Pasha withdrew from further activity on Yemen affairs in protest against the apparent lack of action by the Prime Minister on the Commission's recommendations.[23]

It would in fact have been difficult for the Prime Minister's Office to use the Commission's report as a basis for action, though it contains a useful collection of previous reports and studies. The 1901 Report of Husain Hilmi Pasha, Governor of Yemen during the years 1898–1902, is far better reasoned and sensibly presented.[24] Memduh Pasha dismissed it as 'impractical under the present circumstances'.[25] The personality of Memduh likely had something to do with this statement and with the reception of the Commission's report; he was a palace politican 'known for servility toward his superiors and for the *hauteur* he showed his subordinates'.[26]

In the meantime, while the Prime Minister's Office and the Council of State reviewed and discussed action to take on such reports as these, provincial officers in Yemen waited impatiently and often angrily for some sign of action by the capital. The perspectives on priorities for resolving problems and initiating development programmes in Yemen were worlds apart between field headquarters in San'a' and the Palace walls of Constantinople.

> I wrote a great many strong cables and reports for the Field Marshal [wrote Aziz Bey, Deputy Director of Military Supplies and Communications Officer in San'a' in 1901], but the fact is, I moderated his opinion and words by more than half, to the point where, upon my submitting a draft to him he would say, 'Has the nobility of the pen struck again, friend? Why won't you ever write it all?!'[27]

There were many Syrians among the many thousands of Ottoman officers assigned to or volunteering for civil or military service in Yemen.[28] One such was Abd al-Aziz al-Azmah, who served in several military capacities in San'a' between 1898 and 1902. His career in Yemen culminated with his appointment to the post of Deputy Governor (*mutasarrif*) of Hodaida, where he served between 1902 and 1904.[29]

Aziz Bey, as he was known, made no major changes in administration during his Yemen years. The notes he took down then, however, together with the brief autobiographical sketch he attached to them describing this period, offer us a distinctive personal view of how Ottomans in the field, as opposed to the Palace, saw Ottoman Yemen's problems and future. Aziz Bey's views of administrative problems contained no thoughts on provincial restructuring. For him, personnel was a major issue:

> The administration [*memurlar*] of Yemen could be divided into two parts: the foreigners and the locals. The foreigners were small camp-follower types who could not make a living in their own countries and so came to Yemen, where even there most were incapable. The locals, though there were bright ones, hadn't sufficient education and so hadn't the means of carrying out their tasks. A third group are the children and relatives of officers. They chose to accompany the head of family to Yemen, then found no escape when their head died; or they chose to stay. These are the ones who produce the most work.[30]

The notebook contains thoughts on the perennial deficits run by the provincial government. Aziz Bey's first concern focused on the deplorable state of personnel and supply accounts and records, his first official responsibility:

> Shakir Efendi [he notes disapprovingly], Director of Records and well-known as the most knowledgeable person for accounting and business, set up the accounts for 1896 and 1897 on just two or three forms. When asked for an accounting he simply changed the income and expenditure lists with discounts and the like until they balanced . . . I checked the cashier's account, and although there was 810,000 kurus recorded, there was in fact no more than thirty-five kurus in hard cash. The rest was in the form of standard 'payable' chits [*senedat-i adiye*].[31]

The same budgetary problems applied to the province as a whole, as well as the makeshift methods of their resolution. According to Aziz Bey, the province never produced more than 30 million kurus in income, while military expenditures alone absorbed 20 million at minimum.[32] In 1899 provincial income on paper reached 35 million while military expenditures topped 25 million. The military figures were real; the income figures were not, since more than 5 million in taxes could not be collected. Since military expenses took precedence, very little money was left for school and other civilian expenses.[33]

The tax notes taken by Aziz Bey during his first year of office in Hodaida document the problem of collection. In that sancak, the tax assessment base was 15.5 million kurus. However, in 1901 only 10.3 million were actually collected, and in 1902 only 9 million.[34] The *kaza* of Abu Arish was the best — or worst — example. With a tax base of 1.1 million kuruş, 70,000 was collected in 1902, all but 6,000 of it in market taxes.[35] Why the discrepancy? The entire kaza was in rebellion. Jizan, the seat of kaza government, was itself but tenuously held, while Jizan port business was conducted from Farasan Island.[36]

Further complicating all of these financial matters, Ottoman coinage was refused by most of the countryside, save in the large cities; the Maria Theresa riyal, minted in Trieste, was the standard market coin. Taxes assessed in Ottoman currency always lost when paid in riyals, because of the unfavourable exchange rate.[37]

In budgetary circumstances such as these there must have seemed little point in considering grand schemes of improvement. Ironically, the sancak of Hodaida contained Yemen's only major source of large capital to fund such projects — the salt works of the Salif region. If Aziz Bey's figures are correct, exports of salt to India and Djibouti in 1902 brought in an impressive 78 million kurus gross, nearly eight times the real tax income of the sancak. It could not be touched; the income belonged to the Ottoman Public Debt Administration, to be used to pay off European investors in the Ottoman government. Other state monopolies attached to the Public Debt Administration such as tobacco and general salt tax drained off another 2 million kurus in 1902 (3.8 million in 1901).[38] Other taxes peculiar to Yemen at the disposal of the province, such as the Qat tax, could not begin to match this production.[39]

Aziz Bey offers us no comments on railroad or dams projects, and precious little on roads, save to note their state of disrepair.

Education, however, was of special interest to him; he was very conscious of the role it had played in his own advancement.[40] He copied into his notebook the decrees of 1899 concerning educational funding, and maintained detailed accounts of the education budgets of Hodaida. In 1902, a total of 357,102 kuruş was collected in Hodaida sancak for schools: 306,624 kurus from the coffee-tax collections of Hodaida and Luhayya ports, and 50,478 kuruş from zakat.[41] This amounts to about 4 per cent of the total sancak budget — low, but not insignificant.

But while Aziz Bey spoke hopefully in 1904 of the recent establishment of primary schools in Hodaida, Zabid, Bajil, Raima and Bait al-Faqih, 'allowing the Tihamah to participate in the benefits of education', his overall assessment was, if not sombre, then at least subdued:

> The level of education is extremely low. Though one cannot fault the education of the likes of al-Sayyid Muhammad Bari of Hodaidah, or the Mufti of Zabid Abd al-Rahman al-Anbari, unfortunately they are not training successors . . . A town like Zabid has long been known for its learning and scholarship, . . . but in general, teaching is done in the old way, first learning the Qur'an and a little writing, then continuing with classes in the mosque on some *fiqh* and *hadith*. No more than five per cent of the population ever comes into contact with education, leaving most in ignorance.[42]

The Memduh Commission spoke of reform and development projects; Aziz Bey spoke of taxes. The two contemporary Turkish histories dealing with Turkish Yemen described war. The legacy of Ottoman Yemen was a little of all of these, and a few more things besides. The first printing press came to Yemen in these years, and produced the provincial yearbooks, complete with almanac, and Yemen's first newspaper. For the first time all Yemenis shared a common source of national information. A few thousand Yemenis experienced a secular approach to education. Roads and ports and telegraph lines, though ill-maintained, physically knit the country together. The introduction of a common and semi-secularised court procedure and law, applied to all throughout Ottoman-controlled territories regardless of religious persuasion, undermined the traditional sunni/shi'i divisions of the population.[43] The experience of modernised government service shared by both sunnis and Zaidis in the Gendarme Service, local, municipal, district and provincial councils and the army militia, further helped to lay the manpower foundations for a national government. Many of these features were dismantled in the first decades of modern Yemen's independence, but the experience remained to draw upon. That, and the experience of the thousands of Turks who elected to stay when the Turkish government was gone.[44]

There was more to this experience than the ability to direct modern artillery or drive an automobile. Less immediately obvious, but implicit in all of the projects, new taxes and battles, there was the inexorable movement of Yemen towards a market economy, with all the social changes which followed from it.[45] Already the development of Aden had its effect on the economic patterns in the south. With the flow of troops and capital into Hodaida, San'a' and other Turkish administrative centres, market demand rose. At the same time, pressure from tax collectors for cash payments further encouraged the planting of cash crops. Ultimately, this shift to commercial agriculture, in a land where agriculture dominated the lives of the people, was a factor for change more firmly set than any administrative reform dreamed by Constantinople or attempted by Aziz Bey and his fellow officers.

Finally, there was also the matter of changed attitudes towards the world, towards knowledge and the potentialities of man. Perhaps only a few were affected by this — but they were the first generation of Yemen's modern leaders and carried an influence far beyond their numbers. Aziz Bey, Memduh Pasha and the Turkish soldiers each had their own experiences in Yemen; it was for the people of Yemen to apply the experience of the Ottoman period to Yemen's future.

Notes

1. For this Cairo-Constantinople rivalry, see Faruq Uthman Abazah, *Al-Hukm al-Uthmani fil-Yaman: 1872-1918* (Cairo, 1975), pp. 68–80.
2. The delegates were al-Shaykh Ali Efendi and al-Sayyid Muhammad Efendi; see Robert Devereux, *The First Ottoman Constitutional Period* (Johns Hopkins University Press, Baltimore, 1963), p. 265. Devereux offers no information beyond their names.
3. G. Wyman Bury, *Arabia Infelix* (Macmillan, London, 1915), p. 205.
4. Ibid.
5. Memduh, *Yemen kitasi hakkinda ba'zi Mutalaat* (Istanbul, 1324/1908), p. 51.
The perception of the Yemen problem primarily as a military issue was reinforced by the two standard Turkish histories of the nineteenth-century reoccupation, in Atif Pasha, *Yemen Tarihi* (2 vols., Istanbul, 1326/1910) and Ahmed Rashid, *Tarih-i*

Yemen ve San'a (2 vols., Istanbul, 1291/1875). Both were written by military officers who had served in Yemen. The only recent Turkish scholarly approach to the problem is broader in its approach than the title implies, however; see Ihsan Sureyya Sirma, *Osmanli Devletinin Yikilisinda Yemen Isyanlari* (Istanbul, 1980).

6. Ibid., p. 39.
7. Ibid., pp. 40-2.
8. The two Yemeni leaders were in agreement on the need for immediate amnesty. Naqib Salih bin Yahya favoured enrolment of tribal leaders into government service, and governmental support for succession by rule of primogeniture in tribal leadership. Al-Sayyid Yahya al-Qibsi spoke strongly of the need to show no mercy to the rebels. He also suggested forgiveness of back taxes; ibid., p. 42.
9. Ibid., pp. 45-6.
10. Ibid., p. 47.
11. Ibid., pp. 55-6.
12. Ibid., pp. 54, 58.
13. Ibid., pp. 58, 65.
14. For both, see Roderic H. Davison, *Reform in the Ottoman Empire, 1856-1876* (Princeton University Press, Princeton, 1963), pp. 251-6, 141-60.
15. Not a secular law, the Mecelle was in fact no more than a codification in European format of the Hanafi school of shari'a law.
16. Memduh, *Yemen kitasi*, pp. 48-9.
17. Ibid., pp. 60-1.
18. Ibid., p. 63.
19. For the 1898 Report on this, see Memduh, *Yemen kitasi*, pp. 51-2.
20. Ibid., p. 56.
21. Ibid., p. 81.
22. Ibid., p. 82.
23. See ibid., pp. 82-3, for his personal note to the Palace explaining this.
24. Its complete text is published in Atif Pasha, *Yemen Tarihi* (Istanbul, 1326/1910), vol. II, pp. 211-28.
25. Memduh, *Yemen kitasi*, p. 75.
26. Carter V. Findley, *Bureaucratic Reform in the Ottoman Empire* (Princeton University Press, Princeton, 1980), p. 251.
27. Notebook MS of Abd al-Aziz al-Azmah, 'Aziz Bey', Syrian Ottoman officer who served in Yemen between 1898 and 1904. The MS is currently being prepared for publication.
28. Too much has been made of Syrian resistance to military service against fellow Arabs in Yemen (e.g. Abazah, *Al-Hukm al-Uthmani*, p. 117). By the 1880s, no foot soldier, whether Turk or Arab, was anxious to serve in Yemen. For officers, however, there were attractive opportunities of pay rises or advancement.
29. The Imperial Yearbooks list him in that position in 1903 and 1904: *Devlet Salnamesi* (Istanbul, 1321, 1322AH). Aziz Bey was perhaps better known in Syria, where his brother Yusuf died at Maysalun fighting the French as Amir Faisal's Minister of Defence. His sons Muhammad Nabih and Umar Adil served respectively as Ministers of Defence and Interior under Quwatli.
30. Aziz MS, fo. 41. Aziz Bey brought his family with him to Yemen.
31. Ibid., fos. 40-1.
32. Note the discrepancy between this and the figures reported in the provincial yearbooks: Klaus Kreiser, 'Der Haushalt der Provinz Jemen zwischen 1877/8 and 1910/1' in *Osmanli Arastirmalari* (Istanbul, 1980), pp. 213-17, where average provincial income is given as 40 million.
33. Aziz MS, fos. 45-6.
34. Ibid., fos. 13-14.
35. Ibid., fo. 15.
36. Ibid., fo. 54.

37. Ibid., fo. 37.

38. Ibid., fo. 10. The figures seem high, but not impossibly so. The Indian market was huge, and the Aden salt works had not yet been developed (see Great Britain, Naval Intelligence Division, *Western Arabia and the Red Sea* (London, 1946), pp. 529-30). For the workings of the Public Debt Administration, see Donald C. Blaisdell, *European Financial Control in the Ottoman Empire* (New York, 1929).

39. The Qat tax income was fairly substantial, however, averaging 209,000 kuruş per year in Hodaida. It might be compared with the average 273,000 kuruş collected for education from the coffee tax in Hodaida township: Aziz MS, fos. 5-6.

40. He describes in detail his early studies in his autobiography; see ibid., fos. 9-14.

41. Ibid., fos. 6-7.

42. Ibid., fos. 43, 45.

43. The court records of Yemen dating from this period show the success of this system under both Turkish and Yemeni judges.

44. These Turks, and the military system they introduced, are cited as the major contribution of the Turks to modern Yemen by Robert S. Stookey, *Yemen* (Westview Press, Boulder, Colorado, 1978), pp. 164-6.

45. For the further extension of this process in recent times, see Richard Tutwiler and Sheila Carapico, *Yemeni Agriculture and Economic Change* (American Institute for Yemeni Studies, San'a', 1981).

3 THE FREE YEMENI MOVEMENT: 1935-62[1]

Leigh Douglas

The political movement has traditionally played an important role in Arab politics. One only has to reflect on the role of the Arab Nationalist Movement (ANM), the Ba'th, the Nasserists and the Muslim Brotherhood (al-Ikhwan al-Muslimun) in the politics of Egypt, Syria and Iraq to appreciate this. However, the Arab political movement is an extraordinarily difficult concept to define. Most movements developed from a commonly held idea, aim or value, but are otherwise fairly diffuse entities. Rare exceptions are the Muslim Brotherhood in Egypt under Hasan al-Banna's leadership, Ahmad Husain's Young Egypt Party (Misr Fata), and the Ba'th parties of Syria and Iraq, which have adopted fairly rigid party structures with a clearly defined membership, chain of command and unifying ideology (or 'party line'). The Free Yemeni Movement (FYM) (Harakat al-Ahrar al-Yamaniyin) did not share any of these characteristics.

The Free Yemeni Movement was an active participant in North Yemeni politics from the mid-1930s until the 1962 revolution. For much of this period it represented the only opposition to Imams Yahya and Ahmad Hamid al-Din who ruled the Mutawakkilite Kingdom (as North Yemen was then known) from 1918 until 1962. It was not a cohesive entity like the Muslim Brotherhood or the Ba'th parties and, indeed, it ought to be asked at the outset whether the FYM constituted a political movement at all. In part the problem is one of semantics: *haraka* ('movement') represents a different meaning from 'movement' in English. The latter denotes something finite, cohesive and 'tangible', whereas 'haraka' suggests a meaning much more diffuse — more an intellectual force or spread of ideas than a formal 'party-type' structure like the Ba'th and the Muslim Brotherhood. In exploring the role of the FYM as a political movement use should thus be made of Rudolf Heberle's definition that the political movement is 'a special kind of social group' that has constituent parts which are organised, although 'the movements as such are not organised groups'.[2] This chapter is an attempt to define the 'constitutent parts' of the FYM.

Hai'at al-Nidal (1935-6)

The political organisation that was established in Yemen following the Saudi-Yemeni border war of 1934 was Hai'at al-Nidal (the Committee of the Struggle) and it is regarded as the original 'founding spirit' of the FYM.[3] It was founded by Sayyid Ahmad al-Muta' and was a secret movement dedicated to the introduction of reforms. It was not a formal political organisation since it lacked both office-holders and a formal membership, and can perhaps best be described as a group of like-minded intellectuals who shared certain views and attitudes concerning the desirability of introducing material reforms (roads, schools, hospitals and a 'modern' administration in Yemen). Al-Muta' founded the Hai'a during a tour of Yemen on behalf of the Ministry of Education and succeeded in linking a number of individuals, such as Muti' al-Dammaj, Abd al-Salam Sabrah, Abdullah al-Azab, Abdullah al-Shamahi, Abd al-Rahman al-Iryani, Khadim Ghalib al-Wajih and Muhi al-Din al-Ansi, from different regions and confessional backgrounds, who would subsequently remain at the forefront of the FYM. After only a few months the existence of the Hai'a became known to Imam Yahya, who opposed the introduction of any reforms fearing it would challenge his rule, and in 1936 he imprisoned most of those involved.

Fatat al-Fulaihi (*c.* 1935-?)

Contemporaneous with the Hai'a was Fatat al-Fulaihi (the Youth of al-Fulaihi). Al-Fulaihi was a mosque/*madrasa* in San'a' which attracted scholars from all over Yemen. Ahmad al-Shami was a pupil there in the mid-1930s, along with Qadi Yahya Muhammad al-Iryani, Qadi Abdullah al-Jirafi, Qadi Husain al-Maghrabi, Sayyid Abd al-Khaliq al-Amir and Sayyid Ahmad Abd al-Wahhab al-Warith.[4] Scholars would typically spend four or five hours a day smoking the *mada'a* (water pipe) and chewing *qat* while discussing poetry and such books by contemporary Arab authors as they could obtain. One book in particular — Taha Husain's *Ma' al-Mutanabbi* published in 1936 and prohibited in Yemen by the Imam along with other foreign books — was smuggled into Yemen by one of the al-Fulaihi scholars and borrowed by each of the others for two or three days. Each would then study it in the secrecy and privacy of his home. It was just this sort of activity, undertaken in secret and using books and magazines smuggled from abroad by returning Yemeni *émigrés*, that crystallised the opposition to Imam Yahya.

Nadi al-Islah/al-Madrasa al-Ahliya (1934-5)

Both Hai'at al-Nidal and Fatat al-Fulaihi were based in San'a' and drew most of their support from the Zaidi north of Yemen. In al-Hujariya district of Ta'izz Province the situation was a little different. There, Ahmad Muhammad Nu'man began Nadi al-Islah (the Reform Club) and al-Madrasa al-Ahliya (the People's School) in 1934 in the village of al-Dhubhan. The Club functioned as a meeting place for local villagers to read books, newspapers and magazines smuggled into Yemen by local *émigré* workers returning from Aden, which was only a few hours' walk away. The School, which like the Club was conducted in secret, offered a secular education in arithmetic, sciences, geography and history, in contrast to the traditional Islamic education which was the norm in the village *kuttabs* (Quranic schools) sponsored by the Imam. However, whereas those associated with Hai'at al-Nidal and Fatat al-Fulaihi were urban intellectuals, the supporters of Nadi al-Islah and al-Madrasa al-Ahliya were farmers and labourers. This division in the social composition of the early elements of the FYM is an important explanation for the subsequent political development of the Movement.

Al-Katiba al-Ula (1939-40)

In 1937 Ahmad Nu'man and Muhi al-Din al-Ansi (who had earlier been associated with Hai'at al-Nidal) left Yemen and settled in Cairo where they joined a number of other Yemenis including: Muhammad Salih al-Masmari, Yahya Ahmad Zabarah, Ahmad Abd al-Rahman al-Jifri, Muhammad Ali al-Jifri, Ali Muhammad Luqman, Muhammad Mahmud al-Zubairi and Ahmad Hasan al-Hawrash. Most were students at al-Azhar and all were concerned at the lack of economic development in Yemen which they attributed to Imam Yahya's neglect. Thus, in 1939 Nu'man and al-Zubairi formed al-Katiba al-Ula (the First Battalion). Like Hai'at al-Nidal, Fatat al-Fulaihi and Nadi al-Islah, it functioned to promote discussion of the need for reforms in Yemen and contrasted Yemen with the situation they found in Egypt. It also functioned to throw its supporters into the midst of Cairo politics. Ahmad Nu'man became the secretary to Shakib Arslan, the Druze Arab nationalist, and he wrote articles on Yemen for a number of newspapers owned by Muhammad Ali Tahir, the Palestinian publisher. He also wrote several pamphlets, such as *Al-Anna al-Ula* (*The First Moan*), criticising the backwardness of Yemen and calling for the introduction of reforms. Several other members of al-Katiba wrote articles with similar messages in the Egyptian magazines *Al-Rabita al-Arabiya* and *Al-Sadaqa*. At the same time some of those who had been associated a few years earlier with Hai'at al-Nidal launched a magazine in San'a' — *Majallat al-Hikma al-Yamaniya* (*The Yemeni Review of Wisdom*) — as a forum for a similar debate.

Shabab al-Amr bil-Ma'ruf wal-Nahi 'an al-Munkar (1941)

Nu'man returned to Yemen in February 1941 and several months later al-Zubairi changed the name of al-Katiba al-Ula to Shabab al-Amr bil-Ma'ruf wal-Nahi 'an al-Munkar (the Youths for the Enjoining of Good and the Forbidding of Evil). The change in name also signified a change in tactics since the group was by this time closely involved with the Muslim Brotherhood and, in particular, with an Algerian Muslim Brother called Fudail al-Wartalani. Both the Shabab al-Amr and the Muslim Brotherhood shared the desire of returning to the fundamentals of Islam. Thus when al-Zubairi returned to Yemen in July 1941 he carried with him copies of the manifesto of the Shabab al-Amr urging the establishment of cells throughout Yemen to promote Islam and launch an Islamic revival.[5] The Shabab al-Amr advocated a Yemeni *nahda* (renaissance) and, like the Muslim Brotherhood, saw Islam as the vanguard of that renaissance and as the means of raising Yemen from its state of chronic backwardness.

Following al-Zubairi's return to Yemen the former members of Hai'at al-Nidal, Fatat al-Fulaihi and those who had been associated with *Majallat al-Hikma al-Yamaniya* greeted the manifesto enthusiastically and Shabab al-Amr cells were established in San'a' and Ibb. However, Imam Yahya was not so enthusiastic and imprisoned all those associated with the Movement in December 1941, again fearing that it challenged the nature of his rule.

Hizb al-Ahrar al-Yamaniyin (1944-5)

By the time al-Zubairi and the other Shabab al-Amr were released the centre of Free Yemeni activity had shifted to Ta'izz where the Crown Prince, Saif al-Islam Ahmad, had his court. Saif al-Islam Ahmad was perceived by some of the Free Yemenis as a potentially more open-minded ruler than his father, the ageing Imam Yahya. Nu'man, al-Zubairi, Ahmad al-Shami and Zaid al-Mawshki and others who had been associated with the FYM gathered at his court to try and impress upon him their views on the need to introduce reforms since they felt that he was likely to become the Imam after Yahya's death. Until May 1944 Saif al-Islam Ahmad appeared to be fairly responsive to their views but after a particularly stormy argument that month he is alleged to have declared: 'I ask God that I do not die until this sword of mine has been coloured by the blood of the modernists [meaning the Free Yemenis].'[6] Nu'man, al-Shami, al-Zubairi and al-Mawshki thus fled to Aden in early June 1944 and, with the financial help of some Yemeni merchants and the Luqman family, they established Hizb al-Ahrar al-Yamaniyin (the Free Yemeni Party — FYP).

The FYP was the first attempt to organise Free Yemeni activity on party lines and it sought to gather support from among the village associations (*nawadi qarawiya*) that then existed in Aden.[7] Rudimentary elections were held within the first few weeks and Ahmad Nu'man was made President; Muhammad Mahmud al-Zubairi, Director; Zaid al-Mawshki, Vice-President; Ahmad al-Shami, Secretary; and al-Hajj Abdullah Uthman, Treasurer.[8] However, after this auspicious start the FYP failed, largely because of a lack of financial support, and by early 1945 it had virtually ceased to exist. In February of that year al-Shami and al-Mawshki returned to Yemen leaving Nu'man and al-Zubairi to carry the banner of the FYM in Aden.

Jam'iyat al-Islah (1944)

Jam'iyat al-Islah (the Reform Group) was established in Ibb by those Free Yemenis who, in 1941, had briefly formed a cell of al-Zubairi's pro-Brotherhood Shabab al-Amr until its members were arrested. By 1944 most had been released and in June of that year they formed Jam'iyat al-Islah in response to Nu'man's and al-

Zubairi's flight to Aden and the establishment of the FYP. According to the Group's manifesto its aim was nothing less than the 'elimination of the rule of Imam Yahya and his sons'.[9] It also sought the introduction of reforms. The founder of the Group was Qadi Muhammad Ali al-Akwa' and the members included his younger brother, Isma'il, Abd al-Rahman al-Iryani, Muhammad Ahmad Sabrah, Ahmad al-Mu'allimi and Abd al-Rahman Basalama. All were imprisoned in the summer of 1944 and the Group ceased to exist, the Imam having discovered its existence.

Al-Barid al-Adabi (1945–?)

When al-Shami left the FYP in early 1945 and returned to Yemen he established al-Barid al-Adabi (the Literary Post). It was not a formal organisation and, as its name suggests, involved little more than exchanging opinions on literature, poetry and ideas for reform through the post. Its main purpose was to keep alive the links that had been forged over the preceding decade between the former members of al-Muta''s Hai'at al-Nidal and those associated with *Majallat al-Hikma al-Yamaniya*, who were now scattered throughout Yemen as a result of Imam Yahya's policy of breaking up the opposition to his rule. This function was particularly important after the dissolution of Shabab al-Amr and Jam'iyat al-Islah.

Al-Jam'iya al-Yamaniya al-Kubra (1946–8)

Following a series of meetings with the leaders of the Yemeni community in Aden in December 1945, Nu'man and al-Zubairi launched al-Jam'iya al-Yamaniya al-Kubra (the Grand Yemeni Association — GYA) in January 1946. Organisationally it was a much more substantial entity than any that had hitherto been established under the auspices of the FYM and had both a constitution and its own newspaper, *Sawt al-Yaman* (*The Voice of Yemen*).[10] Using the columns of *Sawt al-Yaman* Nu'man and al-Zubairi began a regular correspondence with the Imam and, while unsuccessful in their quest to see the introduction of reforms, succeeded in making their demands known. These were:

(1) the formation of a Cabinet responsible to a Consultative Assembly as in other Arab countries;

(2) the formation of a Consultative Assembly drawn from the 'ulama' and tribal leaders, charged with drawing up plans for reform;
(3) prohibiting the sons of the Imam from interfering in the running of the country.[11]

In November 1946 the GYA's fortunes received a further boost when Imam Yahya's ninth son, Saif al-Islam Ibrahim, arrived in Aden and pledged his support for the organisation. He was immediately proclaimed *za'im* (leader) of the GYA and henceforth was referred to as Saif al-Haqq (Sword of Truth) to distinguish him from his brothers who were all known as Saif al-Islam (Sword of Islam).[12] As a Zaidi, a sayyid and a member of Yemen's Royal House, Ibrahim's leadership was to represent a focal point for all the disparate elements of the FYM.

Although Saif al-Haqq Ibrahim's leadership was essentially nominal — effective leadership remaining in the hands of al-Zubairi and (especially) Nu'man — under his auspices the GYA's activities were essentially fourfold:

(1) The strengthening of ties with the village associations in Aden by sponsoring the establishment of new associations. During 1947, for example, new associations were created for *émigré* workers from Rada', al-Nadira and al-Shaiban.[13]
(2) The establishment of links with other groups of overseas Yemenis. In the mid-1940s there were perhaps as many as three-quarters of a million Yemenis living overseas, mostly in Africa, the Middle East, Europe and America.[14] Some, such as the community in Cardiff, Wales, were fairly well organised whereas others were not. Most, however, generally supported the GYA. As it developed the GYA relied on the overseas communities both as a source of finance to enable it to continue its activities and to add weight to its demand for the introduction of reforms.[15]
(3) The development of contacts with Arab governments and movements. Like many of their peers in other Arab countries the leaders of the GYA were attracted by appeals for Arab unity, perhaps seeing it as a way of ending Yemen's isolation and opening it up to the material and political advances evident in Syria, Egypt and Iraq. The GYA thus conducted a regular correspondence with the Arab League, the Egyptian government

and the Muslim Brotherhood. In seeking contact with other movements the GYA was hoping first to publicise its cause and secondly to encourage other Arabs to write to the Imam appealing to him to introduce reforms, since it was felt that he was more likely to react to foreign criticism than to that of his own subjects.

(4) The maintenance of contact with Free Yemenis in Cairo and San'a'. In particular this meant maintaining contact with Muhammad al-Masmari, Ahmad al-Hawrash, Yahya Zabarah and Muhi al-Din al-Ansi who regularly published articles in the Cairo press, and Ahmad al-Shami, Abd al-Rahman al-Iryani and Abd al-Salam Sabrah in Yemen.

From late 1947 the GYA was eclipsed as the main forum for Free Yemeni activity by developments in Yemen. In September the Algerian Muslim Brother Fudail al-Wartalani, with whom the members of al-Katiba al-Ula had been in contact in 1940, visited Yemen on behalf of the Brotherhood and assisted Free Yemenis in San'a' — among them Ahmad al-Shami, Abd al-Salam Sabrah and Zaid al-Mawshki — to draw up a document known as 'al-Mithaq al-Watani al-Muqaddas' (The Sacred National Pact — SNP) and select Sayyid Abdullah al-Wazir as Imam Yahya's successor. The SNP was designed to ensure that whoever succeeded Imam Yahya would introduce the material and political reforms the Free Yemenis had long desired. A Parliament (Majlis al-Shura) and a Constitutent Assembly (al-Jam'iya al-Ta'sisiya) were to be established to direct the government's policies, thus reducing the post of Imam to a constitutional role, and to oversee the establishment of ministries as in other Arab countries.

At midday on 17 February 1948 Imam Yahya was assassinated and the next day Imam Abdullah al-Wazir was elected.[16] In the immediate aftermath of his election Imam Abdullah pledged his intention to abide by the SNP.[17] However, he was given little chance to prove his word since on 14 March San'a' and the al-Wazir regime fell to Imam Yahya's son and heir, Saif al-Islam Ahmad, who had declared himself the rightful Imam on 25 February. Imam Ahmad executed most of those associated with the al-Wazir regime, including a large number of Free Yemenis. Those of the latter spared execution were imprisoned in the dungeons of al-Nafi' and al-Qahira jails in Hajja and included Ahmad Nu'man, Ahmad al-Shami, Abd al-Rahman al-Iryani, Isma'il and Muhammad al-Akwa', Abdullah al-Sallal, Hamud al-Ja'ifi and Ahmad al-Mu'allimi.[18]

Al-Ittihad al-Yamani (1952–62)

Bereft of leaders following the 1948 al-Wazir *coup*, the FYM went into abeyance. Only two 'voices' of the Movement remained: *Jaridat al-Fudul* (*Superiority*), a weekly newspaper published by Abdullah Abd al-Wahhab Nu'man in Aden from December 1949 until October 1953 and *Jaridat al-Salam* (*Peace*) published by Abdullah al-Hakimi, the head of the Yemeni community in Britain from December 1949 until May 1952. However, in 1951 the Movement was resurrected in Aden when Abd al-Qawi al-Kharbash, a long-standing supporter of the Free Yemenis who had worked on their behalf throughout the 1940s in Ethiopia, held a meeting of former GYA members and proposed the establishment of al-Rabita al-Yamaniya (the Yemeni League).[19] The British authorities in Aden vetoed the proposal, however, fearful that their permission for any movement based in Aden and directed against the rule of Imam Ahmad would adversely affect Anglo-Yemeni relations. Thus it was not until July 1952 that permission was given to establish al-Ittihad al-Yamani (the Yemeni Union).[20] It was declared to be a 'higher council' of the village associations and was presented to the British as a social and welfare organisation representing the interests of the Yemenis in Aden rather than as a political organisation opposed to the situation in North Yemen.[21] Al-Zubairi, who had been in Saudi Arabia at the time of the al-Wazir regime's collapse in 1948 and thus avoided capture, also opened a branch of the Yemeni Union in Cairo with the help of Yemeni students living there.[22] The main branch, however, was in Aden where elections were held and the main posts distributed as follows: Abd al-Qadir Alwan, President; Ali al-Ahmadi, Secretary-General; Ahmad Ashish, Deputy President; Ahmad Haji, Deputy Secretary-General; and Abd al-Rahman Abd al-Rabb, Treasurer. Most were leaders of individual village associations — Alwan, for example was the Vice-President of Nadi Ittihad al-Aghabira (the al-Aghabira area association). However, despite strong personal ties such as this, formal links between the Yemeni Union and the village associations remained weak and the Union was a 'higher council' of the associations in spirit only.

Reluctant to involve itself in Yemeni politics while the leaders of the FYM remained incarcerated in Imam Ahmad's prisons in Hajja, the Yemeni Union concentrated on sending students on educational scholarships to Cairo for the first few years of its existence. However, in the summer of 1955, following the release of most of the Free Yemenis from Hajja in the wake of the al-Thulaya *coup* attempt, Ahmad Nu'man joined al-Zubairi as the leader of the Cairo branch, and his eldest son, Muhammad, took over the leadership of the Aden branch. From then on the Yemeni Union took over from the GYA as the most organised and vocal expression of the FYM. *Sawt al-Yaman* was re-launched as the voice of the Movement, al-Zubairi began regular broadcasts on Cairo Radio's 'Voice of the Arabs' programme in which he reiterated the Free Yemenis' hopes for the introduction of reforms, and Muhammad Nu'man launched an impressive series of Yemeni Union pamphlets.

In line with Nasser's aims of ridding the Arab World of the 'twin evils' of reaction and imperialism, al-Zubairi's broadcasts denounced both the Hamid al-Din and the Yemeni imamate, which predictably upset those Free Yemenis who supported its continuation.[23] His broadcasts and the apparently new (and pro-Nasser) direction that they indicated heralded a three-way breakdown of the FYM between (a) those who supported the Hamid al-Din and the Zaidi imamate *per se*, (b) those who favoured the succession of Muhammad al-Badr (Imam Ahmad's son and heir) and (c) those who were dissatisfied with what they considered the essentially conservative outlook of the Yemeni Union and the 'established' FYM, and were influenced by newer pan-Arab political movements such as the ANM and the Ba'th. As a result of these contradictory divisions within the YU, the organisation virtually ceased to exist as a political organisation in the late 1950s and the impetus for heralding change in Yemen switched to the military, who successfully overthrew the imamate on 26 September 1962 and established the Yemen Arab Republic.

Notes

1. This chapter is extracted from a study of the Free Yemeni Movement submitted to London University's School of Oriental and African Studies as a thesis for a PhD in August 1983. The study was financed by the Social Science Research Council.
2. Rudolf Heberle, *Social Movement: An Introduction to Political Sociology* (New York, 1951), p. 8. Cited in P. Wilkinson, *Social Movement* (Pall Mall, London, 1971), p. 22.
3. A. al-Shamahi, *Al-Yaman: Al-Insan wal-Hadara* (Dar al-Huna, Cairo, 1972),

p. 176. There is some doubt whether an organisation of the name Hai'at al-Nidal actually existed since it is only used by al-Shamahi and those who have obviously read his book. Nevertheless, some sort of organisation existed at this time and to avoid possible confusion I have retained al-Shamahi's name for it.

4. Unpublished interview with Ahmad al-Shami (American University of Beirut, 1969), p. 13.

5. M. al-Zubairi, *Al-Barnamaj al-Awwal min Baramij Shabab al-Amr bil-Ma'ruf wal-Nahi 'an al-Munkar* (no publisher, Cairo, 1941), pp. 15-16. Al-Zubairi perceived the Shabab al-Amr in the same manner as the Brotherhood's 'Rovers' (Firaq al-Jawwal).

6. A. al-Thawwar, *Thawrat al-Yaman* (Dar al-Huna, Cairo, n.d.), p. 47.

7. The village associations were loose groups of *émigré* workers who remained in contact with each other in Aden for purposes of housing, employment, etc. They varied according to size and one of the largest was Nadi al-Dhubhan, composed of *émigré* workers from Ahmad Nu'man's home village of al-Dhubhan.

8. Uthman was the President of Nadi al-Dhubhan.

9. Al-Shamahi, *Al-Yaman*, p. 192.

10. Al-Jam'iya al-Yamaniya al-Kubra, *Qanun* (Matba'at Fatat al-Jazira, Aden, 1946). *Sawt al-Yaman* was published from October 1946 until March 1948.

11. *Majallat al-Sadaqa* (Cairo), no. 69, 5 June 1946, p. 4.

12. *Sawt al-Yaman* (Aden), no. 4, 28 Nov. 1946, p. 4.

13. *Sawt al-Yaman* (Aden), no. 19, 13 Mar. 1947, p. 3; no. 20, 20 Mar. 1947, p. 2; no. 53, 20 Nov. 1947, p. 3.

14. M. S. al-Attar, *Le Sous-développement Economique et Social du Yémen* (Editions Tiers-Monde, Algiers, 1964), p. 66, estimates that there were a million *émigrés* in the 1950s.

15. Unpublished interview with Ahmad Nu'man (American University of Beirut, 1969), p. 152.

16. It is not proposed here to go into the details of the 1948 *coup* which led to the election of Abdullah al-Wazir as Imam, or the attempt to assassinate Imam Yahya a month earlier. (For details of this see Leigh Douglas, 'The False Announcement of Imam Yahya's Death' (in Arabic) in Markaz al-Dirasat wal-Buhuth al-Yamani (ed.), *Thawrat 1948* (Dar al-Awda, Beirut, 1982), pp. 250-62; R. W. Stookey, *Yemen: The Politics of the Yemen Arab Republic* (Westview Press, Boulder, Colorado, 1978), pp. 213-23; M. W. Wenner, *Modern Yemen: 1918-1966* (Johns Hopkins University Press, Baltimore, 1966), pp. 97-104; and A. Hamza, *Lailatan fil-Yaman* (no publisher, Cairo, 1948), pp. 58-87.) Suffice it to say at this stage that the evidence suggests that the plotting of the assassination of Imam Yahya and the 1948, *coup* had less to do with the free Yemenis than with traditional sayyid rivalry for the imamate.

17. British Broadcasting Corporation, *Summary of World Broadcasts: Part 3*, no. 39, 26 Feb. 1948, p. 60.

18. A. M. al-Shami, 'Yemeni Literature in Hajja Prisons: 1948-55' in *Arabian Studies* (G. Hurst, London, 1975), vol. II, pp. 43-60.

19. A. M. Abduh, 'Al-Ittihad al-Yamani min al-Mahd ila-Lahd', Part 1 in *Majallat al-Kalima* (San'a'), no. 47 (May 1978), pp. 22-38.

20. *Jaridat al-Salam* (San'a'), no. 6 (Apr. 1978), p. 7.

21. See constitution of the Yemeni Union in *Jaridat al-Nahda* (Aden), no. 133 8 Jan. 1953, p. 9.

22. There were about 100 Yemeni students in Cairo at this time studying at various secondary schools and Cairo University, including Ali al-Janati, Muhammad An'am Ghalib, Muhsin al-Aini, Muhammad al-Ra'di and Yahya Jughman (*Jaridat al-Nahda* (Aden), nos. 113 14 Aug. 1952, p. 15, and 116 11 Sept. 1952, p. 13).

23. Al-Zubairi's broadcast criticisms of the Hamid al-Din abated in 1956 when Nasser needed Imam Ahmad's support for the anti-British Jeddah Pact and again in 1958-61 when Yemen acceded to the United Arab States. The Yemeni Union's close

identification with Nasser's foreign policy earned it the reputation in some circles of being a mere tool of the Egyptian intelligence service. (Z. al-Wazir, *Muhawala li Fahm al-Mushkila al-Yamaniya* (Mu'assasat al-Risala, Beirut, 1971), p. 101 (footnote 1), p. 104.)

4 THE RISE OF THE NATIONAL LIBERATION FRONT AS A POLITICAL ORGANISATION

Helen Lackner

The development of political movements in Aden took place mainly in the 1950s. Most of these were urban-based both in terms of their membership and their political orientation, paying scant regard to the interior Protectorate which the elite regarded as essentially primitive by comparison with the urban sophistication which it claimed for itself. Only two of these movements drew their support from the hinterland: they were the South Arabian League (SAL) and the National Liberation Front (NLF). The South Arabian League was founded in 1952 and throughout its existence remained an insignificant force, always failing to gain substance, largely because of its association with the rulers of the dominant Sultanate of Lahej and, therefore, its inability to draw support from ordinary tribesmen on two counts: firstly its connection with Lahej and secondly its connection with the ruling group.[1] Its failure left the field wide open for a political organisation based on the interior. This was to be the National Liberation Front which, within four years, developed into a force which overwhelmed the entire country, defeated its rival the FLOSY (Front for the Liberation of Occupied South Yemen), the Federation of South Arabia and all its component statelets, and finally forced Britain to hand over the country to it on independence. It achieved all this without any substantial support from abroad as it lost the support of Egypt in late 1965 when it refused to merge with the more Nasserite urban-based FLOSY. The success of the NLF in the 1960s and the fact that it has remained in power since independence are both excellent reasons to examine its origins and development in some detail.

Looking back at the history of South Arabia, the NLF considers the conflict between the Irshadis and the Alawis as the first manifestation of a 'class'-based conflict in the region, and therefore the Irshadis as its spiritual ancestors. This conflict, which took place in Indonesia in the first twenty years of the century within the Hadrami community, opposed the 'aristocratic' *sada* to the commoners who organised themselves into the Jam'iyat al-Irshad (the Guidance Association) and became known as the Irshadis.[2] The conflict centred on the Irshadis' challenge of the Alawi (i.e. sada) right to transfer all the social rituals traditionally associated with their status to Indonesia where the two groups were not differentiated economically in the way they were in Hadramawt. The bitterness of the conflict can be seen in the fact that it degenerated to the level of street fighting and even deaths due to the determination of both sides. The root of the argument was the Irshadis' challenge of the almost caste-like social structure of Hadramawt where status was inherited and the dominant position of the sada unquestioned and unquestionable, as it was based on religion and manifested itself in all spheres of life, political, economic and social. Although it took place in Indonesia and was over by 1920, the conflict's influence on Hadrami life went on throughout the 1930s and was witnessed by travellers.[3] In the 1930s and during the Second World War, it even took a concrete form when the bin Abdat family of al-Ghurfa asserted allegiance to the Irshadis in their armed struggle against both the Sultans of Hadramawt.

In the post-war period the Movement of Arab Nationalists had a far more direct and substantial influence on the formation and development of the NLF. Formed in Beirut, in the aftermath of the 1948 defeat in Palestine, by a group of Palestinian nationalist intellectuals, the MAN[4] developed in the following decade to include many non-communist nationalists. Its first cells were in the Fertile Crescent, but gradually they extended to the intellectual periphery of the region with branches in Saudi Arabia, Kuwait and Aden. Expansion usually took place through students from these regions joining the Movement while studying in Beirut or Cairo and then forming branches back home when they returned. Although initially anti-communist, the MAN developed into the most radical organisation in the Arab world and it eventually parented all the left-wing movements ranging from the mild opposition in Kuwait to the People's Front for the Liberation of Oman and the Arab Gulf, the National Democratic Front in the Yemen Arab Republic and, most significantly in the Palestinian arena, the People's Front for the Liberation of Palestine and the Democratic Front for the Liberation of Palestine. Of the various movements the MAN engendered, the only one which has yet achieved power is the NLF in Democratic Yemen.

In the 1950s the MAN's main objectives were the recovery of

Palestine, the unification of the Arab world into a single state and Arab liberation, which implied the elimination of Western influence, direct and indirect, from all Arab states. It separated the struggle into stages, the first of which was political, to be followed by a social and economic phase after the success of the first. It was gradually won over to Nasserite socialism in the mid-1950s as a result of Nasser's ability to force the British out of the Canal area, and particularly after the formation of the United Arab Republic with Syria in 1958. The UAR period was the most 'Nasserite' in the history of the MAN. The first signs of a new ideology became apparent in 1960 when the Movement's organ *Al-Hurriya* published an article rejecting the theory of stages and associating political with social and economic struggle. It stated:

> There is no longer a political national question standing separately and posing against a specific social question called 'the workers' question' or 'the question of social progress'. The Arab question has come to mean an overall revolutionary concept which is the melting-pot of the national, political, economic and social ambitions of the progressive Arab masses.[5]

By 1961 the left analysed the breakup of the UAR in terms of class relations, and the differences between the left led by the *Al-Hurriya* group and the right increased in the coming years, culminating at a conference held in May 1964 where they were openly discussed but remained unresolved; thereafter the movement was effectively split between the two groups.

The first public indication of the emergence of the MAN left, i.e. the 1960 article, came only a few months after the formation of the MAN branch in Aden in 1959. It was formed among students and former students, mostly from the interior, who took MAN ideology back into the hinterland and thus formed the first nuclei for a progressive nationalist movement among the tribesmen of South Arabia. The founders of the MAN Aden branch were to play prominent roles in the 1960s in the struggle against the British and in the first years of independence. They were Ahmad al-Salami, Taha Muqbil, Saif al-Dali' and Faisal Abdul-Latif, who were soon joined by Qahtan al-Sha'bi, Salim Rubai'a Ali and Abdul-Fattah Isma'il.[6]

The 26 September revolution and the creation of the Yemen Arab Republic had an immediate and substantial impact on political life in Aden and the Protectorate. Thousands of men rushed to the north to help with the revolution in the earliest days, well before it was known in Aden that the Egyptian regime was shoring up the new Republic in San'a'. Those who rushed north went to join the National Guard (al-Haras al-Watani) to defend the Republic against its enemies, and later remained to fight the Saudi-backed Imam's counter-offensive. These men included tribesmen from the hinterland, northerners who had migrated to Aden as workers, students from Aden and others originating from the interior, as well as tribal leaders from border regions who supported the Republic and Yemeni emigrants to the Gulf states working there in armies and as civilians.[7]

While in the North, the Southern Yemenis soon started meeting to discuss the situation in the South and what they could do about it. A First Conference was convened by the Aden MAN branch and held in San'a' in February 1963. It was attended by over 1,000 representatives of revolutionary organisations in the South, all of which were to join the NLF. This conference formed a Preparatory Committee and in June 1963 a further conference was held in San'a' where the National Liberation Front for the Liberation of Occupied South Yemen (al-Jabha al-Qawmiya li-Tahrir al-Junub al-Yamani al-Muhtall) was officially founded, and later announced on San'a' radio. The South Arabian MAN was its nucleus and thus the NLF reflected the ideological divisions and debates of the Movement. By the end of 1963 it included nine other organisations, some of which represented tribal groups, like the Formation of the Tribes, the Mahra Youth Organisation and the Yafa'i Reform Front, while the rest represented Arab political tendencies which were significant at the time: the Nasserite Front, the Secret Organisation of Free Officers and Soldiers, the Revolutionary Organisation of Free Men of Occupied South Yemen, the Patriotic Front, the Aden Revolutionary Vanguard and the Revolutionary Organisation of Youth in Occupied South Yemen.

At that early stage in its development, the NLF as a whole had no particular ideology beyond its commitment to armed struggle and it accepted anyone committed to armed struggle to gain full independence from Britain. The creation of the NLF marked the beginning of a serious decline in support for the politically oriented Adeni-based organisations like the Aden Trade Union Congress and its political adjunct, the recently formed People's Socialist Party, which opposed armed struggle and called for political means to achieve their ends. The mass of workers in Aden turned towards the NLF as they found the concept of armed struggle appealing, sometimes on the basis of clearly reasoned political argument but also possibly as a modernised form of traditional tribal armed conflict. The NLF was also significantly different from existing political organisations in the social composition of its supporting groups and of its leadership. Both included social strata which had not previously been integrated into any political tendency, mainly the tribesmen who had emigrated to Aden and further afield in search of work and thus developed a social and political consciousness while working in the Gulf or Saudi Arabia in construction, or even the armed forces, as well as those who had stayed at home or returned there. The NLF also attracted the support of educated youth, again mainly from the interior, who had studied in Aden but, unlike the Adenis, had retained roots in their home areas and used these contacts to further the aims of the NLF. Being essentially tribesmen, they did not come from the top strata of society, but rather from the social group which included the majority of the population and whose economic circumstances varied from poverty to comparative comfort. In brief, the NLF attracted the support of social groups which had not previously been mobilised and whose interests could be turned towards socialist policies, rather than people who had a vested interest in the traditional social structure.

In its early days, the NLF also benefited from the support of the Egyptian political and military authorities in the YAR. This was not an automatic consequence of Nasserite Egypt's hostility to British colonialism, but rather a considered position taken as a result of historical circumstances. The fact that the Imam was alive and rallied tribal support to join battle with the republicans had a considerable effect on the early days, and indeed on the entire nature, of the republican regime. The Imam rapidly obtained the support of Saudi Arabia for his war against the republicans while the regime in San'a' equally rapidly got Egyptian assistance, an assistance that was soon to become stifling and turn many people against it. However, in 1963 the NLF was promised much help from the Egyptians and the San'ani authorities who waited to see which way Britain's support would go before fully backing armed struggle in the South. Britain hesitated between supporting the Imam and recognising the Republic and during this period neither Sallal, the YAR President, nor the Egyptians provoked them, hoping that Britain would eventually recognise the Republic.[8] It was only after February 1963 when the British decided to support the Imam and to encourage the delivery of arms and supplies through Baihan that Egyptian Intelligence decided to back the organisation which was forming itself into the NLF; for the first, and by no means last, time in this conflict the Egyptians showed that their support was based on their own national interest and not on the correctness of a cause.

The NLF's existence was officially announced on 28 July 1963 on Radio San'a' in a statement which emphasised the Front's concentration on co-ordinating urban and rural struggle:

> Our aspiration in the Occupied Yemeni South has now entered a phase which demands a fundamental change in the methods of the struggle to win complete independence and to overcome imperialism. The weakest point is the lack of co-ordination in the struggle in the Yemeni South as a whole. The major reason for that is the lack of a common command for national action in Aden and the Amirates. Another reason lies in the circumstance that the majority of the political organisations limit their activity to Aden . . .[9]

The coming years were to show that the NLF meant what it said. In the summer of 1963 Front members concentrated their energies on training and equipping, while armed struggle was already taking place in Hawshabi and Yafa'i under tribal leadership. The NLF officially launched armed struggle on 14 October 1963 in Radfan. This area, according to the British part of the Dhala' Amirate, had always been a centre of resistance and the British once again treated the problem at first as a merely tribal one. They failed to see that they were dealing with a completely new type of organisation whose appeal and support would strengthen throughout the Protectorate and that, under four years later, it would bring down the structures set up over a century by Britain like the proverbial house of cards. The Radfan campaign has been described in detail elsewhere,[10] mainly from the British point of view, and will not be discussed here. All we need to notice is that the British expected to defeat the rebellion in a matter of days and, in fact, it took them over six months and necessitated the import of SAS elite troops and other reinforcements to achieve no more than a mere foothold in the Radfan area, at the cost of significant defeats and casualties.

In 1964 and 1965 the NLF extended its struggle to Dhala', Dathina and Awdhali, as well as beginning armed struggle in Aden itself in August 1964. What distinguished these clashes from the earlier tribal revolts and attacks on the British in Aden was the organisation behind them. For the first time a single organisation was involved simultaneously both in Aden and the interior, hitting the British and the amirates they supported in a two-pronged attack: armed struggle in the interior had a mainly political impact and went side-by-side with political infiltration and education in the amirates; the objective was to undermine these puppet authorities and this was so successful that, when the time came in 1967, they all fell without any resistance. In Aden, attacks were concentrated on targets carefully chosen for their collaboration with the British. The other major effect of armed struggle by the NLF in 1964 was to gain it enormous popularity among the working people of Aden and the non-privileged classes outside, at the expense of existing political organisations. In response to this loss of support, and as a result of al-Asnag's failure to gain British support for his policies, the People's Socialist Party created the Organisation for the Liberation of the Occupied South in May 1965. This was the fruit of negotiations beteeen al-Asnag and the SAL in Cairo in July 1964 and March 1965, discussions at which attempts to include the NLF had been totally unsuccessful. OLOS finally included the PSP, remnants of the SAL, a few Adeni merchants and ex-Sultans Ali Abdul-Karim of Lahej and Ahmad bin Abdullah al-Fadhli, in an organisation whose stated aim was the expulsion of the British by military means.

The creation of OLOS, and, more important, the developing differences within the MAN at the Arab level, led to the need for the NLF's First Congress which was held in June 1965 in Ta'izz, almost two years after the founding of the Front. The previous year, in May 1964, an NLF delegation led by Qahtan al-Sha'bi had participated in a National Conference of the MAN which had debated the issues which separated the rising left Marxist-oriented part of the Movement from the old nationalist one. As no agreement was reached the Movement was thereafter divided, in fact if not in name. The conference's decisions were confused as, for example, the left distanced itself from Nasserism but wanted financial support from Nasser while the right opposed this; in the end pragmatism won the day and the conference chose financial support.[11] The NLF delegation played no active part in the ideological debate but sided with the right and this was later challenged by other elements in the NLF who had received reports of the debate and found themselves in closer agreement with the YAR branch of the MAN which had sided with the left.

The Rise of the National Liberation Front 53

The NLF held its First Congress between 22 and 25 June 1965 in Ta'izz. By the time it opened the NLF had expelled some tribal leaders and the congress was devoted to the discussion of a long-term programme which was published as the *National Charter*. It also published resolutions which recognised the problem presented by OLOS:

> The Conference affirms that the NLFOS is the sole representative of our people in the South, so it declares . . . the continuation of its armed struggle until the aspirations of the people are fulfilled in full.[12]

Other resolutions indicated the NLF's concern about wider world issues, denouncing imperialist aggression in North and South Vietnam, intervention in the Dominican Republic and oppression in Angola, Mozambique, Guinea-Bissau, the Congo, Southern Rhodesia and South West Africa. The congress also elected an Executive Committee of eight members who included Qahtan al-Sha'bi, Faisal Abdul-Latif al-Sha'bi, Taha Muqbil, Salim Zain, Ali Salami and Saif al-Dali'.

The *National Charter* (*Al-Mithaq al-Qawmi*) is the only document of political analysis produced by the Front before independence, as the next two congresses, in 1966, were entirely devoted to the problem of FLOSY. It is a long analysis of colonialist rule and a programme for NLF rule. Its objectives are worth noting, given the phases which the NLF has been through since then. Its introduction sets the tone for the document; referring to the armed struggle which had been launched in the South, it stated that:

> This revolutionary movement is the expression of a global conception of life which aims basically at the radical transformation of the social reality created by colonialism through all its concepts, values and social relations, which are founded on exploitation and tyranny, and to determine the type of life to which our people aspires and the type of relations which it wants to see installed on the local, regional, national and international levels.[13]

The *Charter* emphasises the need to get rid not only of British occupation and British military bases, but also of the rule of the 'agent reactionary sultans'. Unsurprisingly, given that the document was published after the revolution in the North and that Yemeni nationalists had called for unity since the 1950s, the *Charter* states:

> The Arab people in the Yemeni area, north and south, are part of the Arab nation. The Yemeni area is an integral part of the Arab homeland, and it is a single unit historically through shared struggle and fate. The restoration of unity of our Arab people in the Yemeni area, north and south, on the road towards free Arab unity, is a popular demand and a necessity imposed by the revolution.[14]

In analysing the economic situation the *Charter* concentrates on the great gap which exists between Aden and the under-developed rural areas. In discussing the rural areas, it blames the poverty of the interior on 'feudal landowners, primarily sultans and amirs who exploit the people and plunder their land and wealth'.[15] It points out that small farmers are exploited by the large landowners who are the only ones to extract a profit from the land. The importance it gives to the rural areas is reasserted in the resolutions it broadcast:

> In view of the fact that the tribal sector constitutes a large proportion of our people, and as a result of the imperialist policy which has kept them in a state of ignorance and backwardness, the Conference recognised the need to concentrate on enlightening, taking care of and raising the level of this sector so that it might catch up with the revolution and play its historical part in it.[16]

The NLF's general economic programme is based on the following principles:

> (a) complete economic liberation from foreign exploiting capitalism and colonialist companies; (b) the building of a national economy on a new and healthy basis compatible with the principles of social justice, and achieved through popular control over primary products and the means of production; (c) thorough planning and guidance of material, human and scientific means to achieve this aim, according to a general plan for economic and social development; (d) the private sector can play an important role in the country's development provided it avoids exploitation and monopoly and limits itself to the areas allocated to it by the law; it can operate alone, in association, or in co-ordination with

the public sector, according to the development plan and general economic organisation.[17]

While not advocating solutions associated with Marxist socialism, the *Charter* does challenge programmes linked with capitalism: it does not propose nationalisations but restricts the role of the private sector within limits defined by an overall development plan, and it also suggests social equity and popular control over the economy.

In its sectoral analysis the *Charter* gives considerable attention to agriculture and, here again, while not proposing the nationalisation of land, the programme implies a new social order in the rural areas. After pointing out that the sultans seized the people's land and water by force or by obliging them to sell at ridiculous prices, it calls for the return of land to the small peasants. Tribally owned lands are to be reclaimed, surveyed and redistributed to small peasants. The problem of water is identified as mainly reliance on flood waters which produced endemic drought and famine. The solution proposed is based on the introduction of modern technology, the drilling of boreholes, building dams and better water distribution. Mechanisation is seen as the solution to the problem of productivity. Politically, the *Charter* proposes legislation to improve the conditions of agricultural workers and tenant farmers, as well as to control agricultural production.

The *Charter*'s social programme concentrates on the problem of the rural-urban gap and proposes to close it by bringing electricity to the rural areas, developing modern agricultural machinery, processing agricultural products, planning villages, building houses, schools and health units and providing clean water supplies. The *Charter* proposes to make education freely available to all, as well as health facilities, doctors and medicines. It discusses the position of women, making proposals which must have been considered controversial by the right of the Movement, and holds colonialism responsible for the backwardness in which women have been kept by misrepresenting Islam to keep women in a state of obscurity, ignorance and slavery, and proposes:

> to restore their natural rights to women, and their equality with men in bearing their social responsibility, thus providing the basis for human justice and giving women the position in life which they are entitled to as full participants, developing their utmost social and productive abilities.[18]

Its one clear call for socialism is found in the discussion of internal affairs when the *Charter* says that:

> Social development and progressive transformation from the present backward stage to the stage of socialist construction require that all the working popular forces carry their responsibilities in construction.[19]

The sections of society which are expected to support its aims and fight for them are 'the popular forces of workers, peasants, soldiers, revolutionary intellectuals and students' and in particular the workers and peasants who are to form an alliance which is the guarantor of social progress. On the whole the *Charter*'s ambiguities reflect the debate within the NLF between left and right, and are seen in the fact that it sometimes uses clearly socialist language, calling, for example, for the alliance between workers and peasants, and the construction of socialism, but failing to suggest nationalisation. However, despite its ambiguities, the *Charter* puts the NLF in the vanguard of left-wing movements in the Arab world, and this is important as, even in 1965, its likelihood of coming to power was higher than that of other left-wing groups in the region, given the strength of its position on the ground and British commitment to leaving South Arabia.

The *Charter*'s discussion of foreign affairs was less of a challenge to current progressive Arab opinion, as it did not directly challenge Nasserism, despite the fact that by then differences were already openly emerging between the MAN and Nasserite Egypt and, more specifically, the NLF and their comrades from the YAR had already had the opportunity of noticing that Egyptian policy tended to be motivated more by Egypt's national interests than by the furthering of ideology and revolution: when the two did not coincide the first had priority, as was seen first in 1963 when the Egyptians waited for Britain to side with the Imam before supporting the NLF. Two months later a further example was to take place when Nasser reached an agreement with King Faisal of Saudi Arabia over North Yemen, which, if it had been implemented, would have presented serious problems for the furthering of the revolution. The *Charter* itself praised Nasser and his historic role in the Arab world:

> The Arab revolution of 23 July 1952 in Egypt was the tangible incarnation of the beginning of the process of renaissance of the

Arab Liberation movement . . . Through its revolutionary capacity, its selflessness and its understanding it succeeded in defeating all the colonialist pacts . . . Thus the UAR continues to provide the fundamental support for the Arab revolutionary movement, for unity and progress. The part of the UAR in the support, from the beginning, of our people's struggle, by all necessary means, is a great historic role which deserves to be respected.[20]

The differences between right and left in the NLF reflected those in the MAN and the left were turning towards Marxist socialism, under the influence of Fanon and Guevara among others; they admired Cuba, China and the struggle of the Vietnamese. By contrast, the right favoured continued close relations with Nasser and internally wanted more authoritarian structures within the NLF which would leave the leadership unchallenged and prevent the rank and file from gaining power. The strength of the left and the extent of its support at the grass-roots level were to become manifest in the coming months. Many cadres and members in the South found the *Charter* too right-wing and challenged it in the summer of 1965. Members from Adeni schools sent questions to the leadership, challenging the Nasserite ideology they saw in the *Charter*. This led to a number of smaller meetings which would probably have led to a split had not more urgent problems arisen in the form of the Egyptians' efforts to force a merger between the NLF and OLOS. This pressure was not totally unwelcome to the right-wing NLF leadership who saw it as a way out of the ideological debate. As a result of this, the *Charter* and post-independence policies had to be left to future discussions which, as it turned out, were not to take place till after independence when the NLF was in power. From late 1965 and throughout 1966 the NLF was dominated by the struggle with OLOS.

Given the close relationship which existed between al-Asnag and the Nasserites it was obviously in their joint interests, but specifically in the interests of the Egyptians, to force a merger between OLOS and the NLF after the creation of the former. Ideologically, OLOS was much closer to the Egyptians and its formation came at a time when, as we have seen, substantial elements of the NLF were rapidly drifting away from Nasserism. In order to control them and in the hope of strengthening OLOS with the fighting experience gained by the NLF in its two years of struggle, Egyptian Intelligence, who were responsible for South Yemeni affairs, concentrated their energies on the merger. That it would not be easy was clear as the NLF had already, as we have seen, refused to join OLOS before its formation. The problems which the right-wing leadership was finding within the NLF may have made it more receptive to Egyptian suggestion and on 13 January 1966 three NLF leaders announced in Cairo the formation of the Front for the Liberation of Occupied South Yemen (FLOSY) which was supposed to represent the merger between OLOS and the NLF (and the exclusion of the SAL elements within OLOS). The NLF members and cadres were violently opposed to this and rejected the merger, so three MAN leaders, George Habash, Hani al-Hindi and Muhsin Ibrahim were sent to Ta'izz to try and mediate between the two parts of the NLF, those supporting and those opposing the merger; the first two represented the right of the MAN while the third represented the left. Two months of intensive discussions failed to solve the problem and in March the Egyptians invited the NLF leaders to Cairo, supposedly for discussions. On arrival the leaders were detained and thus missed the NLF's second congress held in June 1966 in Jibla. This meeting rejected the NLF-OLOS merger, expelled the three leaders who had signed the January agreement (Salim Zain, Taha Muqbil and Ali Salami) and elected a new Executive Committee of eleven members who included Abdul-Fattah Isma'il, Muhammad Ali Haitham, Salim Rubai'a Ali, Ali Antar and Ali Salim al-Beedh.

Despite this clear rejection of the merger, the Egyptians did not give up and continued putting pressure on the NLF, thus leading to a new agreement in August signed in Alexandria; this was made by Qahtan al-Sha'bi, Faisal Abdul-Latif and Abdul-Fattah Isma'il. The reaction of the NLF on the ground was, once again, one of clear rejection of any form of merger with the OLOS and they also increasingly rejected Nasserist policies. The NLF membership lost patience with the continued attempts to force the merger and Egypt's many tactics to weaken it, such as attributing all military action to FLOSY and withholding funds from the NLF. They ceased to relate to their central office and started co-ordinating their activities amongst themselves, and also considered other sources of finance and supplies. With the approach of the third anniversary of the launching of armed struggle in October 1966, all the NLF's organisations in Aden threatened to split unless the merger with OLOS was formally ended. They won the argument and the NLF held a Third Congress in November 1966 in Khamr, where it totally disassociated itself from FLOSY, which thereafter was nothing

The Rise of the National Liberation Front 59

more than the armed branch of the PSP. This break with Nasserism meant that the NLF in future would have to rely on its own resources and this, concretely, meant that finances were then raised from bank robberies and expropriation of money from the capitalist companies, as well as increased contributions from political supporters. The congress also added another ten people to the previously elected Executive Committee, most of whom were leaders from the interior who were involved in armed struggle. Thereafter, the relationship between the NLF and FLOSY was to be one of open hostility and conflict for another year, until the final victory of the NLF and independence.

The conflict with FLOSY did not prevent the NLF from continuing the struggle in the hinterland in 1966 and 1967; this mainly involved the political mobilisation of the people, but in Hadramawt a significant left-wing political movement took place in that period, and made socialist reforms in land tenure and social organisation. They held demonstrations and mobilised support from tribesmen; their main contribution to the struggle was their control of an area in which the nationalist movement was under serious threat by Saudi Arabia. It was generally believed that Britain, Saudi Arabia and the sultans were planning the secession of Hadramawt and Mahra from the rest of Southern Arabia, either to form an independent state or to attach it to Saudi Arabia. The presence and activities of the Hadramawt Arab Socialist Party, its ability to gather support for continued unity with the South and its close links with the NLF and participation in its activities were significant factors in the final NLF victory in that area.

The NLF's most important activities were, however, the gradual takeover of the sultanates of the Federation as it collapsed, the British withdrew their forces and the former sultans escaped abroad. The first amirate to fall was Dhala' in June, and they all fell in rapid succession with the fall of the Kathiri and Qa'aiti Sultanates of Hadramawt in September. The occupation of sultanates by the Front while the British were still formally in control led to absurd situations such as the one in Baihan described by the High Commissioner:

We had come to threaten the use of British aircraft against an attempt by a man who was still nominally under British protection, to recover his State by attacking from across the frontier the rebels who had usurped his power with the aid of a battalion which we were helping to pay and arm and which was still nominally under British command.[21]

This was in September, two months before the final withdrawal. The Front occupied Socotra on 29 November, hours before independence, and this was the last outpost to come under its control. The NLF's most spectacular action took place in June-July with the occupation of Crater. This had particular symbolic importance as it was the first Arab victory after the June 1967 Six-Day Arab-Israeli War, which had caused universal depression in the Arab world; thus the NLF's ability to take and control the heart of the city of Aden for two weeks, closing it to all outsiders, represented an important symbolic victory over imperialism, and locally showed its power to the British who had not expected such strength. The actual occupation and battle for Crater have been described in detail elsewhere.[22]

There was little armed conflict between the NLF and FLOSY in the interior, for the simple reason that the NLF was unchallenged except in Wahidi and Awlaqi where FLOSY gained temporary control, but elsewhere FLOSY suffered from its urban orientation and lack of rural support. In Aden where FLOSY had money and arms thanks to its Egyptian support, the conflict was violent and included many incidents of members of one organisation murdering members of the other. Serious fighting took place between the two organisations in January when the NLF called a general strike opposed by FLOSY, who retaliated by blowing up the communist press. Later, in September when the NLF appeared to be the dominant force, FLOSY tried to reverse the balance by organising an invasion from Ta'izz; this was stopped by the NLF in Dar Sa'ad and Shaikh Uthman. Finally, in early November fighting took place in Shaikh Uthman when full-scale battles opposed the two organisations, and the NLF's decisive victory led the South Arabian Army to declare its support for the NLF, thus leaving it the only candidate for power after independence.

By September 1967 the Federation of South Arabia had completely disintegrated and the High Commissioner, Sir Humphrey Trevelyan, recognised this publicly on 5 September when he offered to enter into negotiations with the nationalist movement. As far as the British were concerned at this point there were still three possible contenders for taking over the country on their departure: the NLF, FLOSY and the army. Over the next two months the NLF defeated FLOSY militarily on the ground and the army stated allegiance to the NLF. As Trevelyan put it, 'we only had the choice to hand over to the NLF or to nobody. We were lucky in at last finding someone to whom we might be able to hand over in peace.'[23] The fact that the British had not seriously considered the NLF previously or had any real awareness of the nature of developments in the previous two years is indicated by a further statement of his to the effect that up to November 1967 'We had no direct contact with the NLF leaders, but by this time we were negotiating through senior Arab officers who were in close touch with them.'[24] Within three weeks in November negotiations were started and completed in Geneva and resulted in the signature of an agreement between the British and the NLF on 29 November 1967, in such a rush that the NLF leaders who signed the agreement did not get home till after independence. A distinctly unceremonious and hasty retreat had been completed, and the NLF was left to deal with a particularly difficult internal situation: dissension within itself, attacks from FLOSY, the SAL and the Saudis, and a catastrophic economic situation.

Notes

1. The sociology of the South Arabian League and other Aden-oriented political movements is analysed in detail in A. S. Bujra, 'Urban Elites and Colonialism', *Middle Eastern Studies*, vol. VI, no. 2 (1970), pp. 189-211.
2. The Alawi-Irshadi conflict and its repercussions in Hadramawt are fully discussed in A. S. Bujra, 'Political Conflict and Stratification in Hadramaut — I', *Middle Eastern Studies*, vol. III, no. 4 (1967), pp. 355-75.
3. F. Stark, *The Southern Gates of Arabia* (John Murray, London, 1936), p. 217.
4. Here I am presenting nothing more than a very crude summary of the MAN, concentrating on the features most relevant to the NLF. The most reliable source on the MAN in English is W. Kazziha, *Revolutionary Transformation in the Arab World* (C. Knight, London, 1975).
5. *Al-Hurriya*, 2 May 1960, quoted in Kazziha, *Revolutionary Transformation*, p. 65.
6. Fathi Abdul-Fattah, *Tajribat al-thawra fil-Yaman al-Dimuqratiya* (Beirut, 1974), p. 43; Ahmad Ati al-Masri, *Tajribat al-Yaman al-Dimuqratiya* (Cairo, 1974), p. 188; J. P. Viennot, 'L'expérience révolutionnaire du Sud-Yémen', *Maghreb* (Oct. 1973), p. 74.
7. This account of the formation of the NLF has benefited mainly from the following sources: Abdul-Fattah, *Tajribat*, pp. 48ff; Viennot, 'L'expérience révolutionnaire', pp. 74-5; J. P. Viennot, 'Aden, de la lutte pour la libération à l'indépendance, *Orient* (Paris, 1969), pp. 15-17; Ati al-Masri, *Tajribat*, pp. 246ff.
8. British policies are thoroughly discussed in F. Halliday, *Arabia without Sultans* (Penguin, Harmondsworth, 1974), pp. 178-226. He also goes into far more detailed discussion of the fighting and the political manoeuvres of the 1960s.
9. Quoted in Halliday, *Arabia*, p. 192.

10. Halliday, *Arabia*, pp. 195-9; J. Paget, *Last Post: Aden 1964-67* (Faber, London, 1969), pp. 23-110; T. Geraghty, *Who Dares Wins* (Fontana, London, 1981), pp. 82-100; P. Warner, *The Special Air Service* (Kimber, London, 1971), pp. 232-5.
11. Kazziha, *Revolutionary Transformation*, pp. 74-81.
12. BBC, *Summary of World Broadcasts*, ME 1902, 6 July 1965.
13. Adel Rida, *Thawrat al-Junub* (Cairo, 1969), pp. 85-6. Translation of this quote from Halliday, *Arabia*, p. 194.
14. Rida, *Thawrat*, p. 87.
15. Ibid., p. 88.
16. BBC, ME 1902.
17. Rida, *Thawrat*, p. 90.
18. Ibid., p. 97.
19. Ibid., p. 97.
20. Ibid., pp. 100-1.
21. H. Trevelyan, *The Middle East in Revolution* (Macmillan, London, 1970), p. 253.
22. Paget, *Last Post*, pp. 216-31; C. Mitchell, *Having Been a Soldier* (Hamish Hamilton, London, 1969), pp. 1-16, 169-237.
23. Trevelyan, *Middle East*, p. 258.
24. Ibid., p. 259.

5 THE PDRY: THREE DESIGNS FOR INDEPENDENCE

Salem Omar Bukair

Introduction

The revolutionary experience in the People's Democratic Republic of Yemen is part and parcel of a general Arab and world national liberation movement, and thus can be studied in the light of the general laws and characteristics governing contemporary revolutions in developing countries. Nevertheless, it is one of the objectives of the present chapter to expose local factors that spring from the relevant socio-economic stage of development, tradition, history and culture. As for the scope of my chapter, it confines itself to tackling the main questions pertaining to the early phase, i.e. the beginning and the spread of armed struggle, the social basis of the 14 October revolution and factors leading to the final victory of the National Front for the Liberation of Occupied South Yemen.[1]

On the day of independence, 30 November 1967, when the NLF seized power, many Arab and foreign countries were taken by surprise: some Arab countries went through a short period of indecision, other states issued declarations containing clear denouncements and accusations of intrigue and collaboration between Britain and the NLF, and a third group did not recognise the emerging People's Republic of South Yemen (PRSY),[2] adopting instead a stance of support for counter-revolutionary forces. *Al-Hurriya*, a Lebanese magazine, commented that while an (Aden) Arab delegation had been having negotiations with Britain which would lead to independence, other Arab countries were uncaring about the whole affair, and it stressed that such a situation would certainly weaken the Yemeni cause. Writing a few days after independence the Kuwaiti magazine *Al-Tali'a*, consistent with its policy of support for Yemeni and Arab unity, did not welcome the appearance of the fourteenth Arab state, but rather urged immediate unity with the Yemen Arab Republic (YAR). As for British attitudes, interesting comments were made by two writers. Sir Kennedy

Trevaskis, ex-High Commissioner of Aden and chief architect of the South Arabian Federation, made the curious assumption that South Arabia had been left to its ancient ruler — anarchy.[3] R. J. Gavin said, in the last paragraph of his scholarly and interesting work, 'The initiative then passed to the leaders of the national revolution whose attitudes coincided with those of reforming British officials in more ways than either would have cared to admit.'[4] Such obscure statements and unsustained judgements lead to the confusion of remote observers who can only read or hear about Yemen. For Sir Kennedy Trevaskis, South Arabia is nothing unless neatly organised along British lines, i.e. federation, constitution, consultative committees, legislative council, London conferences, responsible government and maintenance of a military base with the consent of the natives. In appearance only do the attitudes seem to coincide but in reality they are quite diverse. The British in the last phase of their rule planned to unite the area and prepare it for independence; so did the nationalists, but as to what form of unity and the content of independence they differed considerably.

In this study of revolutionary experience in Yemen, I try to give an objective account, mingling narration with analytical exposition. I have drawn extensively from first-hand sources, such as documents of the NLF and other national parties, as well as from local and Arab periodicals. Other Arab and foreign references were also consulted.

The Founding of the NLF and Beginning of the 14 October Revolution

In the fifties the call for national unity and consolidation of revolutionary forces was overwhelming. The United National Front was formed in 1955 and played a significant role in boycotting elections for the Aden Legislative Council, and in the organisation and unification of trade unions. Similar organisations followed suit; the National Congress appeared in 1956, People's Union 1958, National Union 1959, National Block 1960, Block of National Organisations 1961.[5] These unions were a sort of a coalition of workers' trade unions, political parties, cultural societies and sports clubs having common objectives — appeals for a general strike, organisation of massive demonstrations, signing protest memoranda, distribution of pamphlets, etc.

On 28 March 1961 Q. al-Sha'bi presented a paper requested by the periodical *Ahrar al-Yaman* affirming that there was a pressing need to found a national front for the whole Yemeni region, to shoulder the task of liquidating the Imam's regime and liberating South Yemen from the yoke of colonialism.[6] Furthermore, he presented his own suggestions to be worked out as an outline for the national charter of the front. Subsequently, a preparatory committee for a national congress was formed consisting of A. M. Nu'man, M. M. al-Zubairi, M. al-Aini, M. A. Nu'man and A. al-Mu'allimi. Four leading organisations — the Aden Trade Union Congress, Yemeni Union, Arab Nationalist Movement and Arab Ba'th Socialist Party — had been invited to a national congress to be held in Cairo in February 1962 but, busy with their internal conflicts, the Yemeni Union leaders asked for a postponement. The Arab Nationalist Movement from the beginning of 1961 had elaborated its plan for armed revolution and was merely awaiting appropriate conditions: such favourable circumstances were created by the success of the 26 September revolution in North Yemen.

A few days after the beginning of the 26 September revolution thousands of workers, tribesmen, soldiers and officers from South Yemen gathered in San'a' ready to protect the emerging Republic. These nationalists, filled with new ideas and new feelings, began to discuss the political situation in South Yemen and the means of liberating it from colonialism. A meeting was held on 24 February 1963 in Dar al-Sa'ada, San'a', attended by more than two thousand.[7] The meeting nominated a preparatory committee of eleven to work out a national charter. The *National Charter* was approved on 5 March 1963 and a Front for the Liberation of South Yemen was proclaimed. Finally, in August 1963, under the influence of the Arab Nationalist Movement, the name was changed to National Front for the Liberation of Occupied South Yemen, the former charter revised, and a special committee was formed to prepare for armed struggle.[8] The NLF consisted of the following secret organisations: Arab Nationalist Movement; Tribal Brigades; Nasserist Front; Secret Organisation of Free Soldiers; Yafa'i Reform Front; Revolutionary Organisation of Free South Yemenis. However, the leading role was played by Arab Nationalists.[9]

Armed struggle began on the eve of 14 October 1963. On this same day fell the first martyr, Ghalib bin Rajih Labbuza.[10] From the day of that historic event armed struggle in South Yemen did not cease until the achievement of independence in 1967. The immediate cause was the attempt to put Radfan under the rule of the Dhal'a Amir and force it to join the South Arabian Federation.[11] Further, to humiliate the Radfan tribes, they were ordered to deliver their weapons to British authority. The tribes refused the order and shooting was the reply. The start of armed struggle in a naturally fortified region, the Radfan mountains, gave it a good chance of survival, especially in the first phase when it was isolated from the outer world. The British dealt with the armed revolution in a traditional-style punitive campaign — burning villages and fields, demolishing houses, killing livestock and using prolonged siege tactics. For the British, the first impact of the 14 October revolution was violent. In the last three months of 1963 there was shooting every night at British military camps in Al-Thamir, attacks on British patrols and acts of sabotage on the strategic Aden-Dhal'a road.[12] British Intelligence began to notice unusual movements amongst Radfanis, the transfer of families (women and children) from Radfan to other regions or to the north, the arrival of an increased number of uniformed fighters from the north and the signing of an amnesty by tribesmen in Radfan and Yafa'i. Dissidents were estimated to number approximately two hundred with support from a further thousand.[13] It is of some interest to examine the British approach to events in Radfan, the measures taken, changes in policy, etc. The British understood what was going on there as a simple tribal rebellion and dealt with it accordingly. Thus they:

sent a categorical ultimatum to dissident leaders (an estimated twelve) to surrender immediately or leave the region;
besieged the Radfan region;
warned other tribes, e.g. in Halmain, not to co-operate with the Radfanis on pain of being penalised for sheltering government enemies.

On the other hand the 14 October revolution was also understood as a sort of mercenary operation or work of Egyptian agents. In this context we come across statements in British secret reports such as Egyptian commander Murtaji preferring to operate inside the Western Protectorate instead of conducting border operations, or Radfan fighters carrying out as many operations as possible for the sole purpose of collecting money and weapons.[14]

British policy had been influenced by such ideas, so material support to Imam al-Badr was increased. The British government recruited more mercenaries to fight against the republican regime, and granted the royalists subsidies and weapons through the Sharif of Baihan. Moreover, aggressive attacks (mainly bombing) were started against the border towns of Harib, Qa'taba and Baidha. The British government was all this time trying to make a deal with the YAR by the terms of which the YAR would no longer support the armed revolution and would ban the activities of the NLF on its territory. In its turn the British government would recognise the republican regime.[15] The British were taking the events in Radfan seriously, as a threat against their vital interests in South Arabia, and successive military operations were quickly mounted, as follows:

(1) 4 to 31 January 1964 (code-name 'Nutcracker');[16]
(2) 1 February to 13 April 1964 (code-name 'Rustum');
(3) 14 April to 11 May 1964 (code-name 'Radforce');
(4) 11 to 23 May 1964;
(5) 24 May to 28 August 1964.

The objectives of the punitive campaigns were control of the strategic heights and fertile wadi, and the opening of the main road for commerce and military communications. Troops sent to Radfan met unexpectedly strong, self-confident resistance and could not achieve any of the objectives, while the revolutionaries in Radfan gained the support of the whole Yemeni people, and Arab and international solidarity. The NLF decided to extend its operation gradually over all the area whenever conditions allowed, in order to break the siege imposed on Radfan. By mid-1964 fronts were opened in the middle region of Dal'a, Shu'aib and Aden. More fronts were active by mid-1965 — Halmain, Yafa'i, Subaiha, Lahej, Baihan, Awaliq and Wahidi.[17] Fighting techniques were subsequently developed by introducing the elements of planning for the battle, the exchange of light signals and wireless communications. Fighting tactics were gradually learnt — attack and withdrawal, the spread of force, fortifications and camouflage; new weapons were also introduced.[18]

As for Aden, the site of the British military base and headquarters of Middle East Forces, *fida'iyin* operations began in mid-1964 and reached their climax during the visit of Anthony Greenwood, the Secretary of State for the Colonies, in November 1965. He described such operations as 'savage, cowardly terror'. The armed struggle in Aden took the form of 'hit and hide' in the beginning — by attacking patrols and British soldiers. The fida'iyin also organised a brave operation to attack Khormaksar military base, burning some aircraft and bombing certain buildings.[19] Other operations were concentrated in places of gathering such as clubs and houses of British officials, with the result that the British formed a group calling for a return home. Fida'iyin bullets aimed at the heads of those responsible for executing British policy killed Sir Arthur Charles, the Speaker of the Legislative Council, and Harry Barrie, Superintendent of Police. They were also aimed at the heads of British Intelligence, beginning with a brave operation by shooting Fadl Khalil of the Special Branch in a public café. The importance of Aden's battle lay in securing publicity; news about revolution in South Yemen was conveyed to the outer world.

The Social Base of the NLF

The NLF understood itself as fulfilling national unity, i.e. unifying all classes and groups desirous and capable of carrying on the armed struggle against colonialism and its agents, against British designs, for the complete liquidation of military bases and the abolition of treaties and alliances with Britain, and paving the way for Yemeni unity. Studying the NLF declarations, essays and the correspondence of its leaders convinces the reader that it represented 'tribes, workers, soldiers and revolutionary intellectuals, who have a real interest in revolutionary change'. These were considered as the driving forces of the 14 October revolution.[20] Some students of contemporary Yemen have pointed out that the NLF was a loose organisation uniting all national forces including feudals and bourgeoisie. It is therefore essential at this stage to make a precise study of the social basis of armed revolution for the better understanding it gives of the structure of the NLF and the socio-political struggle in the area. Sultan Ahmad Omar[21] put forward the view that the NLF included tribal shaikhs as members, but was able to redress the matter at an early stage, while Naif Hawatma affirmed that the NLF recruited into its ranks some rich peasants ('kulaks') and that its leadership allied itself with high-ranked army officers in the last moments before independence. Indeed, leadership of the NLF in the beginning called for a very wide organisation, but it could not reach what was considered the ideal. Before founding the NLF the leadership of the Arab Nationalist Movement (ANM) had negotiations with al-Asnag, trying to persuade him to contribute to the armed struggle, but he had resolutely refused.[22] Other political parties representing the bourgeoisie were also against the armed struggle but the NLF did not attack them at the beginning. Faisal A. al-Sha'bi in an interview with *Al-Hurriya* explained that slogans were framed to attract what he called 'moderate forces' and to prevent their falling under British influence.[23] The bourgeoisie and feudalists preferred to unite themselves to confront the NLF. So in this early phase of armed revolution one can perceive a clear-cut socio-political differentiation; on one side the alliance of peasants, workers and petty bourgeoisie; on the other, British colonialists, sultans, feudalists and compradors.

The British Design

By virtue of the 26 September and 14 October revolutions, British policies had to be changed to face changing conditions in Yemen. The traditional policy of retaining the base in Aden was still filling the background but new measures had to be taken to secure its success. In order to implement such a policy British manoeuvres ran along three parallel lines.

(1) Making use of its striking force to crush the Yemeni revolution at its very beginning. This plan was fulfilled by punitive operations in the Radfan region and repeated aggression against the YAR.

(2) Pushing a development programme forward with more haste. Thus certain reforms were introduced, i.e. arabisation of civil and military personnel, giving credit facilities to peasants to enable them to buy water pumps etc. and to civil servants to build new houses. All these measures were taken in order to make certain social strata in urban and rural areas tightly connected with Britain.

(3) Preparing to deliver political power in South Yemen to 'responsible men' who were ready to preserve British strategic interests. This third line was of course the most important of all. To serve such a design, the High Commissioner called a constitutional congress in London inviting only the sultans and Ministers of the South Arabian Federation. However, the first congress was postponed because of the incident at Aden airport on 10 December 1963. The congress was later held in June 1964 when the NLF described it as

'London's Congress for treason'. It stressed that the convening sultans and so-called Ministers did not represent by any means the people in South Yemen. 'The sultans and ministers should be penalized', 'Great Britain is negotiating with Great Britain,' commented local and Arab newspapers. The congress has its own internal contradictions: the Protectorates, dreading any social or political change, however insignificant it might be, called for highly centralised, oligarchical rule; the Aden representatives called for democratic, liberal rule securing more freedom and autonomy for Aden within the Federation. The congress, as is well known, was broken up by the withdrawal of A. A. al-Fadli who was at that time Chairman of the congress and President of the South Arabian Federation.

Soon after the success of the Labour Party in the October 1964 election, the new British government found it appropriate to revise, though slightly, its policy. Its inclination was to invite leaders of political parties together with Federation Ministers, i.e. the national forces not taking part in the armed revolution. Anthony Greenwood, visiting Aden in November 1964, met representatives of all legal political parties and during this meeting leaders of parties in the Colony agreed to attend the coming congress to be held in London on 27 August 1965. National parties and independent personalities present at the congress were not satisfied by British proposals about the future of Aden, and the form of rule, and they therefore resorted to Cairo, hoping that the British government would change its policy. The Labour Party declared on many occasions that Britain wished to retain the base at Aden 'with the consent of the people'. Harold Wilson (then Prime Minister) stated that he would discuss with US President Johnson the future of Aden and the US contribution to defence policies East of Suez. The Labour government believed that a deal could be made with Gamal Abdul Nasser and G. M. Thompson, a friend of President Nasser, was preparing to visit Egypt to restore diplomatic relations (cut since 1956) and to come to terms with Nasser about Yemen. However, Thompson's mission ended in failure as Nasser refused to meet him because of the deteriorating situation in South Yemen.

The Arab Design

In the context of the Arab world the years 1964-5 witnessed a 'brotherly Arab reunion' to confront the ambitions of Israel to divert the course of the Jordan river and for this purpose three Arab summit conferences were held. As a preparation for the summit conferences efforts had been made to normalise relations between Saudi Arabia and Egypt, and Nasser suddenly paid a visit to Saudi Arabia where he was cordially received. Negotiations between the two parties ended in the signature of the Jeddah treaty of August 1965 which stressed the necessity of securing peace and order in Yemen, and of letting the Yemeni people decide their own destiny and choose the political system they preferred without any pressure or external intervention. Saudi Arabia would cease to give any material or moral support to the royalists, while Egypt would withdraw its troops from Yemen; it appeared that the agreement contained provisions that the two brotherly states should co-operate in South Arabia. The series of summit conferences in their resolutions had previously approved support for the armed struggle in South Yemen on condition that all national forces should unite. A committee concerned with the case of South Yemen was formed of Saudi Arabia, Egypt, YAR and Kuwait, and this was the first sign of an Arab design for the independence of South Yemen. Then national parties (opposing the armed struggle) were encouraged to ally themselves and the process of unification took the following steps:

(1) The South Arabian League, the People's Socialist Party, the Liberation Association and independent personalities convened in Cairo forming the National Block and signed the *National Charter* on 30 July 1964

(2) A conference consisting of the National Block and NLF was called for in March 1965 on the logical premiss that conflicts could not be resolved by mere goodwill or external pressure. The South Arabian League was demanding that the NLF dissolve its organisations, join the National Block and sign its charter. The NLF was asking the other groups not to negotiate with Britain unless it recognised UN resolutions about South Yemen and was also asking other parties to join the armed revolution. It was clear that they were talking different languages so the conference failed completely.

(3) On the base of the National Block an Organisation for Liberation of South Yemen was founded. A decision was taken that its leadership should be of 21 members of whom 7 were instantly

nominated — A. A. al-Fadli, A. Abdul Karim, M. Aidrus, A. bin Farid, M. A. al-Sufri, A. al-Asnag and M. Nu'man. The First Congress from 30 April to 5 May 1965 was held in Ta'izz. Responses towards it were different in that officials in the YAR government met delegates to the congress, whereas in the streets demonstrations of workers and students opposed it. Participants claimed that OLSY was the sole representative of the Yemeni people, and asked for common action and the dissolution of the founding organisations within two months. They appealed to Arab and friendly countries for support but only one and a half months later, because of acute dissent between the PSP and the SAL, the OLSY broke up and the second congress did not materialise. Nevertheless, attempts to sponsor a design representing an agreeable compromise amongst influential Arab states continued.

The Local Design

The most important event of the 1964-5 period was the First Congress of the NLF, i.e. the local design. The congress, which took place in Ta'izz from 22 to 25 June 1965, was attended by 75 representatives of the fighting fronts.[24] The revolutionary experience during the past twenty months since the beginning of the 14 October revolution was studied with great care and the delegates agreed that the organisational structure should be adapted to rapid changes in the NLF such as an increase in membership and more complicated tasks. It was suggested that a National Council should be formed of 30-35 members representing tribes, workers, students and immigrants. The National Council was to elect an executive council whose members would lead the following departments: military, political, information, financial and mass organisations. For more efficiency it was suggested that certain leading elements should work full-time to direct underground 'cells' and mass organisations. For further reinforcement of the armed struggle and attaining better co-ordination it was suggested that a unified liberation army should be gradually built up consisting of all the existing fighting fronts and those which might exist after the congress. The congress reaffirmed the NLF's former call for complete independence, the liquidation of the military base and abolishing all alliances with Britain. It expressed its opposition to British designs in general and in detail; OLSY was considered an enemy of the people. The most important moment was the approval of the *National Charter* as the theoretical guide of the 14 October revolution. The *National Charter* was considered at the time a progressive radical document for national liberation in South Yemen. We can trace its origin in five main sources.

(1) Nasser's Egypt: Abdul Nasser's call for an anti-colonialist struggle and for Arab unity and dignity was very popular in the fifties and the sixties. Later measures taken in Egypt in 1961 concerning agrarian reform and nationalisation spread as revolutionary slogans in Yemen and to attain socialism was one of the main goals of the national struggle.

(2) The Algerian Revolution: the armed struggle of the Algerian people from 1954 to 1962 and its famous victory captured the people's admiration and raised its morale. The form of the Algerian FLN itself as uniting all national forces was taken as an example, as was its charter. The influence of Frantz Fanon could easily be detected, especially his theory on violence and its role in liberating the country, the oppressed and the oppressor. His evaluation of the political parties in cities and the role of the national bourgeoisie was also adopted to a certain extent.

(3) Experience of national liberation movements: particularly those whose experience was thought to be similar. NLF members were studying the socio-economic situation in these countries, the programmes of their parties and the lessons of armed struggle in such countries as Cuba, Vietnam and China.

(4) The theory of scientific socialism and socialist construction in socialist countries: the theory of scientific socialism was the background of the socio-economic analysis given in the *Charter*. The *Charter* hailed the success of the socialist camp and its support to national liberation movements.

(5) Experience accumulated from the revolutionary struggle itself: the daily confrontation with colonialism helped revolutionaries to know the nature of their enemy, his policy, the types of oppression and political tricks; it helped them know more about monopolistic companies and their relation with rulers. The fida'iyin learnt a lot about organisation, discipline and secrecy, and their political and class consciousness was raised. These so-called sources are not to be regarded as distinct, they are intermingled. But such classification helps to understand certain phrases in the *Charter*.

The *National Charter* described fully the local design — South Yemen would be an independent country without the British rulers and their base, without sultans, with means of production owned by workers and land distributed amongst poor peasants. The *Charter* stated that foreign trade should be in the hands of the state and education should be free for all children having equal chances of access. It also stressed that the design would be achieved by means of armed struggle only and appealed for the building of a revolutionary army. The *Charter* called finally for Yemeni unity, Arab unity and the liberation of Palestine. These statements were a vivid example of the unity of the national and social content of the 14 October revolution.

So it was that by mid-1965 all the forces had, in one way or another, said their piece. In the last three years up to 1967 the three forces were to run a breathtaking race for deciding the destiny of South Yemen.

Notes

1. Later on the NLF.
2. On 30 November 1970 the country was called the People's Democratic Republic of Yemen (PDRY) on the occasion of approving the constitution.
3. K. Trevaskis, *Shades of Amber* (Hutchinson, London, 1968), p. 248.
4. R. J. Gavin, *Aden under British Rule 1839-1937* (Hurst, London, 1975), p. 350.
5. K. M. al-Sha'bi, *British Colonialism and our National Struggle in South Yemen* (Cairo, 1962), p. 228.
6. Ibid.
7. Adel Rida, *Development and Path of the Yemeni National Movement* (Cairo, 1971), p. 244.
8. Documents of the Second Congress of NLF held in Jibla from 7 to 11 June 1966, General Report, p. 4 (unpublished).
9. Little is known about the organisations and further study is required.
10. Labbuza had participated in the meetings in San'a' which founded the NLF. In these meetings a decision had been taken in principle to start the armed struggle against colonialism but the exact time was not fixed and the shooting in Radfan made the historic decision.
11. For a detailed account of the objective and subjective conditions favouring the beginning and victory of armed revolution see Ahmad A. Misri, *Democratic Yemen Experience* (Cairo, 1974), pp. 224-40; NLF, *Charter* (Aden, 1968), pp. 52, 56, 59; and S. O. Bukair, 'Main Phases of the Yemeni Revolution', unpublished dissertation, Moscow University, 1981, PP. 22-5.
12. Ministry of Defence Reports, Aden, Sept.-Oct. 1963; nos. 3 and 4, 27 Nov. 1963.
13. Ibid.
14. Ministry of Defence Reports, nos. 9, 11, 13, 1964.
15. *Al-Hurriya*, no. 265, 21 June 1965.
16. Sultan Nagi, *Military History of Yemen* (n.p., n.d.), p. 376.
17. *Al-Hurriya*, no. 292, 27 Dec. 1965.
18. Ministry of Defence Reports, no. 11, (Oct.-Nov. 1964); also Nagi, *Military History*, pp. 277-8; Misri, *Democratic Yemen Experience*, p. 285.

19. Abdul-Fattah Isma'il, *Revolutionary Experience in Democratic Yemen* (Progress, Moscow, 1978), p. 22.

20. *Al-Hurriya*, no. 225, 22 June 1964.

21. S. A. Omar, *A Glance at Development in Yemeni Society* (al-Tali'a, Beirut, 1970), p. 241; Naif Hawatma, *Crisis of Revolution in South Yemen* (al-Tali'a, Beirut, 1968), p. 55.

22. Ibrahim Muhsin, 'An Attempt to Understand what is Going On in Occupied South Yemen', *Al-Hurriya*, no. 276, 6 Sept. 1965.

23. *Al-Hurriya*, no. 269, 19 July 1965.

24. *Al-Tali'a*, no. 140, 21 July 1965.

6 THE YEMENI REVOLUTION OF 1962 SEEN AS A SOCIAL REVOLUTION

Mohammed A. Zabarah

The Yemeni revolution of September 1962 brought the end of the imamate institution. It was an act profoundly felt by all Yemenis not only because, in its wake, it produced eight years of intermittent civil war, but also because it occasioned regenerative forces that yielded social changes spanning the entire spectrum of Yemeni society. As such, these changes must be classified as revolutionary social changes. The aim of this chapter is to examine the social revolution that occurred after the Yemeni revolution of 1962. The social changes that resulted are seen here as a by-product of the Yemeni revolution. This study will be concerned with, first, defining our terms and concepts in the light of the Yemeni situation; second, examining the impact of the civil war on the social patterns in Yemeni society; and, third, analysing the period of national growth (1971–83) and its involvement in the changing social behaviour of the Yemeni people.

Concepts Defined

Revolutions have as their primary objectives the transformation of society. They aim to change fundamentally the social living, habits and values of the larger part of society. They are distinct from *coups d'état* or palace revolutions in that a *coup d'état* merely changes the people in power or a few laws. The Yemeni revolution of 1962 was a movement that had as its fundamental objective the termination of the imamate system that had endured in Yemen since AD 889. The imamate system was a sacred-collectivity system which assumed that whatever is good for the community is good for the individual. The community in such a system is above the individual. It is an ethical community that adheres to higher laws (kinship, clan, religion) as the basis for its continuity. In such a system, traditional values were to be maintained and promoted. They are, and serve as, the basis for the system.

The Mutawakkilite Kingdom of Yemen (imamate) which came to power when independence was won from Ottoman rule in 1918 was a sacred-collectivity system. The term 'Mutawakkilite' evokes religion. Specifically, it means 'under the guidance of Allah'. The rulers were called imams, hence the term imamate. An imam is a religio-political leader who is granted by Islamic law, shari'a, nearly absolute authority in spiritual and civil matters. When Yemen won its independence from Ottoman rule in 1918, it maintained the sacred-collectivity characteristics of the system. A hierarchical political system was continued, basing its legitimacy on its adherence to Zaidism (a religio-political sect of the *shi'a*) and to traditional values. These two elements were of profound importance to the imamate before and after independence. They were instrumental in inducing Imam Yahya Hamid al-Din (Imam: 1904–48) to adopt the policy of isolationism after Yemen achieved its independence.

The policy of isolationism was meant to safeguard Yemen's hard-won independence and to keep the religious purity of the state from being corrupted by outsiders. In order to secure independence Yemen had to shun international involvement. Consequently, Imam Yahya refused to accept foreign economic investments in Yemen, and rejected becoming involved in regional Arab political movements. Yemen could not be impervious to imperialism or to the competition for outside possessions by the great powers of Europe. It was still crystal-clear to the Yemeni political establishment that Yemen had been geographically partitioned by Britain in 1839. The British had in that year occupied Aden, and begun systematically incorporating areas adjacent to Aden. The British occupation of Aden was construed by the political regime in Yemen as the gravest outside invasion to have occurred, because it was perceived to be a direct threat to the independence and security of Yemen. Yemen was convinced that Britain had designs on it, because it had recently witnessed the complete partitioning of Arab lands by both Britain and France immediately after the First World War. Thus, when France, Italy and the Soviet Union tried to cultivate their economic and political relations with Yemen, their attempts were obstructed by the Yemeni political establishment. However, although the policy of isolationism served Yemen well in the short run, it became a detriment to the development of the state in the long run. During the reign of Imam Yahya, Yemen did not develop any form of an infrastructure. There were no paved roads, no communications facilities, no hospitals, no banks, no telephones and no school system with a standard curriculum. A school for girls, founded by the Turks, was later closed by the Imam. The system seemed inert, lacking in mobility or motion.

An attempt to change Yemen's regional and international positions, and, in so doing, improve the economic and social postures of the state, was occasioned during the reign of Imam Ahmad (1948-62). Imam Ahmad improved his relations with the Arab states, and established diplomatic relations with a number of Eastern and Western bloc countries. In response to Arab nationalism, Yemen became aligned with Saudi Arabia and Egypt when, in 1956, it signed the Jeddah Military Pact. This alignment was followed in 1958 by the creation of the United Arab States, which confederated Yemen with the United Arab Republic of Egypt and Syria. As a consequence of these political developments, Yemen was penetrated by more foreigners that ever before. Egyptians, Russians, Americans, Chinese, Germans and others entered Yemen to undertake diplomatic missions, to train the army, or to help the Yemeni government improve the economic conditions of the state. It was during this era that an infrastructure was developing. Paved roads were being constructed by the Chinese and Americans in an attempt to link the major cities in Yemen. The port of Hodaida was being constructed by the Soviet Union, and Soviet technical and economic assistance were being provided to offset American and Western economic aid. New schools and hospitals were being built in Hodaida, Ta'izz and San'a'. Yet these economic endeavours were largely cosmetic and too late. They also did not conform to the rigidity of the political system, which still revolved around the person of the Imam. The Imam was seen as the personification of Yemeni conservatism and traditionalism. He was the greatest emanating personality in Yemeni society whose personality embodied the Yemeni political structure. As the apex of the hierarchical political system, he was the only one making essential choices and decisions. He presided over the political structure as a parent presides over a household. Nothing was done without his express approval. To compound this, many Yemenis, tribal as well as urban dwellers, believed that the Imams were not only blessed, but also possessed abstract, spiritual powers derived from being descendants of the Prophet Muhammad. This belief was instrumental in pacifying the tribes, and in maintaining stability in the state. However, the factor of emanation as a source of stability had eroded considerably by 1961 because of several factors. Foremost among them are: (1) the huge influx of foreigners to Yemen with ideas and values different from those in Yemen; (2) the cosmetic economic changes the state undertook to improve the economic plight of Yemeni society; and (3) the inability of the political establishment to reform and become more receptive to popular demands. Thus, by the latter part of 1961, Yemen witnessed riots and demonstrations in San'a' and Ta'izz demanding changes and reforms. The Imam's appeal to the people to restore tranquillity and order was not heeded. His aura as a commanding personality had eroded considerably. Thus, one week after he died, the revolution of September 1962 erupted, bringing a definite end to the imamate, sacred-collectivity system.

The Civil War Years and the Changing Social Patterns

When the Yemeni revolution of 1962 erupted there were many Yemenis who wanted to make fundamental changes in their society. As previously noted, many Yemenis came into contact with foreign elements, and were impressed by what they learned of the outside world. The 'Voice of the Arabs' was instrumental in making the Yemenis more aware of their own society. There were reports that between 300 and 400 Yemenis were in Egyptian secondary schools in 1961, and an additional 70 to 80 in European and American educational institutions. These students were instrumental in articulating their country's economic, social and political ills. They, like many others, were demanding changes in their own society. However, the vast majority of the Yemenis went on with their lives as they had for centuries, although that was soon to change in both negative and positive ways during the civil-war period that followed the revolution.

Negatively, the civil-war period was traumatic to Yemeni society. The weapons used by both the revolutionaries and royalists were highly sophisticated and very destructive. The Egyptian intensive bombing of the northern part of the country was devastating and destroyed towns and villages, forcing the inhabitants to flee and seek refuge in caves or other remote areas. This disrupted both the social and economic life of many Yemenis. Another aspect of negative change occurring in Yemen during the civil-war era, which was more disturbing to the pattern of relationship in Yemeni society, was the fact that the internal war was being fought primarily by two factions: royalists and republicans. This fact split tribal allegiance and disturbed the traditional pattern of inter-tribal relationships. The two tribal confederations, the Bakil and Hashid, split into royalist supporters and republican backers. This was the first time in Yemen's contemporary history that the two tribal confederations had split their support. This phenomenon was coupled with the tremendous accessibility of money which was being distributed generously by both Saudi Arabia, the royalist backer, and Egypt, the republican supporter, to the tribes in efforts to win their support. It became evidently clear after a short period that the tribes tended to switch their allegiance to the party most generous in distributing funds or arms. The consequences of this trend brought the tribes, some of which had never come into contact with modern elements, into the current of modern living. Some of the tribes witnessed the emergence in their territories of refrigerators, gas ovens and cine-cameras. The result of these developments was the increased awareness of the village dwellers and tribal members of the shortcomings of their own society. Those tribes that were republican backers from the beginning of the conflict began to view the Egyptians as the new source of emanation, because it was the Egyptians who were the proponents of Arab nationalism, Arab unity, anti-imperialism and social progress. The Egyptians hoped to win over to their side everyone, even the recalcitrant. However, their heavy-handed methods and their inability to understand Yemeni society soon alienated even those die-hard Egyptian supporters.

Positively, the civil-war period helped promote social changes that were not the results of destruction. The roads which were constructed in the latter years of Imam Ahmad's reign became channels by which went vehicles, goods and ideas, reaching the hinterland and areas that had been isolated for centuries. The roads contributed to the creation of a new consciousness on the part of the Yemeni villagers and tribesmen. They were used by both republicans and royalists in their endeavours to propagate political and economic concepts. The civil-war period witnessed the construction of new factories in San'a', Ta'izz and Hodaida. These factories employed women alongside men. What the women earned was used to supplement their families' income. This trend introduced into Yemen a new concept in the traditional male-female relationship, which has since expanded considerably.

National Growth and Social Changes

In 1971 the Yemen Arab Republic, having experienced the trauma of eight years of civil war, and having reconciled with the royalists, felt the time was conducive to introducing plans for national growth. Towards this objective the open-door policy was inaugurated, aimed at improving its relationships with the conservative Arab states and with the Western bloc nations. It was hoped that in so doing Yemen would gain the valuable assistance and interest of those states in its attempts to change. Thus, in the following year diplomatic relations were restored between Yemen and West Germany and with the United States. This was followed by formal recognition of the Yemen Arab Republic by Britain, France and the Netherlands.

Once Yemen's regional and international relations were improved, it turned its attention to addressing its economic problems. The creation of the Central Planning Organisation in 1972 was seen as the first positive effort in that direction. It was followed by the Three-Year Development Programme, 1973/4–75/6, which was immediately followed by the First Five-year Plan, 1976/7–80/1. These two economic plans have laid down the country's infrastructure. More than 1,200 kilometres of paved roads have been completed by the Highway Authority, linking all major cities in Yemen. This has increased mobility and has opened the country not only to the outside, but also internally. Paved roads have facilitated trade, have eased access to markets for agricultural producers and have allowed new industries to be established. Along with the development of a road network, transportation and communication systems have developed rapidly and are being used significantly to integrate the state socially. Television was first introduced into Yemen in 1972 and it has been instrumental in promoting social awareness among the people. Along with television, radio and newspaper dailies are now reaching the most isolated areas in Yemen. Tribes that once relied upon the spread of news by word of mouth are now able to hear or read for themselves about events happening in their own state and abroad.

The industrial sector of the state has also improved and developed. New factories have increased twofold since 1971, employing both men and women. Women have taken an active role in contributing to their family income; they are seen working in factories, in government ministries, in schools, in banks and in business establishments. The female work-force at the time of writing comprises approximately 15 per cent of the total work-force in Yemen. When one considers that before the revolution in 1962 Yemeni women did not work for wages and did not contribute financially to their families' income, the 15 per cent figure must be seen as a major development. The fact that one-third of Yemen's work-force is outside the country has, to some degree, altered the role of women in the agricultural sector. Women are participating more heavily in previously male-dominated agricultural activities such as ploughing, planting and harvesting. This has affected marginally the traditional patterns of male-female relationship in the rural areas of the country. The intensive economic developments in the urban centres in Yemen have strongly affected internal migration from the rural areas to cities in search of work. This trend has been largely a male movement. As more males migrate to urban centres, a decline in the population of rural areas is being felt. This has also strained the traditional values within the Yemeni home, and has added to the altering role of women.

Yemen's socio-economic changes have also been affected by the tremendous improvement in the educational sector. The educational system in the Yemen Arab Republic has been broadened and made to conform to modern standards. Schools were opened in even the remotest parts of the state. The number of schools increased from 700 in 1969/70 to 2,534 in 1979/80. The total number of schools at the time of writing closely approaches the 3,000 mark. The University of San'a', founded in 1971, boasts five faculties: the Faculty of Law and Shari'a, the Faculty of Commerce, the Faculty of Sciences, the Faculty of Arts and the Faculty of Education. The University has planned to open three new faculties in the near future: the Faculty of Medicine, the Faculty of Agriculture and the Faculty of Engineering. San'a' University presently has an enrolment of 7,600 students with more than 120 faculty staff. Of the total student body enrolled in the University, about 20 per cent are women. The state encourages women to enrol in the University, offering them, as incentives, room and board. The educational progress in the Yemen Arab Republic must be recognised as being both positive and remarkable. I have already mentioned that before the revolution of 1962 Yemen's educational sector was backward. There was no curriculum, and the standard of education was, to say the least, poor. Yemeni students going abroad for education had to enrol in high schools in order to take the science courses they had not had in Yemen. Yemen did not have a university. In pre-revolutionary Yemen, secular education was anathema but this attitude changed after the revolution.

The improved educational methods and the fact that education is more readily available to most Yemenis have affected the social outlook of the Yemenis. The view that a woman's place is at home is gradually, with a certain degree of reluctance, changing. As more women are educated, their demands are becoming broader. Their demands on their families have not reached crisis proportions. But they have begun to strain the existing traditional values which have governed the family relationship. This is compounded by the fact that women work and study, even at university level, alongside men. This trend is likely to continue. The consequence will be the erosion of old social values and the introduction of new ones. These inputs, which will eventually alter the social characteristics of Yemeni society, will affect the attitudes of the populace and their outlook on the future. Social cohesion will be maintained so long as valued traditional norms are not disturbed abruptly. They must be changed on a gradual basis. It is one thing to allow a woman to drive a car, it is another to allow her to accompany a man to a cinema. The former can be tolerated, but the latter would be intolerable for a Yemeni family.

Conclusion

Yemeni society has gone from a closed, inward-looking community to an open one. It has changed politically, economically and socially in its attempts to catch up with the modern world. In a political and social sense the Yemeni government has been attempting since 1971 to open up the creative powers of its citizens, by making them become more appreciative of their rights and potentialities as individuals in a relatively mobile society. In order to make them realise their capacities for expression, for happiness and for knowledge, the state has undertaken economic and social programmes aimed at breaking down old social values and replacing them with new ones more compatible with the contemporary world. In order to develop and modernise the state, new inputs into the social, economic and political sectors must be introduced. The road to modernisation involves certain economic, political and social changes, which have been summarised by Charles A. Micaud as:

(1) The authority of the *ancien régime* gives way to the rule of the people, and ideally, to the doctrine that they are equal before the law to which they individually consent. (2) The old social units, such as the family, village, or tribe, become subordinated to a national community; they are replaced as agents of social integration by new voluntary organizations, such as trade unions and political parties. (3) An old elite based on birth either dies out or becomes assimilated into a new elite based on achievement and education. (4) Traditional values are to a large extent undermined by a new faith — essentially the belief in material progress through the efficient use of human beings and technical innovations for maximum production.[1]

In order for modernisation to continue, the Yemeni social revolution, which is a direct by-product of the revolution of September 1962, must be maintained and supported at the rate at which it is now proceeding. We must recall that gradual changes are more suited to Yemen, because traditional patterns need the opportunity to adapt to change. It is through gradual changes that the polity will not be disturbed. Gradual changes in the social structure of a society imply that those changes will retain their legitimacy.

Note

1. C. A. Micaud (with L. C. Brown and C. H. Moore), *Tunisia: The Politics of Modernization* (Pall Mall, London, 1964), p. x.

7 NATION-BUILDING AND POLITICAL DEVELOPMENT IN THE TWO YEMENS

John Peterson

As in many other countries, the impact of modernisation on the two Yemens has been as multifaceted as it has been devastating. Radical change has been induced in many areas of Yemeni economy, society and politics. One area in which this impact has been keenly felt is of particular interest here, that of political change. A principal consequence of political change has been the undermining of the legitimacy of the traditional political order without, however, concomitantly realising a legitimate 'modern' system. Both the Yemen Arab Republic (YAR) and the People's Democratic Republic of Yemen (PDRY) are very new states established in very old communities. They both face the central problem of legitimacy and seek effective strategies for overcoming it.[1]

This chapter contains two major objectives. First, it attempts to sketch the course of political change in the two countries — or more accurately, in the two regions (*shatr*) of Yemen — over the course of the twentieth century. In particular, this involves a brief examination of the record of the various states and governments during this period in such vital areas of concern as nation-building, state-building and legitimation. A second goal is to advance some tentative conclusions regarding the general direction of political development in the Yemens and to suggest some options available for the future.

The Pre-revolutionary Yemeni States

The years 1962 and 1967 have seminal importance in Yemeni history as they, officially at least, mark the establishment of 'modern' — or, actually, 'modernising' — and self-proclaimed revolutionary states in both halves of Yemen. It should be noted, though, that neither of the two existing states before the revolutions of the 1960s could be called 'traditional'. Both regions already had been buffeted by the first winds of modernisation and had experienced a significant degree of political change. Despite this, there were many Yemenis, undoubtedly the great majority, who opposed these changes and who desired a return to the traditional manner and structure of politics or, more precisely, a return to an idealised memory of that traditional past.

In recent centuries there has been only one truly 'traditional' state exercising central authority in Yemen, although its capabilities inherently were severely restricted. This was the Zaidi imamate. In its ideal form the imamate was well constituted to provide the narrow range and scope of functions expected of it by its people. In general, the institution of the imamate served to maintain order, particularly in urban settings, to provide management and mediation of both tribal and personal disputes, to administer such concerns as *awqaf* and *bait al-mal*, and to appoint and supervise judges and deputies in the hinterland. In addition, the Imam was responsible for rallying the defences of the community against external threats.

But the imamate often operated in less than ideal fashion. By its very nature, it was completely dependent on the abilities of a single individual who was expected to be a competent combination of religious scholar, administrator, negotiator and military commander. The consequent dependence on a strong personality to occupy the office of Imam seemed to encourage dynastic tendencies. His effectiveness was subject to the co-operation of the tribes, as the paramount shaikhs exercised considerable influence over Imams, frequently having had a part in their selection in the first place. Most important, the efficacy and legitimacy of the imamate were restricted by the existence of a basic sectarian schism. The imamate was a Zaidi institution while well over half of Yemen's population was sunni. Thus, its legitimacy as a 'national', i.e. supra-Zaidi, institution depended on its ability to (1) control the Zaidi tribes and shaikhs, and (2) maintain order justly and impartially throughout the community. All too often, though, control over sunni areas was maintained through measures of extraction and repression. In the last several centuries this dichotomy, together with the domination of parts of Yemen by outsiders, served to restrict the sway of the imamate to a few areas in the far northern Zaidi mountains. Thus began the schism between North and South and, from this point on, the record of political development must be considered separately for each region of Yemen.

Up to 1962 political change in the North appeared to have occurred much more slowly and far more subtly than it did in the South (or at least in Aden). Nevertheless, parts of the North were directly affected by modernisation in numerous ways. Some of these resulted from innovations introduced by the Ottomans, others from the experiences of Yemenis abroad and in Aden, and still others from the broader horizons introduced through books, newspapers and the radio. The response of the Hamid al-Din Imams to this percolation of change into the country was to attempt greater control over the state in order to maintain the existing nature and values of society. Gradually, these efforts transformed the imamate from a traditional state to a less effective neo-traditional one, resulting in a marked diminution of legitimacy.[2] The homogeneity of what Edward Shils has termed the central zone of society,[3] the shared identification or adherence to traditional goals and values, was shattered. A new split began to appear between traditionalists and modernists, between those who sought to preserve an idealised version of traditional society and those who sought to change or transform society. This division was superimposed on an already fragmented community heavily oriented towards the primacy of local and tribal identifications. The increasing peripheralisation of North Yemeni society caught Imams Yahya and Ahmad in a trap without escape: any changes that they made were anathema to the traditionalists, yet the hesitant and marginal nature of these changes was derided by the modernists as being far too little.

The steady intrusion of nationalist ideas and appeal also influenced twentieth-century political change in North Yemen. Consequently, both Yahya and Ahmad placed considerable emphasis on championing Yemeni and even Arab nationalism. Yahya posed as a nationalist leader in leading the Yemenis' struggle against the Ottomans. Later, he steadfastly opposed the British presence in the South and worked to undermine British authority there, as did Ahmad. This impulse may well account in part for Yahya's determination to extend his authority in the early 1930s to the northern fringe of Yemen (including Najran, Asir and Jizan), a move which ended disastrously in the Saudi/Yemeni war, since when these territories have been thoroughly integrated into Saudi Arabia. Later there was Ahmad's effort to parry the threat of radical pan-Arabism by accepting membership in Abdul Nasser's United Arab States. While the inability of these Imams to dislodge the Saudis from the northern territories or the British from the

South hampered their standing as nationalists, they were successful in nation-building in so far as the incipient right — if not the capability — of the YAR to sovereignty over all the territory of the old imamate has been widely accepted.

The imamate's ability to advance the process of state-building, however, had little permanent impact. In part, this was due to the Imams' heavy-handed actions towards the traditional political elites: Yahya summarily removed many of his contemporaries from their influential and rightful positions, replacing them with his sons. Ahmad later antagonised many prominent individuals and families through his policies of widespread imprisonment and property confiscation after the attempted revolution of 1948, and then later reprisals against a number of shaikhs. Certainly, Yahya and Ahmad did establish some new governmental institutions and adopt responsibility for a limited number of new functions. But these efforts suffered from an inability or unwillingness to co-opt others than Hamid al-Din in the continued maintenance of the regime. Furthermore, both Imams refused to delegate authority, thus denying legitimacy to any of these fledgeling institutions. Finally, those changes that were made were far too limited in scope and number to cope effectively with the emerging challenges and demands.

Consequently, the Hamid al-Din era displayed an eventually ineffectual rear-guard action against the forces of modernisation. Paradoxically, the attempt to exercise greater control in order to halt change actually resulted in less control. By forsaking the traditional basis of authority and attendant legitimacy and relying increasingly on neo-traditional means of rule, the Hamid al-Din imamate forfeited the religious and tribal underpinnings on which the institution had traditionally depended. The result was increasing frustration and the emergence of active political dissidence. While this new source of political opposition was allied with long-standing rivals of the Hamid al-Din in the abortive revolution of 1948, it was not until 1962 that the forces of change succeeded in toppling the thousand-year-old imamate.

Political change in the South was simultaneously more rapid and more protracted than in the North, as a result of the emerging bifurcation between modernising Aden and the stagnating hinterland, especially in the Eastern Aden Protectorate. The cause of this bifurcation and the guiding force in political change there, whether deliberate or not, was the British presence and policies.

In Aden, British actions resulted in the creation of a modern port, one of the busiest in the world, with all its attendant services. Aden was also developed as a principal administrative and, later, military hub. The British eventually consolidated their position by establishing a Crown Colony in Aden from where the Protectorate continued to be administered. Aden's transformation was accompanied by substantial population growth, attracting thousands of Somalis and Yemenis from both North and South to provide labour, and Indians to handle clerical and commercial responsibilities. Eventually, as these new elements were integrated and socialised, provisions were made for a trade union organisation and finally, though tentatively, self-governance.

The consequence of the largely indirect British presence in the Protectorate was to fossilise the existing patchwork pattern of fragmented political authority. Gradually, as British concern with the internal affairs of the Protectorate grew, formal political status was awarded to various shaikhs and notables of minor standing in order to fill in the gaps and provide a symmetric basis for self-administration under the watchful British eye. This process evolved gradually and it was not until the mid-century efforts of Harold Ingrams in the Eastern Protectorate that the complete edifice of British-supervised, stable, indigenous, political entities was finally in place. It should be kept in mind that the emphasis was placed on indirect control by preserving order within the framework of the *status quo*, and minimising the costs and potential risks of even this limited involvement by refraining from encouragement of social and economic development, let alone political change.

The system developed by the British in South Yemen obviously served imperial purposes. But the radical alteration of traditional politics was workable only as long as the British remained. The demographic transformation of Aden not only altered the social, cultural and ethnic composition of the Colony but raised inevitable controversy over the shape of the eventual independent state and whose interests it should serve. The fossilisation of the hinterland led to an 'either/or' situation, preventing any gradations of political expression or inclination. The population of the Protectorate either was forced to co-operate and live within the restrictions of an antiquated system or leave for opportunities outside, in the Gulf or in Aden. Such an experience frequently led to a radicalisation of political beliefs. The net effect of the colonial experience was to sharpen divisions between the centre (here spatially located in Aden) and the periphery, to a far larger degree than in the North.

This is not to overlook certain legacies in both nation- and state-building. Psychologically, an important dichotomy was established between British-controlled and non-British territory. The British presence effectively produced a certain cohesion in the South, particularly through the creation of an administrative and military apparatus responsible for all of this territory. Despite the multiplicity of administrative and military units, a centralised decision-making authority clearly existed.

The British role in nation-building was perhaps even more clearly, if negatively, illustrated by the stimulus that the colonial presence provided for an emerging nationalist movement. The South had experienced an inward percolation of nationalist sentiments similar to the North's but in greater intensity due to the modernisation of Aden where the nationalist response was most acute. Gradually, agitation for self-government and then independence appeared and intensified. The prevailing current of thought seemed to move along an increasingly assertive and unco-operative line, from unfocused modernist goals to pragmatic nationalist goals, to narrowly articulated ideological ones and then to an increasingly radical focus. As ideas and programmes surfaced and faltered because of British prevarication and rejection, the legitimacy of moderate groupings was undermined by the taint of collaboration. Thus the appeal of the South Arabian League waned and was superseded by that of the People's Socialist Party. But the PSP and then FLOSY (Front for the Liberation of Occupied South Yemen) were compromised by their Nasserist connection (Abdul Nasser then being caught in the North Yemen quagmire). The fruits of independence finally fell to the radical National Liberation Front (NLF).

The British role in state-building was rather more successful in producing an effective infrastructure, but it was engineered to meet British needs and thus lacked credibility in the independent state. The attempt to devise an institutional framework for the post-imperial period, the Federation of South Arabia, turned out to be little more than a jerry-built experiment, quite inadequate to hold together the increasingly disparate elements in South Yemen. With independence, the British political framework and conception, and many of the British-trained and influenced elites, were swept away and replaced by a radical structure and direction to state-building and development. While some British contribution to nation-building in the South remained, efforts at state-building came to naught and the new republic began from scratch. In sum, the principal British legacy seems to have been in firmly establishing the political, as well as economic and social, primacy of Aden over all the South.

The Present Republics

The first stages of political change in Yemen, i.e. neo-traditionalism in the North and colonialism in the South, can be very clearly distinguished from more recent developments by the key dates of 26 September 1962 and 30 November 1967. In retrospect, some sort of drastic, even revolutionary, response seems to have been inevitable, given the growing pressures for change and the inadequacy or inappropriateness of existing structures to address those pressures. At the same time, it seems fair to say that there was little predictability or inevitability connected with either the course of the revolutions in North and South or with the composition and basic nature of the resultant regimes. The real revolutions set in motion by the events in 1962 and 1967 were far more profound and protracted than the simple alteration of the states' formal trappings. Both of the new states have committed themselves to policies of socio-economic development, including the consequent restructuring of their political systems to advance that goal. But the official adoption of a modernising course of action is, of course, clearly distinct from the actual establishment of an environment conducive to its accomplishment. It is precisely this gap which in large part is responsible for the crisis in legitimacy faced by many Third World states, the two Yemens among them.

An examination of the short history of both republics allows the identification of a number of distinct stages of political change, most initiated by violent action. Is there any cumulative progression in terms of political development to be discerned in these patterns of change? Or, conversely, is the record simply one of effective stagnation, of a meaningless succession of stationary cycles? A brief assessment of each of the stages occurring in both regions should help to lay a basis for the answers to these questions.

Beginning with the North, the first stage in the YAR was that of civil war (1962–7). Obviously, this was a period of instability, of transition, of searching for a new and viable formula around which to rebuild consensus. Nevertheless, certain tangible permanent steps were taken. First, the attempted Egyptianisation of the fledgeling state was firmly rejected, even though a basic bureaucratic infrastructure introduced by Cairo was largely retained. Second, the strength and importance of Yemeni nationalism were reaffirmed, including an emotional commitment to Yemeni unity. Third, the pervading weariness of war prompted development of amorphous agreement on the general framework of the new YAR, including the rejection of both extremes of right and left. On the negative side, however, the civil war produced a chronically weak and often impotent central government which was fair game for defiance and non-recognition. The war further fragmented the political centre and sharpened existing political schisms.

The second stage was the period of Abd al-Rahman al-Iryani's presidency (1967–74). At the heart of this stage was the process of national reconciliation, including both its promise and its limitations. While the 'national' political elites accepted the YAR as the form of state, this essentially meant little more than rejection of the imamate without clear consensus on the nature of its replacement. These years were characterised by unbridled competition and confrontation over the structure and the direction of the YAR, as well as over the basic allocation of power. The inability of the regime either to mould consensus or, eventually, even wield effective power resulted in the widespread perception of a ship of state adrift. Consequently, military officers, under the aegis of the 'corrective movement', took power, ostensibly to provide the stability necessary for the establishment of a framework favourable to political development. It should be noted, however, that beneath the largely anarchic façade of the Iryani regime, the foundations for state-building were quietly being laid. This was especially true in development planning and organisation, both within the government (with the creation of the Central Planning Organisation) and outside it (in the burgeoning co-operatives movement).

The Hamdi period (1974–7), though the shortest, was arguably the most constructive. While a group of officers acting in tandem initially seized power, it soon became clear that Ibrahim al-Hamdi was the dominant power. There are a number of reasons for Hamdi's relative success: his neutral standing as a qadi; his competent military record and control of key military units; his skill at manipulating the many political factions both in San'a' and the countryside; his charismatic appeal, in large part due to his genuine dedication to development; his strong support for modernists; and finally his ability to see the long-range needs of the YAR and to devise ways in which to accomplish his goals. Consequently, this period seemed to evince considerable progress in political development, but the net effect was limited by excessive reliance upon Hamdi's own position and role, and his gradual alienation of many of the supporters necessary to maintain his position and to carry out his programmes.

Hamdi's assassination marked the beginning of the latest period (1977-present), that of Hamdi's imitators, Ahmad al-Ghashmi and Ali Abdullah Salih. There is a basic thread of continuity in the style and performance of both these leaders which justifies their joint consideration, although Ghashmi's short-lived incumbency has meant that the period has been dominated by Salih. Basic strategy has relied on attempts to appear to be continuing on the broad course that Hamdi laid out: formal emphasis on the modernist conception of the state, including some stated recognition of the importance of state-building, institutionalisation and the leading role of the state in promoting socio-economic development. Behind the rhetoric, similarity also exists in Ghashmi's and Salih's attempts to emulate Hamdi's success in the 'politics of balance', in manipulating the complex forces, both internal and external, affecting the political environment. But the Ghashmi/Salih regime has exhibited far less ability than Hamdi in carrying out these similar general objectives. In part this is traceable to basic differences between Hamdi, and Ghashmi and Salih. The latter leaders suffered from severe personal limitations: they were uneducated, unsophisticated, inexperienced army tank-corps officers with narrow horizons. Their backgrounds were far less likely to appeal to the great majority of Yemenis, since they were both Zaidi tribesmen from minor tribes. Their popular standing was further compromised by their implication in Hamdi's death. Finally, they were heavily preoccupied with regime maintenance and personal survival (although Salih in recent years has made some efforts to broaden his horizons). Consequently, these factors have resulted in a visible weakening of the central government's physical and moral authority over the state. Much of the YAR's territory has fallen prey to the exclusive control of the tribes in the north and east, and the National Democratic Front in the south. The political centre, strengthened and somewhat broadened under Hamdi, has since been weakened, as evidence continues of increased factionalisation and intractable opposition to the regime.

Political change in the PDRY has been more restricted in scope and in its narrower range of participants, but it has been perhaps just as destabilising and inconclusive as in the North. The first stage (1967–71) was one of preoccupation over defining the precise direction of politics in the new state. The primacy of the NLF over internal Southern political forces had been established earlier on in the independence struggle, and British withdrawal in later 1967 left the NLF in secure control of the reins of power. But there still existed considerable diversity within the NLF over questions of ideology and political goals, perhaps reflecting the broad range of opinion within the parent Arab Nationalist Movement and the overriding need for co-operation during the liberation struggle. Only gradually was the radical wing of the NLF able to acquire a preponderant balance of power in Aden and impose a predominantly Marxist view of the state's role, institutions and relations with the outside world. And as the radical wing's influence grew, the position of the party's moderate and centrist wings, as represented by the Sha-'bis and Muhammad Ali Haitham respectively, declined, and the government and the army were purged of the remaining British-trained cadres.

A triumvirate within the ruling Presidential Council dominated the second stage (1971–8). Despite the success of the radicals in the earlier phase, significant differences of opinion were still current even within this wing of the NLF. The result was a long period of uncertainly balanced tension between the pragmatic and ultra-radical factions of the radical wing. Differences were apparent over such issues as: whether the government or the party should constitute the ultimate decision-making authority; whether Soviet-style 'scientific socialism' or a Maoist approach was the proper path for the country to follow (attitudes reflected in the alliances struck by individual politicians with Moscow and Peking); and whether it was proper to accept financial assistance from the Arab Gulf states or to remain poor but ideologically pure. Underlying these disputes was a welter of continuing personal, tribal and regional rivalries. Another divisive element arose over the issue of Yemeni unity, with those South Yemenis of Northern origin being significantly more hawkish than their 'pure' South colleagues. These differences and the internal contradictions and instability of South Yemeni politics were aptly illustrated by the composition of the ruling triumvirate. Salim Rubai'a Ali served as President, deriving his authority from control of the government and army. He appeared to be more Maoist in ideological orientation, particularly reliant on Chinese support and relatively more willing to reach a *modus vivendi* with the conservative Gulf regimes. Abd al-Fattah Isma'il, Secretary-General of the party, made his power base within the party organisation and militia. He was a more doctrinaire Marxist, closer to Moscow and a hard-liner in foreign affairs, being opposed to *rapprochement* with Saudi Arabia, firmer on solidarity with neighbouring Marxist Ethiopia and, being from a North Yemeni family, more determined to force unity. Ali Nasir Muhammad, the Prime Minister, seemed to be the weakest link in the Presidential Council as well as the most pragmatically inclined. He stayed closer to the sidelines as the struggle between Salim and Abd al-Fattah intensified.

The eventual triumph of Abd al-Fattah and the introduction of ideological inflexibility ushered in the third stage (1978–80). The events of June 1978 brought the underlying tensions out into the open and culminated in the deaths of both Ahmad al-Ghashmi and Salim Rubai'a Ali. Seemingly, the ultra-radical faction had finally won in the cumulatively narrowing search for a tight ideological consensus and now stood unchallenged. The party was clearly established as superior to the government, and a number of organisational changes were introduced to reflect this fact formally. Aden grew more isolated from the rest of the Arab world and the fragile link to Riyadh was severed. Relations with the North deteriorated into open warfare and considerable assistance was extended to the National Democratic Front. Ties to the Soviet bloc and allies were progressively strengthened, both through the Soviet/PDRY Friendship Treaty and the Tripartite Agreement (between the PDRY, Ethiopia and Libya), as well as by the near-ubiquitous presence of Soviet, East German and Cuban advisers and training personnel in Aden and the hinterland.

Despite these developments, the consolidation of power within the hands of the ultra-radical core had not been completely secured. Consequently, the fourth and latest stage (1980-present) featured the rise of Ali Nasir Muhammad to the top and a potential return to emphasis on pragmatism in both domestic and foreign policies. Dissension, within and outside the country, continued after the actions of 1978 and centred on a multitude of issues, including ideological differences, the direction of foreign policy, resentment over overwhelming foreign influence and presence in the country, relations with the North, the economic bankruptcy of the South and continuing tribal and regional rivalries, as exacerbated by the rise of Abd al-Fattah and his followers. Abd al-Fattah Isma'il was forced to resign and when into exile, and Ali Nasir Muhammad, the ultimate survivor, took over the positions of President and party chief in addition to the Prime Minister's job. The numbers and power of Soviet, Cuban and East German advisers were reduced, the channel to Riyadh was reopened, goods began to reappear in the shops, talks were opened for the first time with Oman and relations with the North grew more amicable. Technocrats began to appear in key positions alongside the ideologues. The generation of 'founding fathers', those who had led the fight against the British and created the new state, had been nearly decimated in a short decade-and-a-half.

Assessing Political Development in the Yemens

This brief survey indicates that the path of political development in the two Yemens has been anything but straightforward. While no non-violent formula for the allocation of power has been found, both states appear to have made some progress in tackling some of the many problems they face. Gradual improvement in the process of nation-building can be discerned, although it is still complicated by the unsettled matter of unity. Both regions must be seen as actively striving for unity, but given the basic ideological incompatibility of existing regimes there is little likelihood that the problem will be resolved in the foreseeable future.

The status of state-building lags far behind this, since the capabilities of both states to cope with the demands and functions expected of them remain embryonic. At most, attention can be drawn to limited success in creating partially effective governmental infrastructure, some enhancement of basic services in certain areas (with considerable external assistance) and the beginning of key planning and organisation for socio-economic development efforts. Further progress, however, is hindered by a multitude of obstacles.

Some of these obstacles are more tangible and pose immediate problems for existing regimes. These include the problem of financial insolvency and necessary reliance on outside aid; external pressures and interference contributing to this financial dependency; institutional under-development and excessive reliance on vulnerable leaders; the lack of skilled and capable elites in government service; unconstrained and unproductive personal rivalries; and all-too-frequent reliance on violence to solve political disputes and differences of opinion.

Other obstacles are of a more profound character and their removal requires the emergence of a truly national political culture. In large part these obstacles derive from the existing nature of centre and periphery and the wide schism between the two poles. As the above survey has shown, there has been some progress in gaining at least tacit recognition of the legality of the YAR and the PDRY as acceptable vessels of statehood. But the loyalty and identification of the majority of the population in North and South are at best marginal and its participation in national politics tangential.

The difficulty in expanding the centre, and thereby contracting the periphery, is twofold. First, there is a basic dichotomy between modernists and traditionalists which, although more severe in the North, shows no sign of abating in either region. In effect, this is essentially a struggle between a primary, modernising centre, and a secondary, traditionalist centre; a curious reversal of the situation characterising the pre-1960s period. At the same time, there is little cohesion even within the modernising centre. In the North, basic disagreements over the shape of the state and society and the ordering of priorities range from arch-conservative approaches to progressive, even Marxist, outlooks, especially if the dissident NDF is considered. While the historical experience of the South has resulted in a relatively more cohesive political centre, serious differences still exist there as well, particularly when account is taken of the massive number of exiles who share few of the current regime's goals.

The ability of the two Yemeni states to act with legitimate authority founders on a major dilemma. Their political systems are predominantly based on new or 'modern' concepts and institutions and are heavily dependent on Western influences. These systems, however, have been uncertainly superimposed on socio-economic milieus which display traditional goals and institutions and which persistently retain the primary allegiance and attention of most of the people. Because of the difficulty in legitimation encountered in many political systems or regimes, attempts are often made to achieve legitimacy on a personal or ideological basis in the short run, with the hope that this strategy may produce the time to develop structural or institutional legitimacy.

The North has so far placed greater emphasis on personal legitimacy. National reconciliation may not have been possible without the central role played by Abd al-Rahman al-Iryani. Later, much of

Hamdi's success derived from his charisma, which enabled him to remove rivals from key positions, to enhance the central government's authority, both institutionally and geographically, and to hold the Saudis at arm's length. Hamdi's successors have attempted to emulate his popularity by publicising their concern for the co-operatives movement and anti-corruption drives, but have had far less success. The shortcomings of the personal emphasis were clearly illustrated by Iryani's inability to control the YAR's feuding politicians, and then in the assassinations of the following two Presidents.

The South, meanwhile, has relied more heavily on ideological legitimacy. The ability of the NLF to implement its programme of 'scientific socialism', in large part, was due to its nationalist credentials acquired in the liberation struggle against the British. But the record of independent Democratic Yemen highlights the severe restrictions inherent in excessive reliance on rigid, abstract principles. The South has been no more successful than the North in resolving disputes other than by recourse to extraconstitutional measures involving violence.

These considerations should not obscure the fact that both governments have sought to legitimise their exercise of power through efforts at institutionalisation. In the North a principal function of the People's Constituent Assembly has been to elect the President formally. In the South the Yemeni Socialist Party constitutes the only legal form of political expression and, through its control of the Supreme People's Assembly, is intended to provide the guiding direction of the state. Despite these manoeuvres, though, power obviously continues to reside firmly in the hands of a few individuals who maintain their positions through less institutional means.

The above assessment of changes already occurring raises speculation over the future direction of Yemeni politics. Michael C. Hudson, in his *Arab Politics: The Search for Legitimacy*,[4] provides a synthesis of three models to explain the impact of modernisation and the resultant patterns of social change and transformation. One such model is that of social mobilisation, whose proponents, often employing Weberian concepts and terminology, perceive a gradual transformation from a traditional society to a rational/legal one through a process of increasing secularisation which eventually produces a uniform, modern political culture.

The transformationist model, on the other hand, emphasises the necessary, almost inevitable, role of revolution in bringing about a complete or radical transformation of society. Since political revolutions in the Middle East or Third World — with the important exception of Iran — essentially consist of narrowly based *coups d'état*, the necessary cataclysmic effect of revolutionary change must also incorporate a continuing 'social revolution' sponsored and generated by the state.

Finally, there is the mosaic model, which rejects the implicit evolutionary implications of the previous models by stressing the persistence of primordial cleavages even as modernisation and social change are simultaneously taking place. This model introduces the possibility of continuous conflict between traditional identifications and orientations and emerging 'modern' ones, of an enduring schism between centre and periphery. It also poses the threat of a permanent legitimacy crisis.

In applying these models to the Yemeni experience we see clearly that the revolutionary path has failed to accomplish the objectives foreseen by the transformationist model. The September 'revolution' in the North was the work of only a small coterie of modernists and the price for ending the civil war was the official rejection of many of the proclaimed revolutionary goals and means. The 'social revolution' in the South was launched by an unrepresentative faction trading on nationalist credentials acquired by leadership in the anti-British struggle. A pessimistic outlook for the chances of the social mobilisation model succeeding is indicated by the continuing strength of peripheral identities, the overwhelming weakness and poverty of the two states, the troublesome dilemma of sectarian hostility, and the absence of either regime or societal reinforcement for the emergence of a truly national political culture.

It may be only realistic to assume that the mosaic model provides the most likely avenue for future change in the Yemens. This view foresees a long, hard process of political development that must be intimately linked to the traditional concerns of society. Rather than force a transformation of the periphery to conform to the values of a modernist centre, the outlook of the centre should probably expand to encompass many of the goals and values now located in the periphery. For example, rather than an emphasis on urbanisation, light industrialisation, large-scale agricultural schemes, and prominent state sponsorship and control of development (whether socio-economic or political), greater reliance might be placed more constructively on local initiative. The initiative is undeniably there: both in the continuing strength of peripheral affiliations, and in the positive development of the co-operatives movement, spurred in part by the impact of wide-scale labour migration. The ideal role of the central government might be minimal and directed at creating a network to co-ordinate autonomous units and to provide advice, a channel for linkages and a vehicle for conciliation. In some ways, this approach is not all that far removed from the ideal 'traditional' system.

Such a strategy is far easier to discuss or devise than to put into operation. The emphasis of existing regimes is overwhelmingly focused on survival and on personal and factional rivalries. There is little remaining energy — let alone capability — to look beyond immediate horizons. Furthermore, even if the determination were there the outside world presents considerable constraints, ranging from the interference of the Saudis in the North and the Soviet Union in the South to the pressures of pan-Arab and regional concerns, rivalries and threats. Finally, there is the thorny issue of Yemeni unity, which constitutes a key stumbling block to any achievement of legitimacy.

It is perhaps not entirely Utopian to advocate a gradual, incremental approach to the dilemma. One possible scenario for circumventing the existing ideological incompatibility of the two regimes may lie with the functional model of integration.[5] A first step might involve a *pro forma* merger, leaving both regions essentially autonomous. True unity, though, would come about only when a strong and complex web of interdependent functions — economic, social, bureaucratic, technical and legal — have created enough integrative momentum to reduce significantly or even eliminate seemingly irreconcilable political differences. It is a process that would eventually benefit all concerned parties but also requires considerable patience.

Notes

1. Only a few of the numerous worth-while sources on politics in the two Yemens can be mentioned here. Among the more pertinent and/or comprehensive are: Robin L. Bidwell, *The Two Yemens* (Longman, London; Westview Press, Boulder, Colorado, 1983); Abdallah S. Bujra, 'Urban Elites and Colonialism: The Nationalist Elites of Aden and South Arabia', *Middle Eastern Studies*, vol. VI, no. 2 (1970), pp. 189–211; R. J. Gavin, *Aden under British Rule, 1839–1967* (Hurst, London, 1975); Fred Halliday, *Arabia without Sultans* (Penguin, Harmondsworth, 1974; Vintage, New York, 1975); *idem*, 'Yemen's Unfinished Revolution: Socialization in the South', *MERIP Reports*, vol. IX, no. 8 (Oct. 1979), pp. 3–20; J. E. Peterson,

Conflict in the Yemens and Superpower Involvement (Georgetown University, Centre for Contemporary Arab Studies, Washington, DC, Occasional Paper, 1981); *idem, Yemen: The Search for a Modern State* (Croom Helm, London; Johns Hopkins University Press, Baltimore, 1982); *idem*, 'The Two Yemens and the International Impact of Inter-Yemeni Relations' in William L. Dowdy and Russell B. Trood (eds.), *The Indian Ocean: Perspectives on a Strategic Arena* (Duke University Press, Durham, North Carolina, forthcoming); Robert W. Stookey, 'Social Structure and Politics in the Yemen Arab Republic,' *Middle East Journal*, vol. XXVIII, no. 3 (1974), pp. 248-60; vol. XXVIII, no. 4 (1974), pp. 409-18; *idem, Yemen: The Politics of the Yemen Arab Republic* (Westview Press, Boulder, Colorado, 1978); *idem, South Yemen: A Marxist Republic in Arabia* (Westview Press, Boulder, Colorado, 1982); Manfred W. Wenner, *Modern Yemen, 1918-1966* (Johns Hopkins University Press, Baltimore, 1968); and Mohammed Ahmad Zabarah, *Yemen: Traditionalism vs. Modernity* (Praeger, New York, 1982).

2. The delineation of traditional, neo-traditional and modernising (or post-traditional) phases in North Yemen's politics has been outlined in the author's 'Legitimacy and Political Change in Yemen and Oman', *Orbis* (forthcoming). Basically, decentralisation and limited central authority characterised the political system of the traditional phase. On both the national and constituent levels the exercise of power conformed to the goals, responsibilities and constraints long present in a traditional, inward-looking society. The neo-traditional phase produced a political system based on the personal strength and direction of a single individual who introduced certain significant innovations into the system — particularly as they enhanced his own authority — in a defensive and ultimately futile attempt to maintain the traditional goals and values of the society. The modernising phase was initiated by radical attempts to replace the existing regime and redefine the scope and role of the state. With this step the state committed itself to a policy of socio-economic development, including the consequent restructuring of the political system to advance that goal. It should also be noted that discussion in this chapter of political change in the Hamid al-Din imamate is essentially concerned with the reigns of Imams Yahya and Ahmad and excludes that of Imam Muhammad.

3. Shils defined the centre, or central zone of society as 'the centre of the order of symbols, of values and beliefs, which govern the society . . . It is a structure of activities, of roles and persons, within the network of institutions.' 'Centre and Periphery' in *The Logic of Personal Knowledge: Essays Presented to Michael Polanyi on his Seventieth Birthday, 11th March 1961* (The Free Press, Glencoe, Illinois; George Allen and Unwin, London, 1961), p. 117.

4. Yale University Press, New Haven, 1977, pp. 7-16.

5. For a synthesis of applicable theories of international integration see James E. Dougherty and Robert L. Pfaltzgraff, Jr., *Contending Theories of International Relations: A Comprehensive Survey*, 2nd edn (Harper and Row, New York, 1981), Ch. 10.

8 EDUCATION FOR NATION-BUILDING — THE EXPERIENCE OF THE PEOPLE'S DEMOCRATIC REPUBLIC OF THE YEMEN

Saeed Abdul Khair Al-Noban

Its full implementation [Butler's Act] may make all the difference between a happy and glorious future for our country, or an unhappy and inglorious one.[1]

No advanced literary education was required and only enough English was necessary to enable him [son of chief] to have contacts with Royal Air Force officers and others visiting him who had no Arabic.[2]

The above two statements reflect two concepts concerning the purpose of education in two socio-political settings — the first being for Britain, and the second for the Aden Colony and its Protectorates. It is clear how desperate Britain was to reorganise its educational system to cope with the urgent need for social reconstruction after the Second World War. It is natural, too, that education should take the lion's share of developmental investment and, had not the role of education been recognised, the Education Act of 1944 would not have been 'the first of a series of major measures of social reconstruction'.[3] 'Social reconstruction' and 'glorious future for our country' are steps along the path of nation-building, and they imply that through investment in the development of human resources Britain can achieve its goals. Other British thinkers and educationists have expressed the important role which education plays in preparing young people to maintain the place of Britain among other nations. Hutchinson and Young have stated that 'If the Battle of Waterloo was won on the fields of Eton, it is equally true that Britain's destiny is today being hammered out in the classrooms of secondary schools all over the country.'[4]

Again, Percy's committee on evaluating the position of Britain as a leading industrial nation concluded that:

First, the position of Great Britain as a leading industrial nation was being endangered by a failure to secure the fullest possible application of science to industry, and second, that this failure was partly due to deficiencies in education.[5]

We can also refer at this juncture, to the major and comprehensive reports on the British educational system, namely Newsom's Report *Half our Future*, Plowden's Report *Children and their Primary Schools* and Robbins' report on higher education. All these reports emphasise and move in line with the thesis that 'the nation which will stride ahead will be that which best solves the problem of stepping up the supply of scientists, technologists, technicians and craftsmen'[6] who are by necessity a product of a good educational system respondent to the national goals and the social needs of economy, industry, etc.

As for the second concept, the opening quotation implies a great deal:

(1) It was written by one of the pillars of colonialism who played the major role in establishing British rule in the Hadramawt. I think he meant what he wrote, i.e. limited education.
(2) This concept of education, though contemporary with Butler's Act (1939 and 1944, respectively), is contradictory to it. It denies children in the colonies one of their basic rights — education. It reflects the dualism in the mentality of the British.
(3) If the level and quality of education given to the sons of the chiefs of the tribes are such, how would one expect it to be for the sons of the other social classes? We have to take into account that these chiefs and their sons are supposed to be the closest and most reliable friends of the British.
(4) What output would one expect of such education? Is it education for nation-building as we have seen in Butler's Act? Not at all. It is an education in the service of the British Empire.
(5) To what extent does this policy fit in with Lawrence's famous quotation, 'a ring-wall around Arabia, a country which must be reserved as an area of Arabian individualism. So long as our fleet keeps its coasts, Arabia should be at leisure to fight out its own complex and fatal destiny'?[7]

In actual fact this situation was not prevalent in Aden Colony only. It was the general pattern of British colonial policy in education, and was characterised by irrelevance of curricula to social needs, behaviour and values, low rates of enrolment and an imbalance between the different levels of education. In addition there was an over-emphasis on arts subjects, a corresponding neglect of technical and vocational studies and an absence of higher education.

Towards a Theory of the Role of Education in Nation-building

From the brief introduction above we can see that the two concepts can create a good environment for establishing a theory of the role of education in the making of nations — the thesis which is sustained here is that education can flourish and play a remarkable role in the making of nations only when those nations are independent and can exercise their full sovereignty. We can trace this through studying the development of education in the Colony of Aden and its Protectorates on one side, and the emerging People's Democratic Republic of Yemen on the other. In general terms, the two systems of education represent two diametrically opposed patterns as far as educational goals and national objectives are concerned. The components of the two systems can be compared as follows:

(1) A colonial system of education, representing and reinforcing the colonial philosophy of sovereignty, and persuading the local institutions to act in line with colonial policy. Against this, and after independence, there is a national regime which declared a national system of education in the service of economic, social and progressive development.
(2) A colonial system of education which was conscious of the dangers of any policy of expanding educational opportunities, against a national system of education which is convinced that expanding and equalising educational opportunities are rights of every Yemeni child guaranteed constitutionally, and that such expansion of educational opportunities augments national consciousness of social responsibilities.
(3) A colonial system interested in the children of different social classes who would, it was hoped, protect its interests and defend its political targets, against a national system which looks equally at all children whatever their social origins. It considers all children as future citizens having a role to play, and as participants in the implementation of national, social policies.
(4) A colonial system practising hard, selective measures

Education for Nation-building 105

unnecessarily, and discriminating between children, against a national system which looks equally at children, and discriminates only in so far as their mental capabilities differentiate between them and do not permit them to be promoted to higher levels.

(5) A colonial system which imprints in the minds of children the greatness and glory of the British Empire, and the eternity of the Crown to which they should pay homage, against a national system which imprints national unity, national values and international solidarity.

(6) A colonial system whose objectives concentrate on class differences, against a national system which endeavours to wipe out such social differences.

(7) A colonial system which practised a policy of 'divide and rule' even in education, against a national system aimed at creating a consciousness of adherence to one central government.

(8) A colonial system which intentionally established different educational structures, against a national system which rejected such multiplicity and called for one structure which guarantees equal opportunities for every child in the Republic.[8]

Such broad terms epitomise the characteristics of the future citizen of the PDRY in terms of personality and character-building, expected and accepted behavioural traits, development of cognitive faculties, developed attitudes, value acquisition and an internationalist outlook on the world. They also depict the role they have to play in social development. The magnitude of work, the voluminous studies and the training of personnel needed to realise the above targets are as heavy as the tasks bestowed on any Ministry of Education in a revolutionary regime which plans to rebuild society according to drastically different ideological, social and economic strategies. We will discuss the ways and means of approaching this task in detail as we proceed in this chapter.

Comparative Analysis of the Role of Education in Two Sociopolitical Environments

To develop the theory that only in a national political system with full sovereignty can the educational role for nation-building flourish, we have to elaborate the above eight components and compare in detail the practical steps of their implementation in the People's Democratic Republic of Yemen and the Colony. The areas for comparisons may be the following:

(1) Objectives:
   the constitutional tasks bestowed on education;
   the educational objectives laid down in the statutes.
(2) Tools for implementation:
   administrative principles governing the management of education;
   financing of education;
   the educational set-up: structures, curricula, assessment, student participation;
   higher education and research institutions.
(3) Results achieved:
   democratisation of education;
   human resources development.

We have to elaborate on the above topics to give them some depth and meaning. The elaboration will help to make the difference clear, and, more important, to prove the thesis that only in a sovereign state can the role of education for nation-building flourish.

Tasks Bestowed by the Constitution

During colonial rule two constitutions were passed some five years before independence and less than a year before the armed liberation movement was declared on 14 October 1963. One actually wonders how Britain denied these rights for 129 years of colonial rule; one also questions the haste of the belated action. The Colony of Aden had its constitution passed in October 1962 (amended in 1964). In 1963 an ordinance was passed whereby the Federal Constitution for the Federation of South Arabia was declared (Ordinance No. 9 of 1963). One doubts if these constitutions can bear the name of national charters, because they concentrated on political issues and neglected the main and basic rights of the people — education being one of these rights. In actual fact, three factors were behind the haste: (1) the appeal of the United Nations in June 1960 to grant independence to colonies;[9] (2) the revolution in North Yemen and the overthrow of Imam Ahmad; and (3) the high tide of Arab nationalism.

Contrary to the above, the emerging PDRY, led by the National

Education for Nation-building 107

Liberation Front and subsequently the Yemen Socialist Party (YSP), conscious of its social responsibility towards the citizens, and towards society, passed its constitution (revised in 1978). We need not go into discussion of the main principles which the constitution laid down to establish the new society as we are concerned only with education. Three articles of this constitution refer to education, the philosophy behind it, role in society, beneficiaries of it and the different organs responsible for its implementation.[10]

(1) Article 40 of the constitution refers to the right of education and states: 'All citizens have the same right and access to education. The government guarantees that right through expanding educational opportunities for all children . . . Education is free and the government should pay particular attention to technical and vocational education.'
(2) Article 60 refers to the parents' responsibility in bringing up their children according to socialist morals and values, and in preparing them for 'socially productive work'. It aims at opening kindergartens for infants to allow mothers to work as effective members of society.
(3) Article 65 of the constitution refers to the responsibility of the Yemeni Youth Organisation in the educative process and in the preparation of youth for 'socially productive work'.

These constitutional articles express the targets which the YSP (Successor of the National Liberation Front and the Unified Political Organisation of the National Front) aims to achieve during the period of national democratic revolution. Beginning with the Fifth General Conference of the NLF in March 1972 in which the programme of national democratic revolution was adopted, passing through the Conference of Unification of all Progressive Forces in February 1975, and the sixth General Conference in October 1975, and culminating in the First Conference of the YSP in October 1978 and its Extraordinary Conference in October 1980, the politico-economic programmes have emphasised the importance of and concentration on social reconstruction on the basis of scientific socialism. Education, as we have said earlier, has an important role to play in this drastic social change. The report submitted to the First Conference of the party in 1978 stated:

> Considering the paramount importance of education in the ideological formation process, the Conference of Unification of

Progressive Forces (1975) gave special care and emphasis to the necessity to *eradicate illiteracy, maintain democratisation of education and link education with production* . . . Education has expanded horizontally and vertically during the last three years in the direction of its democratisation to all citizens . . . Regarding higher education, we stress the role played by the University of Aden in building up cadres. The founding of this University was a response to the appeal of the Revolution to prepare cadres with high qualifications who are ideologically oriented towards scientific socialism. These cadres *have to participate effectively in the overall development of society and relate scientific research to the needs of material production, social activities.*[11]

Educational Objectives in the Statutes

Looking at the statutes which govern education and elaborate the general constitutional articles, we can trace only one ordinance for the Colony of Aden[12] (Ordinance No. 23 for 1952). However, this ordinance concentrated on the management rather than the purpose of education. It dealt with governing schools, parents' committees, etc. The structure of the Ministry of Education was limited to the Minister, Permanent Secretary, Director of Education and an inspection team: other jobs were clerical. The explanation of this can only be seen in the limited responsibilities bestowed on the Ministry of Education because policy matters and the planning of education were in the hands of the Colonial Office, represented by the Governor of Aden, who had, by the constitution of 1962, almost full power. He could overrule any decisions by the Council of Ministers, let alone a Minister's decision. If we are interested in these policy lines, we have to look at them in other documents, e.g. the document on the Adenisation scheme where it is stated clearly that investments in education should be limited and that the purpose of education should be to prepare clerks for the administration and craftsmen.[13] In the Hadramawt a similar document was adopted in 1944.[14] Nothing is recorded in the other governorates (the then sultanates and shaikhdoms) where the highest level of education was the intermediate level. Secondary education and teachers' training started in the 1960s and were limited to one college of each, situated in Aden.

After independence things were different. Taking into account the directives in the party's programmes and the constitutional articles, the PDRY has passed a number of laws which clarify the role of the Ministry of Education. The PDRY looks at education as integrated from kindergarten to university. Consequently, Law No. 26 for 1972 is the first and major law which organises the educational system, and the Ministry of Education. It is concerned with the general objectives of education, specific objectives for each level of education, levels of education and its duration, the Ministry and its functions and the departments of education in the governorates. Amendments to this law are being formulated so that it can cope with the developments that have taken place in education, and also in society as a whole. To elaborate this basic law, other laws have been passed or are concerned with specific targets:

Law No. 32 of 1973 regarding the eradication of illiteracy;
Law No. 13 of 1974 concerned with care for the Yemeni child;
Law No. 22 of 1975 regarding the foundation of Aden University;
Law No. 23 of 1975 concerning the establishment of the Council for Higher Education;
Law No. 2 of 1980 setting up the Democratic Yemen Youth Organisation.

Supplementary to these laws, regulations have been passed by the Minister of Education to elaborate in more detail the functions of each department, school, headmasters . . . etc. Of these regulations we have:

A Ministerial Order regarding the organisation of the Ministry of Education and the Departments of Education based on the principles of centralisation of planning and major policy issues, and decentralisation of implementation. Amendments to this have been made to cope with the developments that have taken place in education.
A Ministerial Order concerned with school administration.
A Prime Minister's Order which is concerned with the establishment of an Educational Research Centre (ERC) as part of the Ministry of Education. It deals with curricular development and other research projects which may help in developing education. The intention is that this Centre will develop gradually to constitute a specialised academy for pedagogical sciences. Plans are in progress for the preparation of high-level personnel in the different fields and organisation of the Centre.

Regulations for the organisation of the Institute for Audio-Visual Aids to develop into a resource and production centre catering for all schools in the Republic.

Regulations regarding the establishment of the Central Institute for In-Service Training for all cadres working in the Ministry of Education.

When we study all these laws and regulations, we should not forget that scientific socialism is the philosophy behind them, and that democratic centralism is the principle governing all relations in the Ministry, and between the Ministry and the schools.

Administrative Principles in the Management of Education

As we have previously stated, the magnitude of work is great and it cannot be completed overnight. Law No. 26 of 1972 is one of the major social issues in Democratic Yemen, and its implementation required the collaboration of every citizen. And taking into consideration the vast area of the PDRY, rigid centralisation would produce adverse results. There are therefore three general principles which constitute the mainspring for any future regulations or modification in the educational set-up.

Democratic centralism. This constitutes the backbone of the relations between the Ministry and its branches and it usually implies that the Ministry should take the necessary measures for guaranteeing the real participation of all those involved in the educative process, i.e. the educationists, including teachers, students and parents. This participation in decision-making allows workers, parents and students to exercise their democratic right of involvement in issues that relate to their future. As soon as decisions have been made and when these have been passed centrally by the Minister, the implementation is binding and obligatory. This is the essence of democratic centralism. The principle is implemented on two levels.

First, major policy issues are normally discussed in educational conferences, representatives for which come from every governorate in the Republic. Representatives from the Workers' Confederation, Ministries, Students' Association and Women's Federation also attend. Draft documents are sent in advance to the governorates where seminars at the level of the governorate are held. The educational conferences are held every four years. Issues discussed are varied, e.g. change of the educational ladder, comprehensive changes in curriculum, etc. Two conferences have already been convened (1975 and 1979) and preparations are now in hand to convene the third. In May 1981 the University of Aden convened the first conference on Higher Education.

The second level where the Ministry practises this principle is through the Consultative Committee, which is presided over by the Minister of Education and contains Deputies of the Minister, Assistant Deputies and Directors-General in the governorates. Representatives of the Teachers' Association and Students' Association are also members of this Consultative Committee. At this level discussions emphasise the proper ways and means to put into operation party and government directives in the field of education, or perhaps review some of the recommendations of the conference and pass instructions for implementation.

Centralisation of policy-making and planning, and decentralisation of implementation. The Ministry of Education was the first Ministry to delegate authority to governorates. From the beginning of the academic year 1973/4, directorates of education were established in the governorates with full financial and administrative powers. With the issue of the law on Local Government in 1978, the Ministry responded immediately by delegating more powers and giving greater help in back-up and implementation. In 1979 the Second Educational Conference passed a recommendation that more power should be delegated to the governorates, and that the level of authority should be equivalent to that of an Assistant Deputy Minister, i.e. Director-General. As far as policy matters are concerned, the Director-General is responsible to the Minister of Education. He is fed with information through his membership in the Consultative Committee of the Ministry. The Director-General, on the other hand, is responsible to the governorate as he is an elected member of the local council. In that capacity he is responsible to the local council for implementing central policy. However, he can raise points to improve the educational facilities in the governorate to the Consultative Committee and abide by whatever resolutions they arrive at.

Group leadership. This is the third of the principles which govern the administrative process and direct those who are concerned with the drafting of resolutions. The essence of this principle is that consultation with colleagues in the Ministry usually leads to a ripe and useful result. This consultation can be through regular meetings which the Assistant Deputy can organise with the departments under his authority, to discuss with them points concerning their departments which will be discussed at higher levels. Subsequently he may discuss the resolutions and recommendations of the meetings of the Consultative Committee and ask them to suggest ways and means of implementation of those parts which concern their work. Similar steps can be taken by the Director-General of the governorate.

The above three principles have proved very helpful to the Ministry of Education, especially in the light of the fact that there is a dearth of qualified personnel. We can go a step further and consider this process not only as one of the ways through which leadership is brought up, but as a democratic step where participation in decision-making is not limited, but diffused over a wide base. The effect of this is psychological in the sense that everyone feels satisfied that he has a say in the running of his department and is thereby ready to do whatever he can to defend these decisions and achieve the goals of his institution. For this reason, the three principles have been practised not only at the level of administrators in the Ministry and governorate, but also at the level of the school. The regulations concerning school administration refer in detail to the ways in which schools practise the above principles.

Financing of Education

We have in the previous pages referred to Article 40 of the constitution in the PDRY which states that education is a constitutional right and that it is free. Despite the huge financial problems and the incessant intrigues that faced the Republic during its developmental march, the political leadership has never thought of a retreat, and the government has made funds available to expand educational opportunities. Private schools have been closed and the government took full responsibility for education to guarantee:

(1) That all children get the official care proclaimed in the constitution. Democratisation of education cannot be maintained through the issuing of laws only, because some problems may arise which make the parents unable to send their children to schools, e.g. financial limitations. For this reason the government has guaranteed free education, and made boarding

facilities available for children where no education exists in their vicinity. The government has also guaranteed free daily transport facilities from home to school. Text-books and tuition are free.
(2) That development of education should be distributed evenly between the different governorates of the Republic. We must remember that, during colonial rule, education up to secondary level was limited to Aden and Hadramawt only, while some of the other governorates did not have even primary education, e.g. al-Mahra governorate.

Because education was not developed earlier, heavy investments were poured into this sector — some as part of the government's annual budget for recurrent expenditure — while investments on capital expenditure have been found from the resources of the socio-economic development plans. In order to evaluate the magnitude of effort and the strides which the PDRY has made, we should look at some of the financial indicators (see Table 8.1).

Table 8.1: PDRY: Comparison of Education Expenditure in 1972 and 1980

	1972	1980
Percentage GNP devoted to education	2.3 (for 1969)	6
Central government expenditure on education as percentage of total	12.6 (for 1971)	10.5
Percentage of public education recurrent expenditure allocated		
Primary	—	63
Secondary	—	14
Higher	—	8

Source: World Bank, *Comparative Education Indicators*, 1974 and 1982.

The Educational Set-up

So far, we have been discussing points of a general nature which are concerned with educational objectives as the legal sources and the YSP expect them to be in the new society. We have also discussed the administrative guidelines and principles which govern the management of schools, and which are in themselves part of educational development in the PDRY. The question to be raised now pertains to the actual realisation of these objectives in view of the fact that government investments on education are higher than in many of the countries which became independent before the PDRY, and also more than in some countries with greater potentialities and natural resources. What are the achievements of the PDRY in the field of education? Looking back at some of the comparative educational indicators may help us to visualise the actual situation better.

Table 8.2: PDRY: Comparison of Enrolment in Education in 1972 and 1980

	Primary Enrolment Ratio	Completion Rate for Primary Cycle (%)	Primary Students per Teacher
1972	70	—	29
1980	70	53	24

	Secondary Enrolment Ratio	Higher Education Ratio
1972	12	—
1980	31	2.5

Source: World Bank, *Comparative Education Indicators*, 1974 and 1982.

We will discuss this in some detail as we progress in our discussion of participation by governorates.

Structure. The system during the colonial era consisted of two structures which were distinct in Aden (4-3-4) and the Hadramawt (4-4-4), despite the fact that the Colonial Office took over responsibility from the India Office in 1937 for Aden Colony and the Protectorates. The British authorities in Aden sought the assistance of two experts to advise on the best way to organise the educational system: J. P. Attenborough, who then became Director of Education, advised the structure of 4-3-4 for the Colony, while V. L. Griffiths from Bakht ar-Rudha in the Sudan advised a structure of 4-4-4 for the Hadramawt. A third structure was the Quranic schools, which are the traditional institutions prevalent all over the Islamic world. However, this last structure was phased out as the other two expanded. The other Protectorates were not given any consideration at this early stage of direct British rule in the area. We may note that these colonial structures were made for an educational process which was academically oriented up to the time of evacuation of the British forces and the emergence of the new Republic in 1967. We may except from this remark one vocational, industrial or trade school which was constructed by Anthony Besse, one of the leading monopolists of trade and industry in the Colony. However, in the fifties, it was suggested that students in the only secondary school (Aden College) might branch into academic and commercial classes. This was at the request of the monopolist companies which flourished at this period and needed cheap labour to do the clerical jobs.

From 1956 a GCE Advanced Level class was started for some of the best students who completed secondary school with more than six passes in the GCE O Level. Higher education was never thought of except for a handful of bright students of the privileged classes or those children from other social classes with very sharp and intelligent faculties. We can come to some conclusions about this structure:

(1) The educational structure reflected the socio-political system in the Colony and the Protectorates which was itself socially biased.
(2) The educational structure did not meet the socio-economic needs of society as it did not reflect the varied employment needs of the economy.
(3) The educational structure was characterised by sharp selective measures and very few children were permitted to the higher levels. However, the sharp selectivity trait coincided with another characteristic inherent in this biased structure, i.e. no outlet for those drop-outs from schools to train them in craft schools and make them good productive citizens. The result of this high wastage of the system was that children might revert to illiteracy and do jobs they were not prepared for, or migrate.
(4) Because the structure did not respond to social and economic needs, the monopolist companies and the British themselves had to contract top-level managerial and second-class officers from the Commonwealth; this leads us to the conclusion that the structure did not prepare for a level of citizenship capable of taking over full responsibilities.
(5) From the above we may sum up that the structure was not by any means designed to prepare its output for nation-building.

What is the situation after independence? On 30 November 1967 the first Cabinet was formed and the first national Ministry of Education came into existence. It is natural that the new Ministry had to face a great many problems; philosophical as far as the purpose of education was concerned, economic to find the necessary allocations to leap forward and expand education, and, of course, educational. In this section we are concerned with the structure of education and what its philosophy is. Since independence two educational structures have been adopted. The first was immediately after independence and was in conformity with the pattern of the Arab Cultural Pact (6-3-3). There were some sound reasons for adopting it:

(1) The new Republic was made up of a number of sultanates, shaikhdoms and amirates, and the first task of the new government was to create a consciousness amongst the people that they had been one nation, that colonialism had divided them and that with their struggle led by the National Liberation Front they were again back to unity. The educational system had a role to play in this process. To have one Ministry looking after education all over the Republic was the dream, and to make it felt by everybody without any sensitivity was a big responsibility for those in charge of education. The political unity represented by the new government helped to bring to life the historical unity which was destroyed by the British.
(2) The tools which were needed for implementation were not out of reach. Expatriate teachers had left the country but the new structure had Arabic as the medium of instruction and with the aid of Arab governments teachers could be made available. At the same time the Egyptian government supplied us with the books we needed.
(3) The new structure broke the barriers in education — the two structures had been abolished and the new one proclaimed as the official one.

However, this change did not bring the ideal educational structure which would respond to the socio-economic objectives which the revolution had publicly announced. With the 'Corrective Movement' of 22 June 1969 the progressive wing in the National Liberation Front took over power. The programme of this wing was clear. Social revolution after the national liberation of the country. For the educational sector the long-term objectives could be stated as follows:

(1) Education was an ideological sector which should be oriented

on the basis of scientific socialism. It should aim at the building up and development of the multi-sided personality.
(2) Education should produce the different levels of cadres needed. They would form the wide base of the educated working class who could discuss their problems intelligently and defend their rights vigorously.
(3) Education should help in the material production of society as well as the spiritual.
(4) Education is a right of every citizen. Democratisation of education should obtain for all children.

On such basic philosophical grounds the First Educational Conference (September 1975) was convened and a new structure was adopted (see Figure 8.1). The new structure attempts to solve some of the basic issues of the revolution, especially the development of human resources. The new structure is dependent on the integrated nature of the educational system from kindergarten to university where a rational balance between the different levels is sought — this is what Law 26 of 1972 emphasised. However, the realisation of this sought-after balance needs much effort, and it also needs the co-operation of many sectors to attain good results. Those most concerned are the economic sectors which must work hard to generate and increase job opportunities for the new output from schools. So the absorptive capacity of the economy plays an important part in this rational balance. The new structure gives eight years of schooling (Unity schools of grades 1-8) which is considered to be the basic right for every citizen. This is followed by a tripartite system of secondary education: secondary academic which prepares students to pursue studies in the University, technical which leads to technician level, and the craft course to prepare a skilled worker. The duration of study varies: four years for secondary and teachers' training, five years for technician level and two years for the trade school (see Figure 8.1). One has to emphasise that the technician and trade courses are not closed or terminal in nature. Promising students in the technician level can proceed to the University through partial exemption and satisfying the other parts of the University prerequisites. The same applies to promising students in craft courses who wish to proceed to technician-level courses. This structure, in our opinion, serves the present stage of social revolution anticipated by the YSP and hence paves the way for the future development of society. The quality of the output is dependent on

118 *Education for Nation-building*

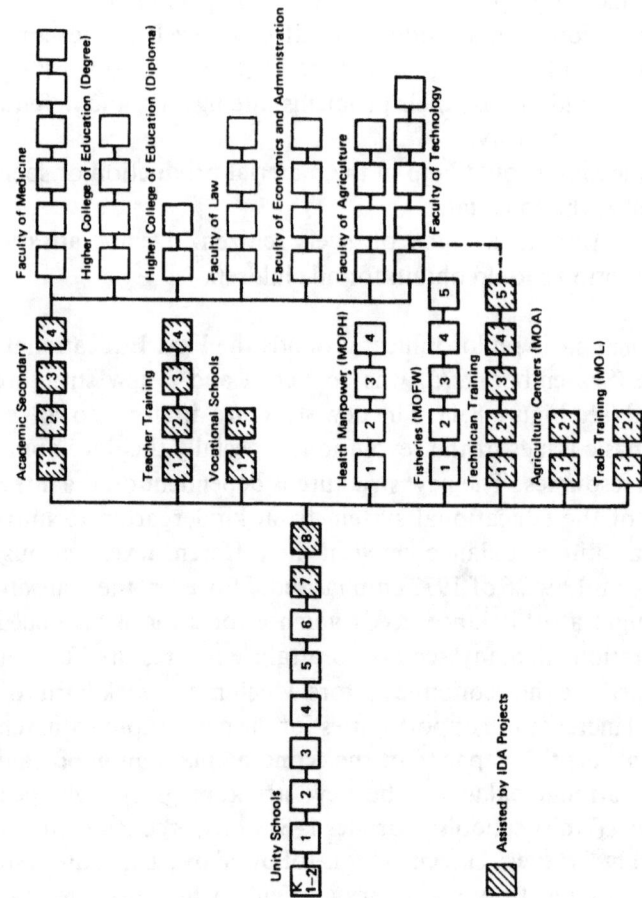

Figure 8.1: People's Democratic Republic of Yemen: New Education Structure, 1980

Source: World Bank

the curriculum which is adopted, and other inputs which will make that curriculum successful.

Curricula and assessment. The basic factors for evaluating a curriculum may best be described as those which answer the following questions:

To what extent does it orient the student towards socialist values, imprint in him solidarity with the world proletariat, and implant a good, firm stand against capitalism and imperialism, and a liking for socialism?

To what extent does it convey solid, up-to-date scientific knowledge, and develop the mental faculties of students through popularising discovery, creative thinking and problem solving?

What possibilities are there to depart from the purely academic, and introduce some polytechnical education (pre-vocational) to develop skills, interests and talents?

To what extent does it take the child's society as a departing point?

How is it relevant to societal needs?

To what extent do the above questions help in the formation and development of the multi-sided personality?

These are the basic issues which concern the Educational Research Centre (ERC) in formulating the syllabus in the Unity schools as well as the secondary. Up to now the experts in the ERC are still making endeavours to issue text-books which will meet the above conditions and take into account experiences from the local environment. Text-books have already been issued for grades 1-11. In the academic year 1983/4 the first batch of the secondary schools' output will leave school in accordance with the new syllabus which was adopted at the First Educational Conference in September 1975.

As far as assessment of students is concerned, the Ministry is now attempting to assess the overall development and thereby follow the student through the year. So daily exercises, monthly tests and final examination together with talent in arts, music and physical education are all components of the students' evaluation. Daily exercises and monthly tests count for 60 per cent and the final examination 40 per cent. It has not yet been decided whether this method of evaluation will one day be adopted in the Ministerial examinations as this method is still in the stage of experimentation and evaluation.

Student participation. In conformity with the party's directives, the constitutional objectives and the government programmes accepted by the People's Council, the Ministry has made its plans to universalise the Unity school level (grades 1–8) and expand the secondary level to the extent which will meet the different categories of manpower requirements. There are many obstacles facing a fully fledged implementation of a manpower approach, most important of which is lack of reliable data for existing employees, classified in accordance with a standard job-classification system. Future forecasts are also not yet reliable.

To conceive the big leap which the PDRY made in educational development and give it its proper magnitude, we have to look back in anger at the situation during colonial rule. Unfortunately, no detailed figures are available for each sultanate, amirate or shaikhdom. The only figures were for Aden Colony and the Hadramawt — the latter being from 1964. However, even these statistics were incomplete in the sense that they do not show age-group participation, or sex, etc. An attempt made by a UNESCO expert in educational statistics suggested a total of nearly 60,000 students in the Republic on Independence Day. Immediately after independence, and for obvious reasons, thousands of young children in towns and villages called on schools claiming their basic educational rights. These reasons were the colonial policy of limiting educational opportunities and depriving the young of their right, and secondly, and contrary to this colonial policy, the national regime which declared education a right for every child of school age. To implement this policy was near to impossible as the educational buildings were also limited. The Ministry had to increase class sizes to 40 and sometimes to 60 children. Had it not been for the people's participation in building schools or additional classes, it would have really been impossible to increase student admissions. Unfortunately no studies of this phenomenon have yet been made.

We now have to turn to the actual enrolment figures after independence. Table 8.3 illustrates the participation rate for each governorate by sex and age group, but we have to admit that there is some unreliability in the rates because we feel that the statistics the Ministry received from governorates are not completely accurate,

Table 8.3: PDRY: Percentage of Participation in Education by Governorate, Sex and Age Group[a,b] (Governorates: Ad: Aden; Lah: Lahej; Ab: Abyan; Had: Hadramawt[c])

Year	Age Group 7-14 Male				Age Group 7-14 Female				Age Group 15-18 Male				Age Group 15-18 Female			
	Ad.	Lah.	Ab.	Had.	Ad.	Lah.	Ab.	Had.	Ad.	Lah.	Ab.	Had.	Ad.	Lah.	Ab.	Had.
1968/9	59	69.6	54	57	46	7	10.5	11	8	0.5	0.3	5	6	0	0	0.1
1969/70	64	68	63	59	53	8	10.6	14.7	10	0	1.0	6	8	0	0.2	0.5
1970/1	79	79	96	62	62	12	13	16.7	21	2	2	9	11	0	0.3	0.3
1971/2	88	85	95	62	66.9	14	15	17	25	0.5	3	12	13	0.1	0.4	0.5
1972/3	86	86	93	64	69	14.5	14	18.7	34	9	5	12	19	0.3	0.8	1.0
1973/4	96	97	81	68	77	14.7	31.6	22	38	10.7	7	15	20	0.5	1	1.5
1974/5	88.6	80	79.5	73	77	27	28	25	41	14	10.7	18	26	1.3	1	2
1975/6	85.8	76	72	72	75	31	38	31	42	14	12.4	22	29	11	0.24	2.8
1976/7	84	72	68	71.5	70	31	38.6	34	40.6	20	16.8	24	32.6	4	0.33	4
1977/8	83.6	74	69.5	72	70.5	29	40.6	35	41.4	23	15	27	38.4	4.5	0.33	8.7
1978/9	76.6	71	66.6	70.5	66.9	25	37.8	36.9	40	27	14.4	27.7	40	5.9	0.37	6.6
1979/80	73.8	87	45.3	66	63.6	31.7	21.7	35.9	40	26	12.4	32.8	43	5	0.42	7.7

Notes: a.   Over-age students are included.
b.   Age-groups prior to 1975 are adjusted to conform with the new structure.
c.   Participation by the governorates of Shabwa and al-Mahra has not yet been calculated.
Source: Ministry of Education annual statistics.

and that these figures also include over-age or under-age children. This is a problem which even international agencies face in developing countries. It is envisaged that by 1995 education in the Unity schools (grades 1–8) will include all of those eligible.

Higher Education. We have already touched on the role higher education plays in the development of the human resources which shoulder the responsibility in the new formation of society on the ideological principles of scientific socialism accepted and implemented by the YSP. In this section higher education means all postsecondary education, and on the basis of this interpretation the PDRY has a three-part strategy:

(1) University education in the University of Aden which comprises six main faculties necessary for developmental planning — Education, Economics, Agriculture, Medicine, Technology and Law.
(2) Scholarships abroad: this was vigorously followed at the initial stage and before the development of the University of Aden. Further studies can be followed in specialisations which are not catered for in the University of Aden.
(3) The preparation of the technician level in the technical institutes (industrial, agricultural and commercial). There are also Colleges of Education in the governorates which offer a B. Ed., as in the Hadramawt governorate, and a two-year post-secondary Diploma in Education in the Lahej and Abyan governorates.

The above university courses lead to the first degree from the University of Aden, and the new regulations which were adopted after the First Higher Educational Conference (1981) have introduced the Special Degree which is a twelve-month graduate course comparable to the Master's Degree. The students eligible to follow this course are those who attain 'Excellent' or 'Very good' in their first degree. This degree was introduced to promote research activities in the University gradually.

It should be pointed out that the curriculum in this university follows the same principles as those in general education, i.e. scientific socialism. The last point to be made is that the University of Aden started with 40 students in the College of Education in 1970, and it now houses over 4,000 students having free education and stipends averaging about a thousand dollars annually.

In conclusion, we have to proclaim loudly that what has been achieved in education since November 1967 is unprecedented, compared with the achievements of 129 years of British colonial rule. Of course Britain could have achieved these targets and maybe more, but this was never to be. The difference can be attributed to the fact that British policy in the colonies was oriented towards the service of the Crown, while education in a national regime is for nation-building.

Notes

1. H. S. Dent, *The Education Act of 1944* (University of London Press, London, 1962), p. 4.
2. W. H. Ingrams, *Arabia and the Isles*, 2nd edn (John Murray, London, 1952), p. 96.
3. Dent, *Education Act*, p. 3.
4. M. Hutchinson and C. Young, *Educating the Intelligent* (Penguin, Harmondsworth, 1962).
5. G. A. N. Lowndes, *The English Educational System* (Hutchinson University Library, London, 1964), p. 84.
6. Ibid., p. 85.
7. W. H. Ingrams, 'Political Development in the Hadhramaut', *Journal of International Affairs*, vol. XXI, no. 2 (1945).
8. S. A. K. Noban, *Spotlight on the Development of Education in the PDRY*, vol. II (forthcoming, in Arabic).
9. United Nations Document OPI/66-13187, June 1961.
10. Constitution of PDRY — amended 1978.
11. Political report submitted to First Conference of the Socialist Party of Yemen, 1978.
12. *Laws of Aden*, Vol. I (1955).
13. Document on Adenisation, 1964, Library of the Colonial Office, London.
14. Archive of the Department of Education, Mukalla.

124 *Education for Nation-building*

Figure 8.2: People's Democratic Republic of Yemen: Education Pyramid, 1979/80

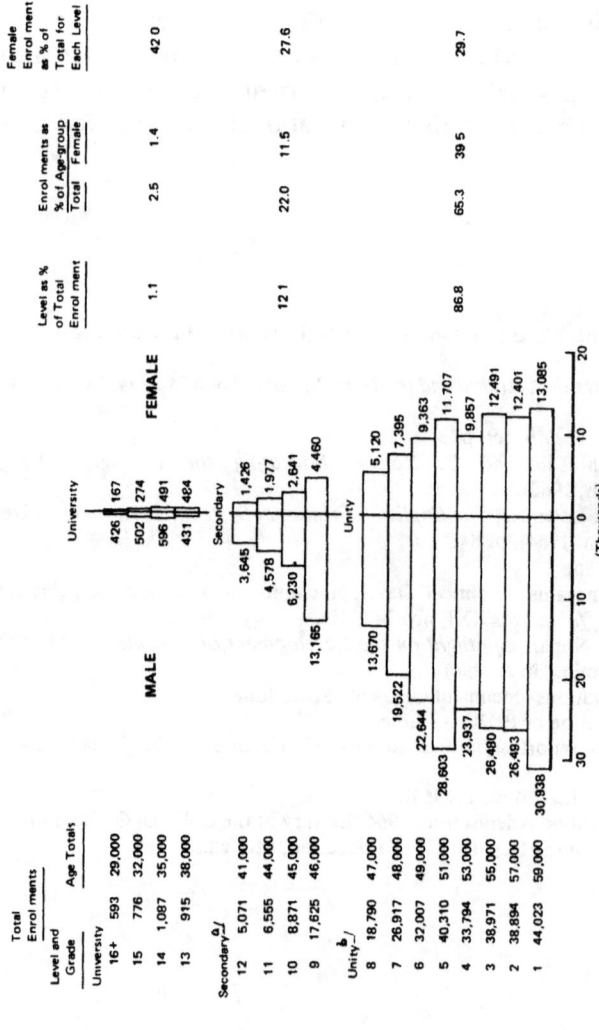

Notes: a. Includes bedouins, teacher training, vocational and technical enrolments in MOE institutions.
b. Includes bedouin enrolments.
Source: Compiled by the World Bank from statistics prepared by the Directorate of Planning and Statistics, MOE, and the University of Aden, May 1981.

9 SOUTH YEMEN SINCE INDEPENDENCE: AN ARAB POLITICAL MAVERICK

Manfred Wenner

Introduction

The southern rim of the Arabian Peninsula has been of politico-economic, and therefore military, interest for as long as we have any records of human activity in the area. Some four thousand years ago, when the city-states which ruled in this region controlled the world trade in frankincense and myrrh, as well as a variety of exotic East African and Asian commodities, there were efforts by the European powers (notably the Roman Empire) to alter existing arrangements. And one of the reasons for doing so, aside from the control of the trade routes and the commodities involved, was control of Aden — certainly one of the best ports on the Arabian Peninsula. Once the wind and water patterns of the Indian Ocean were known and capable of being effectively exploited, the politico-military importance of the harbour at Aden increased further.

In more recent times, that is since the advent of the modern Europeans, the port has generally continued to be important, though it has occasionally slipped into insignificance. It was deemed important to the trade patterns which characterised the British Empire; these patterns, especially after the opening of the Suez Canal in 1869, made Aden the major port between Western Europe and the Far East. It was, in fact, the opening of the Canal which made Aden and its owner an automatic 'player' in the contest for influence and ascendancy in the Red Sea and Horn of Africa region. In part, however, this is because the political ownership of the port of Aden has historically been associated with control over two other strategically placed items: (1) the island of Socotra, about 120 miles south-east of Aden and therefore capable of exercising some influence over access from the Indian Ocean to the Strait of Bab al-Mandab; and, (2) the island of Perim, located in the Bab al-Mandab Strait itself.

Although it is possible to argue that too much has been made of the location and military advantages which possession of these islands bestows (and, in fact, much that is inaccurate or irrelevant has been published), there is little doubt that they could be used in ways which would markedly increase their strategic role and influence.[1] It is far more accurate to argue that it is the Strait of Bab al-Mandab itself which is of greatest geo-political relevance in the region. It derives its strategic role from being the southern access point to the Red Sea, and therefore is a potential 'choke point' for Red Sea traffic with its origins to the East (and therefore presumably bound for ports in the Red Sea or wishing to transit it on the way to Europe). This means that one could, by controlling Bab al-Mandab:

(1) affect access to the Suez Canal from Asian points of origin;
(2) affect traffic patterns to Israel's port-city of Eilat;
(3) affect traffic patterns to Saudi Arabia's major harbours on the Red Sea, i.e. Jeddah, Yanbu' and Jizan;
(4) affect traffic patterns to Sudan's ports;
(5) affect traffic patterns to Egypt's Red Sea maritime facilities;
(6) affect traffic patterns to Eritrea and Ethiopia; and,
(7) in more general terms, perhaps effect a change in the trade patterns of one or more of these Red Sea riparian states.

Logically, one must ask: are there states, or even non-state actors, which are interested in any one or more of these outcomes as policy objectives?[2] The answer has so far always been 'yes' — one of the reasons for the concern of the riparian powers expressed at the Ta-'izz Conference of March 1977,[3] as well as the continued interest on the part of the United States and its allies in the region ever since the revolution against Haile Selassie in Ethiopia. The current owner of Aden is the People's Democratic Republic of Yemen, usually known as South Yemen.

South Yemen: the Historical Background

Since one can argue that the politico-military and economic significance of Aden is a result of the (re-) emergence of world trade patterns after the period of European expansion, it is instructive to review briefly the interests of the major powers in the region, primarily because some of the intellectual as well as emotional motivations for contemporary policies rest upon developments during this period. In the past two centuries, two powers have been of exceptional importance: the Ottoman Empire, whose re-emergence as a power in the southern Red Sea was directly related to the opening of the Suez Canal; and Britain, whose interest stemmed directly from its interests in Asia in general, and India in particular. Though some have argued that Britain's entry into Aden in 1839 was more accidental than intentional, this is difficult to accept in view of Britain's conscious policy of acquiring strategic entrepôts between Europe and its areas of imperial ambition and concern. Although it must be admitted that Aden was in one of its low points in importance at the time of the British takeover, it took only a short period of British administration and activity, combined with the opening of the Canal, to bring about a rapid increase in population, trade and general importance. With the revival in the Ottoman Empire's concern, the British decided to guarantee their own presence more effectively. They did this by establishing a (at first) very rudimentary and tentative presence in the Adeni hinterland which, at the time, was an incredibly complex set of principalities, shaikhdoms and other statelets of various sizes, powers and wealth, most often organised on the basis of some form of tribal affiliation (or tribal confederation).

This decision turns out to have been of momentous importance: it eventually required Britain to play an ever-increasing role in these territories, as provider of subsidies to specific tribal leaders (thus altering existing political relationships), as arbiter of tribal disputes, as an ally when the Imams of North Yemen sought to expand their political influence towards the South in an attempt to regain what they saw as their traditional patrimony, and, eventually, as the organiser of new forms of political organisation and associations. As often occurs in such situations, certain tribes or tribal confederations are more inclined to associate themselves and co-operate with the foreign power. Thus British rule in turn tended to favour certain tribal groupings and leaders more than others. In order to facilitate their administration of the hinterland, the British created two distinct administrative sub-divisions, known as the Eastern Aden Protectorate (EAP) and the Western Aden Protectorate (WAP). In general, those closest to Aden itself (in the WAP) were most affected by British administration, and were, later, to play a more important role in political developments.

All the while, the economic importance of the port continued to grow: the result was a growing cultural, economic, social and political gap between Aden, which was separately governed as a Crown Colony, with its cosmopolitan and diverse population of more than 250,000, and the sparsely settled, essentially tribal and agricultural population of no more than 500,000 spread over an immense area and governed indirectly through subsidies and along traditional lines.

In the 1950s, in an effort to control Aden as long as possible, the British sought to amalgamate these disparate parts into one whole — the South Arabian Federation. Utterly out of temper with the times, this policy brought about the inevitable reaction: the growth of a multitude of organisations which sought to resist British policy, especially the incorporation of the world-city of Aden into a system of administration which gave the upper hand to the traditional hinterland. Just as inevitably, the leadership of these organisations tended to devolve into the hands of the far more politically sophisticated people of Aden, whose leaders came from the trade unions and political parties which had sprung up in the more cosmopolitan and urban tradition which characterised the port and its complex of military, berthing and bunkering facilities and petroleum refinery, as well as the extensive commercial and business communities. Of no mean significance, however, was the fact that a substantial portion of Aden's population was of *North* Yemeni origin — individuals who had left their homeland either in search of employment, or, just as often and simultaneously, to escape the government of the Imams because of their political activities. Aden, with its relative political freedom (in fact, unmatched anywhere else in the region at the time), became the focal point for extensive political organising on the part of these North Yemenis (as well as others).

The outbreak of the revolution in North Yemen in 1962 provided an important impetus to events in the South: it now became conceivable to bring about a re-unification of the two parts of 'historic' Yemen, a combination which in fact had not existed for more than 250 years, and a revolution in the South as well. With the entry into the civil war in North Yemen of a number of outsiders,[4] it was probably only a matter of time before local organisations of various kinds were being encouraged and supported by a similar variety of foreign powers large and small. The result was that, by the mid-1960s, the whole of south-western Arabia was at war. (The South Yemenis, with some poetic licence, take the Radfan uprising of 1964 as the beginning of their national liberation efforts.)

By 1967, the cost of the pacification efforts in South Arabia, combined with the decision to retreat from 'East of Suez' led the British to decide to withdraw completely. At the time, the domestic group with the most effective organisation (especially in the Protectorates), and by far the dominant group in the constellation of anti-British organisations, was the National Liberation Front. So it was that in November 1967 the NLF took over the reins of government in what is now known as the People's Democratic Republic of Yemen.[5]

The National Liberation Front and Independence

The *total* withdrawal of the British was an economic blow to the new state: not only was the extensive set of British subsidy payments eliminated, there was also the loss of the indirect income from the British-operated military and maritime facilities. And, as if that were not enough, a few months thereafter the Suez Canal was closed. The result was that Aden, which a few months earlier had still been one of the busiest ports in the world, suddenly found itself receiving as many ships in a year as it formerly had in a month.[6]

Under its new leadership, the South Yemeni government sought to obtain economic assistance to cover operating expenditures, and, in addition, some economic development and assistance grants and loans from the major providers of such financing — the United States and the major Western states. The United States, which had already indirectly provided economic assistance to those groups and individuals which had opposed the NLF, decided for its own reasons (one of which was the contemporary involvement in Vietnam) that it was uninterested in providing any economic assistance; moreover, it seems to have effectively communicated its lack of interest (opposition?) to other potential Western suppliers of economic assistance. The result was that a political party which was less than enthusiastic about Britain, the United States and their allies and friends on the world stage began to move in the opposite ideological direction, with all that that implies for the social, economic and political characteristics of the society.[7] In fact, it is possible rather easily to treat the development of the NLF and South Yemeni foreign policy — from its accession to power to the present day — as well as some major internal policies as, at the very least, closely related to if not dependent upon events and developments elsewhere.[8]

The first two years of independence were characterised by the political ascendancy of Qahtan al-Sha'bi and Faisal Abd al-Latif — both of whom were considered moderates within the party's ideological and organisational orientation. Both were evidently prepared to associate the new state with the economic patterns and associations which had been dominant in the pre-independence period, as long as certain essential reform measures to transform South Yemen into a more modern state were not, as a result, watered down or abandoned. In general, it is fair to characterise these as no more 'socialist' than some of the patterns of state intervention and ownership found in such Western European countries as Britain, West Germany or contemporary France.

Despite the fact that al-Sha'bi and Abd al-Latif controlled a substantial part of the NLF's machinery, and their opposition to major changes, the 1968 Party Congress which met at Zinjibar adopted the most radical programme of nationalisation, collectivisation, state initiative and control over the various sectors of the economy, as well as a series of related social and socio-economic goals, yet publicly advocated in any Arab Middle Eastern state.

The NLF, 1969–78

The result was that both al-Sha'bi and Abd al-Latif were forced to resign, and a so-called 'hard core' of left-wing ideologues assumed control. This period is characterised by the political ascendancy of Salim Rubai'a Ali and Abd al-Fattah Isma'il. It is of some relevance that this particular wing of the party was in the hands of North Yemenis. In any event, though agreed on many things, the two new leaders began to differ on foreign policy, i.e. South Yemen's relations with North Yemen (where the civil war had now ended), with other Arab states, and especially with the major powers who were either capable of, or interested in, giving economic aid or military assistance — both of which were desperately needed. Salim Rubai'a Ali began to associate himself more closely with a clique favouring closer relations with the People's Republic of China; Isma'il, on the other hand, began to associate himself with and develop a pro-Soviet clique within the party. In South Yemeni terms, this made Isma'il the moderate, despite the fact that the Western press generally reported these developments as a sign that the Soviet Union had suddenly succeeded in obtaining a new 'ally' for itself in the Arab Middle East.

Under the leadership of Ali and Isma'il, however, there is little doubt that the government adopted policies which eliminated the supporters of the previous government, which sent literally thousands of South Yemenis into exile (many of these elected to migrate to nearby North Yemen); and which can be best described as 'aggressive anti-imperialism' on the foreign front. This included becoming intimately involved in a number of revolutionary movements, including the one aimed at altering the political *status quo* in neighbouring Oman (the Dhofar Liberation Front, which later become the Popular Front for the Liberation of Oman, and then, as its goals widened, the Popular Front for the Liberation of the Occupied Arab Gulf (PFLOAG); and, last but definitely not least, the government sought the radical transformation of domestic society, including various agrarian reform programmes, nationalisation of all industrial enterprises, promotion of collectivisation schemes among the agricultural population, the fishermen, and just about every occupation in the social hierarchy, as well as a radical transformation of the status of women. The immediate result was that the economic situation deteriorated even further, making it less likely than ever that Western sources would be found to assist in meaningful economic development programmes, or fund, much less operate, any significant technical assistance programmes. Moreover, additional elements of the population chose to leave, most especially the remnants of the middle class, the entrepreneurs in Aden, and those with technical or industrial skills, which could now be easily and profitably marketed in North Yemen.

Despite these developments, the fact that major members of the South Yemeni elite were of North Yemeni origins (while many former South Yemenis now held major political responsibilities in North Yemeni governments, e.g. Abdullah al-Asnag) made possible some preliminary and meaningful discussions on the terms for some form of political association (if not outright union immediately) between the two countries. It was these discussions which led to the next major change in the South Yemeni government.

In late 1977, the day before he was going to South Yemen to participate in a round of union talks (encouraged by some other Arab states), the North Yemeni President, Ibrahim al-Hamdi, was assassinated; it was widely believed then, as it is now, that this act was carried out by agents supported by the Saudi Arabian government, which feared (as it continues to fear) any real movement in the direction of union between the two Yemens. Al-Hamdi's successor was Ahmad Husain al-Ghashmi, who, it was believed by Salim Rubai'a Ali, had at least tacitly approved of the act (for his own personal political ambitions). For a complex constellation of reasons, among which the above appear to be the most important, Rubai'a Ali elected to have al-Ghashmi assassinated in turn, in mid-1978. One can only assume that Ali presumed that it would serve as a warning to Saudi Arabia, and strengthen his domestic position as well. Unfortunately for Ali, the assassination did not have the desired or expected consequences: instead of bolstering his position, it led other members of the NLF to turn on him, and after a brief trial, have him executed.

His replacement as President was Abd al-Fattah Isma'il, whose accession, in foreign-policy terms, led to a pronounced pro-Soviet Union turn, with little if any attendant change in domestic policies, except perhaps more clear use of Soviet models for certain domestic issues, including the relationship between the civilian and military functions, etc.

The NLF, 1978-80

Under President Isma'il, himself of North Yemeni origin, a more active campaign to change the relationship between the two Yemens was instituted. He appears to have believed that active support of the major opposition force in North Yemen, the National Democratic Front, as well as some judicious encouragement of tribal and local discontent in the southern areas, would provide him with the leverage needed to change the orientation of Yemen's new leader, Colonel Ali Abdullah Salih. Once again, results did not meet expectations: the minor skirmishes which took place and the increased activity of the NDF suddenly and unexpectedly escalated into a major confrontation over which the local participants soon had little or no control. Other regional as well as extra-regional states saw far more important and wider issues involved, and used these outbreaks of violence for their own purposes.[9]

Among these additional participants, and their motives, one would have to include (but not limit it to) the following:

(1) Saudi Arabia, with at least two interests: (a) to isolate South Yemen in so far as possible with respect to Peninsular affairs because of South Yemen's rather consistent opposition to Saudi

interests and policies; and (b) to ensure that North Yemen remained a reliable 'satellite', i.e. supported Saudi interests and objectives, and would not get too friendly with or co-operate too extensively with South Yemen.
(2) The United States, also with multiple interests: (a) the Carter administration — then in power — wished to appear able to stand up to what was being depicted as another Soviet threat to the Middle East, and it wished to be seen domestically as able to cope effectively with developments in the Middle East; this was an especially important motive in view of the fact that the hostages were still in the hands of the Iranian Islamic Republic; (b) to enable the United States to move military *matériel* into the Peninsula quickly (without Congressional approval if necessary) in order to act quickly to protect what is ultimately the most important interest: (c) the continued movement of large quantities of Saudi oil into the market and at a stable price.
(3) North Yemen, which expected to obtain more than $300 million in military equipment which it could probably not have obtained otherwise, and which hoped that these supplies, and the assistance of the United States, would enable it to be less dependent upon Saudi Arabia, i.e. gain somewhat greater flexibility in its foreign and domestic policy options.
(4) The Soviet Union, which for a relatively small investment had developed another friendly state in the Red Sea region which it seems to view as of considerable strategic and political value (see below).

In the event, some military equipment was transferred, and the policy objectives of the United States and Saudi Arabia were probably largely accomplished, though one might be permitted some doubts about the long-run effects and advantages. With respect to developments in South Yemen, however, the consequences were rather less positive: after some months of internal disputes, occasioned at least in part by the failure of Isma'il's policies, the latter was deposed as President.

The NLF, 1980 to the Present

The current period is characterised by the political ascendancy of Ali Nasir Muhammad (al-Hasani), who was Prime Minister under

Isma'il. He succeeded in replacing the latter in April of 1980, and within days there appears to have been a tangible relaxation in the extremely tight controls which had previously existed over nearly all aspects of South Yemeni society, including, for example, the prohibition of conversations between South Yemenis and any 'foreigner', which term extended to other Arabs.

Although the first signs of a modification in South Yemen's 'hard line' on various issues began to appear in 1979, the most interesting changes have taken place in 1982–3. Perhaps one of the most important indicators was the decision to co-operate fully with the World Bank in an analysis of the South Yemeni economy. Although the final report[10] was remarkably frank in its assessment of the achievements and shortcomings of the regime's policies, the most important fact was the decision to let such an obviously Western financial institution undertake the assessment in the first place. (It is even possible that the report itself played a role in later internal developments, though I have no evidence for this presumption.)

In any event, many observers began to note a 'thaw' in South Yemen's attitudes and policies; the relevant developments which contributed to this perception would include the following:

(1) The willingness of the government to undertake diplomatic missions to various Arab states in the effort to re-establish normal relationships after the 1978 decision to, essentially, 'censure' the government of South Yemen.[11]
(2) The decision to establish a number of new diplomatic missions with major industrial states in Western Europe.
(3) The decision to accept Arab mediation in the effort to end the dispute with neighbouring Oman over the conflict in Dhofar.
(4) The inability of many of South Yemen's 'bloc' advisers and experts to promote effectively the development of local resources at the same speed and with the same technology which such Western states as West Germany, France, Japan and even Britain were capable of providing and implementing.[12]
(5) The discovery of a deposit of high-quality crude in the Hadramawt;[13] however, the important factor is not so much the reported discovery (about which further details are lacking) but the fact that the Italian firm which undertook the exploration charged nothing for the effort and was successful, whereas the Soviet team had been searching for a number of years without success, and had been charging the South Yemenis for their work.

South Yemen since Independence

(6) The speedy, and on the whole rather generous, efforts of a number of Western states and financial institutions to come to South Yemen's assistance after the disastrous floods of spring 1982; in fact, it was Western and/or Western-controlled funding agencies which provided the overwhelming bulk of the assistance which was provided.[14]

It would appear possible to suggest that the South Yemeni regime, in a word, is considerably more pragmatic in its orientation towards the outside world than many Western observers have been prepared to admit. In order to understand how such misconceptions may have arisen, it is instructive to review briefly some other aspects of South Yemen.

The Bases of Politics in South Yemen and the NLF

Politics in South Yemen is a complex and constantly changing combination of a number of elements, many of which are characteristic of other developing states and/or the Arab states, among which at least the following are important:

(1) personal origins: essentially we are here concerned with whether or not the individual is from North or South Yemen; for example, Ali Nasir Muhammad is the first major political figure in the NLF in some time to be of South Yemeni origin.
(2) 'tribal' affiliation: although this may also be of importance to those of North Yemeni origins, the concern here is only with those of South Yemeni origins. In theory, the possibilities number in the dozens (and a quick glance at the old political configurations under the British will give the modern observer some inkling of the major groupings); in reality only about six are or have been relevant during the past two decades. Nevertheless, a couple of additional comments are in order: (a) the South Yemeni government has made some inroads into the relevance of tribal affiliation as a result of its administrative restructuring of the country and its determinedly secular programmes; on the other hand, long-time observers of South Yemen would not be too surprised to learn that Ali Nasir Muhammad, for example, is from the old Dathina state, whose members have played a particularly important role in the

military ever since the departure of the British.[15]
(3) personal loyalty, usually the result of previous associations in political, economic, or social endeavours of various kinds, as well as the links created by the patrimonial system which characterises nearly all Middle Eastern politics, and which even the NLF has not been able to eliminate completely from South Yemeni affairs.
(4) opportunism, i.e. taking advantage of opportunities for personal advancement, as well as the interests of one's social grouping, whether on traditional or more modern grounds.
(5) ideological orientation; in contemporary South Yemen this variable has undergone a pronounced leftward shift, but still encompasses such orientations as the kind of moderate socialism which characterises, for example, Sweden, as well as the more radical strain which emphasises world revolution, and the more standard contemporary Soviet version of Marxism-Leninism. In this connection, it might be worth noting that the modern era is not the first time that South Yemen has adopted a radically different ideology from the rest of its Middle Eastern counterparts: in the Middle Ages it long was a supporter of such disparaged and radical ideologies as Ibadism, and, most important for a possible link with the past, the Carmathian (Qarmati) movement, with its strong emphasis on communalism.[16]

Even this list does not do justice to the complexities of South Yemeni politics, because it does not recognise the more specifically South Yemeni elements, such as:

(1) the various links between North and South Yemen, and the long history of efforts to forge some kind of association since the departure of the British and the overthrow of the Imams in the North.
(2) the influence of outside powers with specific interests in South Yemen, whether direct or indirect; the list would include the Soviet Union, Cuba and East Germany on the one hand, and such peripherally associated states as China, and the Western states of West Germany, Japan, Britain and even the United States on the other, as well as the regional cohorts of some relevance,[17] such as Oman, Saudi Arabia, Ethiopia and Somalia to mention just a few.
(3) the rather straightforward economic interests of the business

community in Aden, the agricultural workers, the burgeoning fishing industry, etc.

The point, of course, is that, in this writer's view, it is a horrendous oversimplification to attribute the policies and actions of South Yemen since independence solely to the relationship which has developed between South Yemen and the Soviet Union (and its allies). Here, as in so many other instances which involve the description and analysis of contemporary political events, it is likely that the preconceptions of the observers will ultimately determine the interpretation given to available information and events (not to mention their presentation for others). The issue which has been raised — by the press and some academics, as well as by some government — is whether South Yemen today represents another case of the Soviet Union expanding its influence beyond its 'traditional' post-war limits (by 'leap-frogging' the southern rim states); whether it represents a part of a deliberate Soviet effort to create a ring of 'satellites' in major strategic areas (e.g. the Red Sea and the Horn of Africa); or whether South Yemen may be more accurately described and analysed in terms of its desperately poor economy and lack of natural resources, its conflicts with its regional neighbours, the ideological and pragmatic circumstances surrounding its birth as a state and the development of its ruling party and political elites.

Contemporary South Yemen

In view of recent events involving the Soviet Union in the general area of the Middle East, which in this case include the invasion of Afghanistan and the presence in Ethiopia, as well as the commitment to South Yemen, a number of questions become pertinent. The Western press, in particular in the United States, has been quite effective in portraying South Yemen as the latest dependency of the Soviet Union, and the result has been that the American public, and to some extent contemporary policy makers in the United States, appear unable to distinguish South Yemeni interests and objectives from those of the Soviet Union — either in the Middle East or in other regions of the world.

This strikes me as a dangerous oversimplification of the politics of a region where political analysis has never been particularly easy to begin with. In part, I believe, the problem lies in the terminology which the West, and particularly the Western press, employs to describe relationships between states — in this case, the relationship between the Soviet Union and other states. Among the terms which have won widespread acceptance are the following:

satellite	proxy
puppet	ally
client	surrogate.

Even so, this list is not complete, since other terms with the same general connotation continue to be used in works by journalists, as well as academics and political analysts of the Congressional and Executive branches of the United States government.

The problem essentially lies in the fact that we have no objective criteria *whatever* for the use of these terms. In fact, the terms used by the Soviet Union to describe its relationship with other states are somewhat more precise, though it would not be possible systematically to distinguish among alternatives over time. For example, although the so-called Brezhnev Doctrine provides us with some criteria for some states, it also is not an objective nor quantitative measure, and a number of problems arise if one tries to use its terms to describe states which do not border on the Soviet Union, and whose historical experience with the Soviet Union and the Communist Party are very different.[18]

One possibility would be to tally such items as the presence of 'bloc' technicians and advisers in various fields; the number of indigenous military personnel sent for training to 'bloc' states; the number of economic and development-project advisers from 'bloc' states providing assistance and direction; the number of students sent to 'bloc' universities — all these and related quantitative measures (whether on an absolute or *per capita* basis) might help to distinguish between states, but will remain unsatisfactory because they do not discriminate effectively between countries we generally do not consider to be 'satellites', such as India, and those we do, such as Poland.[19] Furthermore, such quantitative measures do not take into account the specific policy goals and orientations of the individual policy maker, especially if these change over time. In political systems with high personalistic characteristics, this presents a significant methodological problem. Moreover, a simple recitation of the type of quantitative measures suggested above would not explain the decision of the Egyptians to dismiss their Soviet techni-

South Yemen since Independence 139

cians and sever the Soviet 'connection', and reorient their trade and other policies towards the West.

To resort to the use of these terms without clearly specifying the criteria being used to make the judgement(s), then, does not contribute to our understanding of the multifaceted ways in which relationships between countries and governments, not to mention personalities in certain governments, may develop over time, or eventually end. Perhaps, then, the questions alluded to above are what policy makers actually take into account in making their assessments:

(1) What may we presume to be the motives and objectives of the Soviet Union in becoming involved in the southern Red Sea area, including South Yemen (and Ethiopia)?
(2) What may we presume to be the motives and objectives of the South Yemenis in, first, establishing close relations with a number of states clearly linked with the Soviet Union and, second, continuing such relationships over time?

Soviet Objectives in the Red Sea Region

The motivations ascribed to the Soviet Union in specific locations around the globe would seem to be a function of one's established notion of what objectives it pursues in general. For example, among the less militant and aggressive ideas of what the Soviet Union is seeking in the Red Sea region one might include (but not necessarily be limited to) the following:

(1) developing 'leverage' which could be employed in future negotiations or agreements with political opponents (e.g. the United States) with regard to the status of a region;
(2) actively seeking to decrease the influence and prestige of the United States and its allies (in the military and economic sense);
(3) obtaining a long-term and reliable lease on a maritime facility from which naval operations and trade relations could be maintained.

Someone with this view of Soviet objectives would be able to support this viewpoint by citing Soviet support for South Yemen since 1970, and suggesting that the level of such support was quite minimal in comparison with the potential gain. Furthermore, one could further suggest that the level of Soviet support which was given to the PFLOAG indicated clearly that the Soviet Union was unwilling to be dragged into any protracted Peninsular conflict. Even so, these are not the only items which could be adduced for this viewpoint.[20]

On the other hand, one can suggest a considerably more militant and provocative list, which would include (but not necessarily be limited to) the following:

(1) disrupting, and then eventually controlling, regional trade through control of major strategic points such as the Straits of Hormuz or Bab al-Mandab;
(2) controlling all Middle Eastern oil, from extraction to distribution;
(3) actually taking over the Middle East in its entirety, and incorporating it into the Soviet 'sphere'.

Someone with this view of Soviet objectives would be able to support it by noting the Soviet attempt to obtain the United Nations Trusteeship for Eritrea in the immediate post-Second World War era; by noting the willingness of the Soviet Union to provide more than just adequate supplies of military equipment, but the battle-hardened troops and trainers of a major (military) ally, Cuba; or the willingness of the Soviet Union to invest substantial amounts of money and *matériel* in regimes of doubtful longevity if their location is of strategic significance.[21] The point deserves repetition: the interpretation of the motives and actions of the Soviet Union (and its allies) in this region is more than likely to have been decided upon in advance, i.e. before an investigation of the 'facts' in such potential 'case-studies' as South Yemen. Furthermore, it is highly unlikely that such preconceived notions are going to be subject to easy (and publicly admitted) change.

South Yemeni Objectives

Much of what has been said concerning Soviet motives and actions holds for the analysis of South Yemeni motives and actions. The first analyst will suggest that the economic hardships which South Yemen has had to cope with since independence, and the pronounced unwillingness of the Western states to provide assistance, have combined to drive South Yemen into the opposite camp in the search for both economic and military aid, as well as friends and allies in the international arena. His opposite number will insist that the ideological predilections of the NLF, from its very birth out of the Arab Nationalist Movement, set it on the path towards subservience to Soviet policy objectives and methods of policy implementation; furthermore, only South Yemen has been so forthcoming in its willingness to sign military agreements of the type recently widely publicised (including the Tripartite Treaty between it and Ethiopia and Libya).

In this writer's view the South Yemeni government's views and orientation since 1967 have undergone a number of rather clear changes; these have been associated with a change of leadership (in the NLF and the Yemeni Socialist Party), as well as with other events in the region, e.g. the Yemeni civil war (from 1962 to 1970), the war in the Ogaden, the Dhofar issue, relations with Saudi Arabia and the Gulf Co-operation Council, etc., etc. The recent decision of the government to relax the regulations on foreign participation in investments and to open its doors to the World Bank and related institutions, as well as some flexibility in the implementation of other 'revolutionary' social and economic programmes would appear to indicate a greater flexibility in the regime's ideological stance than had previously been the case.[22]

Summary and Conclusions

In my view, the review of the Soviet Union's policies on the southern fringe of the Arabian Peninsula shows a pattern of *reacting* to opportunities which, for one reason or another, presented themselves as exploitable — at first, perhaps only for short-term objectives, and later, occasionally, for longer-term ones. In brief, then, I do not detect a clear and deliberate policy, slowly developed and implemented, in order to further a set of specific objectives in the Red Sea region.

Perhaps the major reason for this conclusion is that the Soviet Union appears to me to have embarked upon a set of *bilateral* arrangements in the area; I find no evidence of a co-ordinated multi-lateral programme. Rather, it would seem that the Soviet Union has managed skilfully to exploit grievances based upon past misgovernment, incompetence and injustices, not to mention poverty, ignorance, disease, an uncaring administration and the other unnumbered ills of less developed societies (as we call them). But, and this is precisely the point, each of the affected governments (at least in the Red Sea region) tends to judge the success or failure of its association with the Soviet Union precisely on the basis of its own limited resources, interests and objectives, not in terms of some global programme to alleviate social ills, modify reactionary social systems, or restructure the world economic system (no matter what some of the leaders claim). And, if we may use such other states in the area as Egypt, Somalia or Iraq as indicators, when the bilateral arrangement is no longer to the satisfaction of the local partner, it is substantially modified, or even completely severed.

Afghanistan, clearly, represents a different case: for one thing, it borders on the Soviet Union (and therefore could in any event conceivably have fallen under the terms of the so-called Brezhnev Doctrine). For another, it has been directly occupied by Soviet troops, who now guarantee that Soviet policy objectives are implemented. None of these conditions applies in the case of either Ethiopia or South Yemen; furthermore, neither of these states is as important to the development of the Soviet economy, or the continued rate of Soviet development, as Afghanistan appears to be; and, last but not least, neither of them has presented the Soviet Union with a direct threat of Western economic expansion into what was seen as 'neutral' territory (between East and West). Moreover, to suggest that the presence of Cuban advisers (and even some troops) is the equivalent of the Soviet occupation of Afghanistan is neither accurate nor logically defensible.

Therefore, there does not seem to be any way in which the Soviet Union can effectively hope to control completely the foreign and domestic policies of these states, despite whatever current overlaps (either pragmatically or ideologically) may exist. Though American influence specifically, and Western influence generally, has unquestionably been eroded, this would seem to have been an inevitable by-product of the fact that the Western states (not necessarily the United States) were intimately associated with the *ancien régime* (in both Ethiopia and South Yemen). The West, therefore, was logically going to bear both popular and governmental blame — rightfully or wrongfully — for the ills, injustices and problems associated with these regimes. On the other hand, it is worth suggesting that both of these countries continue to suffer from a long list of economic (and even social) problems which the intimate association with the 'opposite side' has not managed to cure. It does not seem too far-fetched to believe that the pendulum will begin to swing in the opposite direction in the near future.

Policy Implications

For these reasons, I must conclude that Western policy in the Red Sea region has been ill-informed and dangerously short-sighted. Perhaps the best single instance of this is the 1979 decision to accept the Saudi version of events in south-western Arabia, and therefore argue adamantly (in the United States) to the public, the press and the US Congress that events showed that an 'aggressive Communist-inspired South Yemen was attempting to expand militarily'. While it may be true that South Yemen has supported the NDF, has contributed weapons to North Yemeni dissidents, etc., it is also true that the unquestioning acceptance of one particular version of events, and reactions to them, results in precisely the kind of policy which was adopted in the case of the Shah's Iran: one which is blind to changes taking place below the level of governmental awareness, and/or blind to significant changes in the orientation of relevant groups and individuals. The result is the inability to effect changes in policy in time to take advantage of altered circumstances.

For the moment, then, I must conclude, first, that South Yemen is best characterised as an Arab 'political maverick' rather than as a Soviet 'satellite'. Second, I find that argument that the Soviet Union has tended to act with caution in the Peninsula more persuasive than its counterpart.[23] Therefore, to continue to make policy and act as if South Yemen were a satellite is to guarantee that it will become one. It should be appended immediately that the perception of change has apparently reached the level of policy-making in the United States in recent months. For example, the Reagan administration, although it specifically denied that its actions constituted a real change in its position on South Yemen, eased its controls on the sale of aircraft to that country in the late spring of 1982.[24]

Theoretical Implications

Since the terminology which is used to describe an event, a person or a relationship can *per se* influence the perceptions of those being informed, it would seem to be of some importance to be clear on what is meant by certain key terms. This particular study of the political orientation of South Yemen since independence encountered a bewildering set of terms to describe the relationship between it and the various countries which have provided assistance or political support in that time (see above).

Contemporary Sovietologists are probably willing to accept the categories and statuses assigned to various states by the Brezhnev Doctrine as a reasonably useful definition; although not completely satisfactory on many grounds, it has the virtue of according with the Soviet definition of where its interests and concerns lie, and therefore has some predictive capability. My own suggestion for the English terminology is that we adopt some rudimentary quantitative measures in order to ensure greater precision in the use of our terms. If we were to construct a broad-scale index, which would include the items mentioned above, as well as certain obvious additional ones (trade, loans, etc.) we might be better able to sharpen our analyses of such relationships, and even be considerably more knowledgeable in undertaking *comparisons*, from one region to another, or over time.

Notes

1. The first press reports on Soviet military installations on the Red Sea coast appeared in the 1950s (concerning North Yemen). It was presumed at the time that these were for the purpose of interfering with traffic through Bab al-Mandab. In fact, no such fortifications ever existed. In the past few years, similar installations were alleged to have been built on Perim as well as Socotra; indeed, the latter has been said to be the site of a major Soviet military base which includes submarine 'pens'. I have been unable to locate a reliable account which adduces acceptable evidence for these allegations. The best description of Bab al-Mandab and its importance is John Duke Anthony, *The Red Sea: Control of the Southern Approach* (Middle East Institution, Problem Paper no. 13, Washington, DC, 1980).

2. It would probably be very difficult to carry out only *one* of these, that is to the exclusion of the others. I am, therefore, inclined to suggest that this is precisely why no systematic effort to do so has taken place: it is highly unlikely that anyone (state, non-state actor, etc.) would have either the motives or the means to attempt all of these simultaneously (or even any significant number of them), though this does not discount the possibility that more limited objectives could or would be achieved through the judicious (i.e. limited) application of pressure.

3. Ferdinand Hurni, 'Counter-Movement on the Red Sea', *Swiss Review of World Affairs* (May 1977), p. 7.

4. The major external participants were Saudi Arabia, on the side of the royalists, and Egypt, on the side of the Republic. However, at one time or another, the Jordanians, the Iranians, the British, the Americans, the Soviet Union and a miscellaneous collection of others, including mercenaries, also participated to varying degrees.

South Yemen since Independence 145

5. There is an extensive literature on the development of the British presence in Aden and their policies in the 1950s and 1960s, as well as their eventual departure. No attempt has been made here to document each event adequately, as it did not seem necessary. The best contemporary account is the one by Tom Little, *South Arabia* (Praeger, New York, 1968), which also contains a good bibliography. See also the account and the bibliography in M. W. Wenner, 'The People's Republic of South Yemen' in Tareq Y. Ismael (ed.), *Governments and Politics of the Contemporary Middle East* (Dorsey Press, Homewood, Illinois, 1970), pp. 412-29.

6. This statement contains a bit of poetic licence to make the point; in fact, the number of ships calling at Aden began to decline once Aden had become a battleground between opposing groups and the British. As the level of violence escalated, so the number of cruise and other ship berthings declined. According to Fred Halliday, 'Yemen's Unfinished Revolution: Socialism in the South', *Merip Reports*, no. 81 (Oct. 1979), p. 5, the figure went from 6,000 yearly to 1,500 yearly in the mid-1960s.

7. John Duke Anthony, 'Relations between the United States and the PDRY: Problems and Prospects' in *Diego Garcia, 1975: The Debate over the Base and Island's Former Inhabitants*, 94th Congress (GPO, Washington, DC, 1975), p. 86.

8. The following summary of events and developments between 1967 and 1981 draws largely from the following sources: Wenner, 'The People's Republic of South Yemen'; Anthony, *The Red Sea*; Halliday, 'Yemen's Unfinished Revolution; Joe Stork, 'Socialist Revolution in Arabia: A Report from the People's Democratic Republic of Yemen', *Merip Reports*, no. 13 (Mar. 1973); Fred Halliday, *Arabia without Sultans* (Vantage Books, New York, 1975); Mordechai Abir, *Oil, Power and Politics* (Frank Cass, London, 1974); Richard F. Nyrop *et al.*, *Area Handbook for the Yemens* (GPO, Washington, DC, 1977); and Robert W. Stookey, *South Yemen: A Marxist Republic in Arabia* (Westview Press, Boulder, Colorado, 1982).

9. Probably the best illustration for this is the Congressional hearings which dealt with the subject of arms transfers (*Proposed Arms Transfers to the Yemen Arab Republic*, 96th Congress (GPO, Washington, DC, 1979). It later became increasingly clear that a good deal of misinformation had characterised some of the testimony (cf. the testimony of Colonel John J. Ruszkiewicz in *US Interests in, and Policies Toward, the Persian Gulf*, 96th Congress (GPO, Washington, DC, 1980). A brief overview of the popular press's coverage, easily gleaned from the major bibliographical references, makes clear the fervour which surrounded the American government's 'decisive action' in this instance:

'How the West is Losing a Strategic Mideast Crossroads' (*Business Week*);
'Making a Stand in Yemen' (*Wall Street Journal*);
'More than Just a Border Clash: Saudi Fears about Subversion' (*Time*);
'Yemen's War: Big Meaning for the US' (*US News and World Report*).

10. World Bank, *People's Democratic Republic of Yemen: A Review of Economic and Social Development* (The World Bank, Washington, DC, 1979).

11. 'South Yemen Seeks to Widen Arab Ties', *New York Times*, 15 June 1980.

12. David Shirreff, 'South Yemen Leadership Favours a Little Free Enterprise', *Middle East Economic Digest*, 23 May 1980, pp. 6-8; 'Aden is Perking up under New Leader', *New York Times*, 22 June 1980; Chris Kutschera, 'South Yemen: A Slow Move towards the West', *The Middle East* (Aug. 1982), pp. 20-1.

13. *Financial Times* (London), 2 Apr. 1982.

14. Chris Kutschera, 'South Yemen Counts the Cost of Flooding', *The Middle East* (July 1982), p. 51.

15. Information on the tribal affiliation of major leaders is now difficult to come by; for the significance of tribal affiliations in the past (i.e. under British rule) see

Wenner, 'The People's Republic of South Yemen'. Among the more recent writers who have, at least indirectly, acknowledged the relevance of such designations and affiliations, see Halliday, 'Yemen's Unfinished Revolution' and Abir, *Oil, Power and Politics*.

16. 'Karmati', *Encyclopedia of Islam*, 2nd edn (Brill, Leiden, continuing).

17. Major recent works which have discussed this subject are: Adeed Dawisha, *Saudi Arabia's Search for Security* (International Institute for Strategic Studies, London, 1980); Christopher Lee, 'Soviet and Chinese Interests in Southern Arabia', *Mizan* (Aug. 1971), pp. 35-47; and Stephen Page, *The USSR and Arabia* (Central Asian Research Centre, London, 1971).

18. Apparently formulated by one Prof. S. Kovalev, the 'Brezhnev Doctrine' is today understood to cover such matters as damage to the fundamental interests of other socialist countries; damage to socialism; threats to the defence capabilities of the Soviet Union, etc. See *Current Digest of the Soviet Press*, Vol. XX (16 Oct. 1968), pp. 10-12.

19. Data of this kind have been collected and tabulated by such organisations as the Central Intelligence Agency and the Department of State in the United States, the International Institute of Strategic Studies in Britain and the Peace Research Institute in Stockholm. Unfortunately, there is no consistency in the data, in their method of presentation, in the subjects covered, in the dollar values assigned, etc. The result is that it would take a considerable effort to research and collate adequately what would be required for a thorough presentation.

20. Page, *The USSR and Arabia*, and Shahram Chubin, *Soviet Policy towards Iran and the Gulf* (International Institute of Strategic Studies, London, 1980).

21. Although dated, the article by Stanko Guldescu, 'Marxism Comes to Yemen', *Communist Affairs*, vol. V (Sept./Oct. 1967), pp. 9-13, is an appropriate example.

22. See Anthony, *The Red Sea*, as well as Shirreff, 'South Yemen Leadership', and Kutschera, 'South Yemen'.

23. Page, *The USSR and Arabia*, p. 133, and the conclusions immediately following.

24. *New York Times*, 4 Mar. 1982.

10 MODERNISATION OF GOVERNMENT INSTITUTIONS 1962-9

Ahmed Al-Abiadh

In order to assess, appreciate and evaluate the modernisation effort after the 1962 revolution we must go back to the pre-revolution era. The Imam held absolute authority — without any limits — in running the country. There was no structure or organisation which could be called a government, in spite of the fact that he retained some Ottoman officials to assist in building an administrative machinery to run the government. But these retainees did nothing[1] more than organise the army. In 1931 a Cabinet was set up, albeit without ministries with the sole exception of the Ministry of Foreign Affairs. That Ministry was located in a four-room building; its personnel was composed of the Minister, Deputy Minister, a Chief of Protocol, a clerk and two typists. But the Imam still held the authority to grant entry visas and, in addition, he acted as chief administrator of finance, military affairs, education and justice. He was the sole employer, i.e. with the authority to hire and to fire all government workers.[2] In short, there was a very primitive foundation of public administration in terms of structure, functions or procedures.

Public administration as a concept and as an approach had been put into practice only after the revolution of 1962, when the theocratic regime was replaced by a revolutionary and constitutional government. That is why, in the early months of 1963, eleven ministries were established. Other ministries and agencies followed. These government institutions were accompanied by two republican decrees which reflected the government's concern and its concentration on modernisation of the administration. The first decree was No. 8 of 1963, which established the General Commission for Employees' Affairs under the President of the Republic's supervision. The second decree was issued for the establishment of the National Institute of Public Administration (NIPA). Those two decrees reflected the enthusiasm of the government for establishing new organisations and administrative structures. Also, it was considered an urgent task to train and prepare civil servants for new functions in the revolutionary era.

With the establishment of the new organisations and the new functions, the problem of public administration started to manifest itself as follows:

(1) The organisational structures were designed by Egyptian experts who had no background or knowledge about the Yemeni environment; they merely transferred a duplicate of the Egyptian organisational structures and by-laws which did not fit the needs of Yemeni institutions.
(2) The designers of the organisational structures did not have the basic information which was objectively necessary for any organisation to be established, such as capital and manpower resources as well as the required skills, etc.[3]
(3) The new institutions set about performing the new functions by utilising the groups of people who were employed before the revolution, and most of them continued to occupy high leadership positions after it. They brought their traditional values and concepts into the new institutions, which created some kind of resistance to the modernisation of the administration, directly and indirectly.
(4) Despite the enthusiasm of the government in establishing the new administrative institutions, it could not reach its goal of modernising the administration since it faced one important and urgent task that had to be completed, i.e. to win the civil war, 1962–9, and preserve the Republic.

Therefore, preserving security and public order under the republican flag was the main goal for which all people, resources and efforts were mobilised and recruited. In other words, modernisation of the administration as an important goal was over-shadowed by a more important goal whose achievement was a matter of life and death. That does not mean that the government had neglected modernising the administration as an important goal; a great deal of attention was paid to developing the Civil Service Commission and the National Institute of Public Administration (NIPA) as important organisations carrying out the responsibility of modernising the administration, even during this critical period.

We should now briefly discuss how the Civil Service Commission and NIPA progressed.

The Civil Service Commission

It has already been mentioned that the Civil Service Commission was established by republican decree No. 8/1963, by which its functions were stated as follows:

(1) To follow up the execution, implementation and processes of laws and instructions concerning government employees and government labourers.
(2) Designing systems which must aim at increasing productivity and improving performance at the lowest cost.
(3) Designing a system to test candidates for certain positions to be occupied only after passing that test.
(4) Determining the number of positions, the number of employees needed for those positions, and the number of government labourers, their salaries and wages. These matters to be discussed and approved through a co-ordination process between the Commission and the ministries and other agencies, in accordance with their functions.
(5) Discussing the annual budgets of the ministries and agencies connected with employment affairs.
(6) Designing the training programmes for the ministries and other agencies.
(7) Suggesting the status and other systems concerning government employees and labourers, and proposing others or modifying them.[4]

Those functions reflect the true desire of the government to regulate and clarify relations among government organisations. They also reflect government aspirations to modernise the administration. However, those functions which were assigned to the Civil Service Commission were too much for that organisation to accomplish and went beyond its capability, particularly in view of the fact that the number of CSC employees was not more than seven.[5] It would have been beyond its capability even if the number had been doubled many times because time was needed to train them for the new functions. Therefore, and because of the scarcity of skilled people, the government issued a decree, No. 25, on 10 October 1963, that established a committee for organising government institutions. This committee never held a meeting, for unknown reasons, so another decree was issued to modify the first one by broadening its authority. It seems that the decision makers during this period were uncertain; that is why they were prepared to do what they were told, even though this meant that the actual decision makers were people whose interests were not served by a stable environment.

On 17 April 1966 republican decree No. 22/1966 was issued to establish the Supreme Committee for planning, follow-up and supervision. In addition to its responsibilities in those fields the Supreme Committee absorbed the Civil Service Commission. In the light of responsibilities of such magnitude, the Supreme Committee was, in its turn, inadequately staffed: it suffices to say that its total staff numbered only forty.[6] With this number of people it was impossible for the Committee to achieve vital national goals such as planning, training, staffing, directing, etc. The CSC was therefore separated from the Supreme Committee again by decree No. 11/1967 on 15 March 1967 when the Supreme Committee for planning, follow-up and supervision, together with the committee for organising government institutions, were abolished. For the first time, the Civil Service Commission acquired an organisational structure which consisted of four major departments:

(1) the National Institute of Public Administration;
(2) the committee for foreign appointees;
(3) governmental assignments and training missions;
(4) retirement department.

The new Civil Service Commission was successful in some aspects of public administration such as manpower planning, training and the amendment of some regulations. However, modernisation of the administration as an objective was very far from being reached and one of the reasons for the failure was the low status of the Civil Service Commission. In other words, you cannot influence someone over your head. That is why the Civil Service Commission, in its relations with the ministries and other government agencies, did not have the respect and attention it needed.

NIPA

NIPA, established in 1963, is considered as one of the oldest government institutions, and it has a better record than the Civil Service Commission.[7] During the period of the civil war, NIPA was struggling to attain its objectives in training, research and consultation but, despite that struggle, its achievements were modest because of the lack of skilled staff and other materials.

Modernisation of Government Institutions, 1970-82

It is very important to indicate here that administrative modernisation as a goal was not a first priority during the civil war. However, the seeds of modernisation grew during this period (the sixties) and the bases of the government administrative foundation were built then. For instance:

The Monetary Control Agency and the Currency Board. These bodies, which participated in laying the foundations of financial and banking systems, and rules governing imports and exports, were established during this period. As a product of these, the Central Bank of Yemen was established. A similar evolution took place and resulted in the establishment of the Ministries of Commerce and Supplies and other commercial and financial public institutions.

The Technical Office. This office was affiliated to the Cabinet and was created to promote the use of planning in modernising the administrative apparatus. This office was later transformed into the Central Planning Organisation which today plays an important role in administrative development.

The effect of these two institutions was evident, directly and indirectly, and they succeeded in building several ministries and agencies. By the end of the civil war and the achievement of political stability, the government was paying special attention to the creation and modernisation of government institutions. That was made possible through UN assistance sought by the government for that particular purpose: a UN Development-Programme-sponsored project to develop Yemeni human resources and to train civil servants was established with NIPA as the executing agency. This project also intended to establish research and consultation services in public administration within NIPA. Additional international assistance was solicited from the World Bank and friendly governments and this attempt at seeking expert assistance from abroad through international and bilateral aid speeded up the transformation and led to a more modern and effective government machinery. It also speeded up the Yemenisation of the charters and by-laws of many government organisations. This whole administrative effort was greatly helped by the Central Planning Organisation through the role it played in co-ordinating economic and social policies.

In spite of all these successful efforts, however, some problems remained which impeded progress towards more responsive and effective organisation. Major among these problems were traditional and informal influences from outside the government organisation itself. However, the fact remains that any objective comparison shows that substantial progress has occurred during the seventies in terms of scope and quality of government services. The highlights of such a comparison are given below:

(1) New ministries have been added to service new needs.
(2) Some previous ministries and agencies were abolished, e.g. Ministry of Unification and Ministry of Tribal Affairs, and were replaced by small offices.
(3) Some of the main departments within the old ministries were expanded to become independent agencies affiliated to ministries, e.g. Taxation Department, Survey Department, Tourism, Banking, etc.
(4) A similar and parallel development occurred in the field of education and training. Some of the old training offices grew into specialised independent training centres, e.g. Justice, Taxation, Customs and Banking institutions.
(5) In the civil service, education and training, and human resource development, NIPA played a leading role. Out of about 35,000 government employees in 1982, NIPA alone trained about 13,000 between 1970 and 1982. Out of this total, 1,077 attended top-management seminars and conferences; those who attended middle-management programmes numbered 3,565; participants in office-management programmes were 879; the remainder attended NIPA's languages programmes.

Conclusion

The concept of modern public administration has been introduced only during the past two decades in Yemen. During the imamate era there were no government institutions and no limits to the Imam's authority. Yet, when the 1962 revolution took place, the government recognised the importance of modernisation in the field of administration as one of the most important requirements to develop the country. During the sixties there were no significant achievements in modernising the administration except for the establishment of some ministries and agencies shaped along the lines of foreign models. However, the problems of public administration in the country remained. Since the early 1970s, after the civil war, the government started to plan and organise its efforts to develop the country: among these efforts were serious attempts to reform the administration. Some of these efforts have failed and some have succeeded. That is why the current five-year plan concentrates on public administration more than the First Five-year Plan, particularly on manpower planning. Finally, the importance of modern public administration has been reiterated in the National Charter which guides all national efforts.

It seems to me that we have a perfect diagnosis of the problem. And it has been realised that the solution to it lies in adopting techniques of planning, follow-up, appraisal, evolution and information training, and developing an effective approach to administering the country.

Notes

1. J. E. Peterson, *Yemen, the Search for a Modern State* (Johns Hopkins University Press, Baltimore, 1982).
2. El-Azizi, *Lectures in Economic Development* (Dar al-Fikr al-Arabi Press, San'a', 1979).
3. Ministry of Civil Service, *The Civil Service in Twenty Years* (San'a', May 1982).
4. *Al-Akhbar* (Cairo), 23 Oct. 1966.
5. *Official Gazette* (1966).
6. *The Civil Service Publications* (1982), p. 6.
7. Publication of NIPA (1981).

11 TRIBAL RELATIONS AND POLITICAL HISTORY IN UPPER YEMEN

Paul Dresch

From south of San'a' to the Saudi border, Upper Yemen is dominated by a series of major tribes. With the exception of Khawlan bin Amir (five tribes around Sa'da) most of these belong to one or other of two famous confederations; Hashid and Bakil. This pair of names is extremely ancient. In pre-Islamic times they became aligned, as they are now, as referring to two halves of a larger entity called Hamdan. A set of genealogical connections was later elaborated, according to which Hashid and Bakil are the sons of Jusham bin Hubran bin Nawf bin Hamdan, and Hamdan is a lineal descendant of Qahtan. Few of the tribes which make up each confederation are mentioned as early as the confederations themselves, but many are referred to by al-Hamdani (early tenth century AD), at which point they occupied much the same geographical positions as they do now.

The tribes have been an important source of armed strength throughout the Islamic period and they remain so today. They have been the basis for successive attempts to form a state, usually led by the Zaidi Imams, but they have seldom been closely integrated in the structure of government, and, indeed, tribalism has often been seen as inimical to the state's interests. There is something of a paradox involved: the tribes have always been politically important, and yet tribalism forms no part of the language of statecraft. The paradox is of very long standing. If it now seems that tribalism and the affairs of a modern government belong somehow to different worlds, the difference itself is not really new.

The Tribes and the Rest of Yemen

The population with which we are concerned is nowadays in excess of half a million, divided rather unevenly among some seven major Hashid tribes and perhaps fourteen from Bakil. The territory of these major tribes occupies the northern plateaus and the eastern

Tribal Relations and Political History in Upper Yemen 155

Figure 11.1: Tribes of Upper Yemen

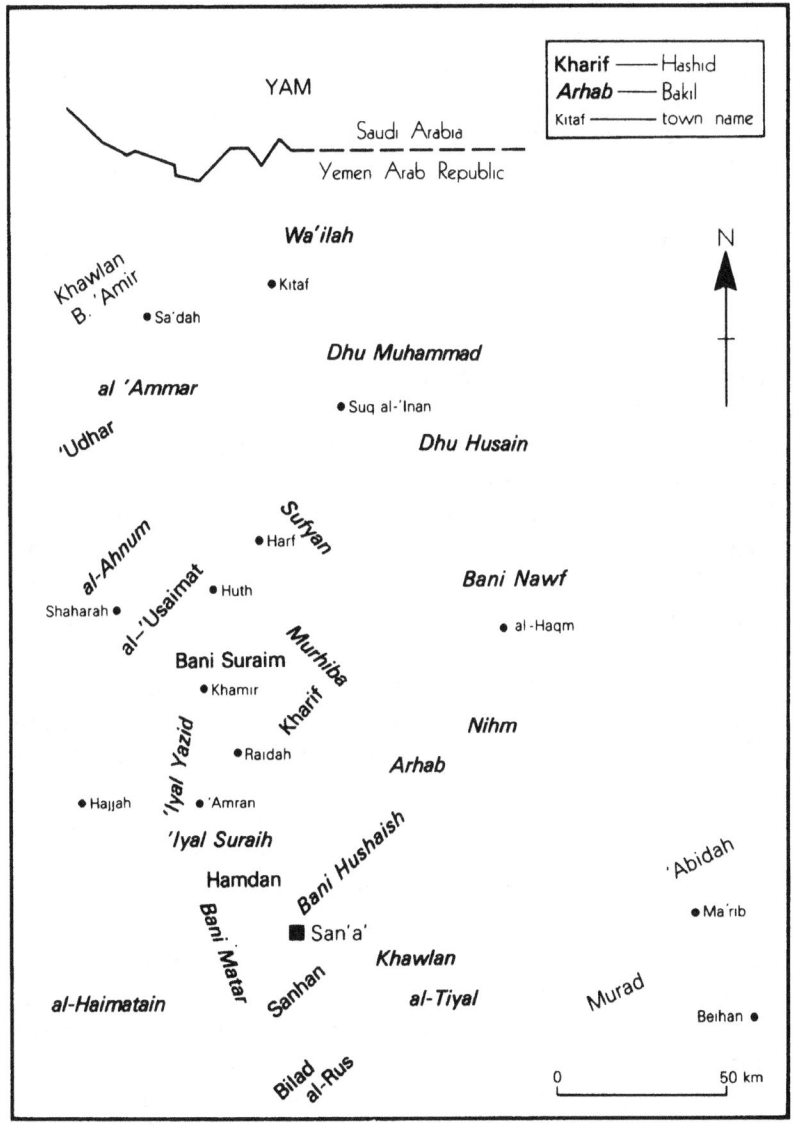

slopes.[1] The classification of tribes as Hashidi or Bakili in fact extends west of the plateau to the mountains which border the Tihama, but these western areas are rather marginal to the web of arbitration and dispute in which the plateau tribes are constantly involved. Bani Suraim and al-Usaimat (Hashid), and Iyal Yazid and Sufyan (Bakil), for example, are all liable to become involved in events which concern the confederations as wholes, but al-Ashmur and al-Sharafain, in the west, are not. Some such difference between the plateau and the Western Mountains has probably existed since at least al-Hamdani's time. Similarly, the distinction between Upper Yemen, with its major tribes, and Lower Yemen, where large-scale tribal organisation is scarcely in evidence at all, is of very long standing.

The tribesmen in the north are mainly villagers, who grow sorghum, barley and wheat by 'dry' (rain-fed) cultivation. There are nomadic and semi-nomadic *badu* in the east and in the more low-lying areas of the far north-west (for example, in Udhar). On the other hand there are a few areas of cash-crop cultivation on the plateau, notably the grape plots of Wadi Dhibin and the Sa'da region. Most tribesmen, though, are grain farmers who produce very largely for their own use. It is difficult to assess the productive potential of the land at all accurately but plainly one is not now, and never was, dealing with the kind of surplus production to be found in Lower Yemen and the west. The land of Hashid and Bakil would provide a poor economic basis for any elaborate exploitative class.

Land tenure in the tribal areas is fairly equitable.[2] It is essential that a man own land in the tribe if he is to be a tribesman at all, and in most cases where a man's own holding is insufficient for his needs the additional land he works belongs to his relatives or fellow tribesmen, among whom the exchange of labour may not be equal but remains none the less an exchange. In the south and west of the YAR the picture is quite different. There one finds that the great majority of the population in many areas are sharecroppers who work on the property of a few large land-holding families. A number of these families have their origins among the northern tribes, and some maintain active links with the areas they came from. Bait Hubaish, for example, are noted shaikhs in Sufyan and at the same time own large areas in Mahwit province. Such great shaikhly families as al-Ahmar, al-Juzailan and al-Sha'if have for a long time owned large estates in Hajja province, which reportedly

Tribal Relations and Political History in Upper Yemen 157

were a bone of contention between them and Crown Prince Ahmad in the years after the First World War.³ At a less elevated level, one finds many land-owning families in the west who came originally from such plateau tribes as Arhab, Nihm and Bani Suraim. Some of those who still live on the plateau own land in the west, and in the extreme north-east (among Dhu Muhammad and Dhu Husain) one meets men who remember how, as children, they walked the breadth of Yemen to areas near al-Mahabisha in order to collect part of the rent in cash.

The historical relation of economic dependence or interdependence between the plateau tribes and the rest of Yemen is now almost impossible to assess. There is no doubt, however, that the tribesmen have often spilled over into the west and south. They did so under the first Zaidi Imam (al-Hadi, d. AD 911) and they continued to do so until the end of Imam Yahya's campaigns to conquer all of what is now the YAR during the 1920s and 1930s. Often large bodies of tribesmen (in the nineteenth century Dhu Muhammad and Dhu Husain were particularly conspicuous) would move into the west or south despite an Imam's express orders to the contrary and descend on these other parts of the country, as more than one chronicler says, 'like locusts'.⁴

It is no surprise to find nowadays a certain fear and distrust of the tribes in the areas they used once to invade. Muhammad Nu'man elaborates a historical model of Yemen's politics which revolves around the tribes' supposed greed and poverty:

> When the area of grazing [in the north] was reduced by scarce rainfall, and its extent was thus insufficient for the number of inhabitants, who multiply year after year, then there was a temporary migration from their arid homelands to the fertile plains of the West and South.

The imamate, according to Nu'man, aided and abetted this process which mere ecology underlay:

> The escape of the fertile areas from the Imam's control, or more properly from harsh and unjust exploitation by the mountain people, at certain historical periods, provided the motive for persistent new attempts. These took the form of constant struggles which on many occasions tore Yemen into a number of petty states each trying to gain control of the rest of the country, to the

point where the country as a whole has been unable to unify under a central government more than three times in the past eleven centuries.[5]

By the terms of modern political rhetoric, of course, the accusation that the tribes have spoiled 'unity' is very serious. As a historical thesis it has its drawbacks; not least, that the Qasimi expansion of the seventeenth century would have to count as an episode of 'unification', although it was the product of a succession of strong Imams backed by tribal armies. The rather similar expansion of the Hamid al-Din Imams in this century also brought or imposed a large measure of 'unity', whatever its other faults. To the modern nationalist there must also be a measure of ambiguity in the fact that the tribes played a major part, as they did just before these Imams' further conquests, in expelling the Turkish invader. To reverse al-Wazir's phrase, 'The sword which has sometimes pierced the body of the community' is also 'the armour which has protected Yemen against every aggressor'.[6] Historically, though, there is certainly a marked contrast between the image of the tribes as a chaotically violent force elsewhere in the country and the remarkable stability of formal divisions within the tribes' own territory. Tribes do not absorb or displace each other as clans did among the Huns or Mongols. The borders between tribal divisions change only slowly, and then by alliance, not conquest.

What, then, are these divisions? Every tribe has borders which are carefully maintained. Even if land within these borders is bought by men from the next-door tribe, the borders themselves remain where they were unless villages or sections from elsewhere formally renounce membership of their own tribe and 'become brother' (*yukhawi*) to this one. Within its borders a tribe is answerable for whatever happens. If, let us say, a man from tribe A is robbed in the territory of tribe B by someone from C, it is B which is answerable and honour-bound to extract amends from the culprit. If it fails to do so, B and A may be set at odds. Moreover, it is B's prerogative to right the wrong, and if outsiders presume to do so B is insulted. The responsibility and the prerogative of upholding the peace generally within given borders, as well as defending the borders themselves, are comprised in the idea of 'inviolability of territory' (*hurmat al-watan*). It is on this inviolability that the honour of the tribe depends.[7]

The relation is always problematic between a tribe as such (the supposedly ancestral name which applies to a given territory) and the mass of tribesmen who for the moment make the tribe up. They are not identical. Men may refuse to become involved in events that, abstractly conceived, concern them because they concern the name those men share. It is not unusual for sections of a tribe to refuse support to their 'brother' sections at odds with another tribe, or even to turn on them and actively oppose them. Tribes are not solidary groups. Moreover, even though a dispute may be carried on in terms of an opposition between whole tribes or confederations the number of men actively involved is usually quite small: the rest of the men who share the tribe's name may be simply not interested. Tribal divisions are not to be thought of as groups, therefore, but as moral spaces within which various obligations exist that are recognised by all but may or may not be met in particular circumstances. Groups may demand support from other groups on the basis of the ancestral name they share (the *da'i* or *da'wa*, 'summons'), or may demand on the same basis that their 'brothers' settle with outsiders, but whether the demands are met depends on any number of considerations in addition to shared membership in the tribe or confederation.

The moral space which a tribal name defines is bound up first of all with territory. Within that territory falls arable land, which is privately owned (*milk, mal*), and land which is not farmed but which is available to all members of a village or tribal section for such purposes as grazing (*faish, ard baida'*). The tribal territory also contains particular people, places and events for which the tribe is responsible; 'weak' people such as Jews and those born into degrading occupations (the *muzayyina* for instance), respected people who are *hijra* from the tribe ('elevated' and 'protected' like the sayyids and certain qadis, certain villages particularly associated with these respected people, and the weekly markets held in tribal territory.[8] The honour of the tribe depends upon the successful protection of all these. They are, as it were, marked elements. The call to right wrongs committed against them will generally be answered by large numbers of men from the tribe in question, whereas the call to support a fellow tribesman may be far less compelling.

It is important to note that, although a tribe may be responsible for the safety of protected people, markets and so forth, it has no monopoly over their services. Conventionally, for example, any tribesman has access to any market, and the market on market-day is 'secure and guaranteed' (*amin damin*) for all comers. At the new *suq* of Bait Harash near Raida, for instance, one now finds men from the Jawf selling firewood, traders from surrounding Bakil tribes and from the towns, even men from as far away as Bajil on occasion selling tomatoes, and buyers from throughout the surrounding region. If the market-peace is in any way broken, responsibility for repairing the breach devolves on the protecting tribe alone; in this case, Kharif. The pattern of responsibility and the pattern of commerce linking different markets are not congruent.[9] They never were. Rather similarly, a particular sayyid house may be under the protection of a particular tribe, but historically their services as learned men would have been open to anyone. Even shaikhs who are identified with particular sections or tribes operate in such a way that their domains of influence are seldom congruent with tribal divisions.[10]

This disjunction, or difference in type, between structures of commerce or political influence and the structure of tribal divisions no doubt accounts in large part for the latter's longevity. Trade may change, the fortunes of sayyid or shaikhly families may rise and fall, but the tribal divisions themselves are seldom at stake. The political history of Upper Yemen is turbulent. Through it all, though, there survives a system of intelligibility which revolves around the idea of a moral equilibrium between tribes. This does not mean equity between tribesmen: the casualties in intestine disputes may sometimes have been very serious, families may have died out or been driven out by want, groups may have changed tribes in despair of help from their 'brothers'. The formal structure of the tribes, however, changes very little and provides almost fixed points of reference against which the fortunes or misfortunes of groups of men are worked out and make sense to their fellows.

Outside the tribes' territory this system of intelligibility and the practical constraints which go with it do not apply. When a horde of tribesmen descended on a non-tribal area they appeared to those faced with them as an irrational force almost comparable to plague or drought. They were simply the antithesis of order; 'evil ones' (*ashrar*) or 'depraved' and 'corrupt' (*ahl al-fasad*).[11] San'a' has been starved or sacked by such hordes more than once. A shaikh of the city, Muhsin Mu'aid (elected about 1860), is still remembered for closing Bab Sha'ub, the northern gate from which, until last year, the taxis to Khamir and Sa'da ran, saying, 'Nothing comes through here but evil.' This is not merely ancient history. In 1948, after the collapse of al-Wazir's rising, San'a' was again sacked by tribal forces at the instigation of Imam Ahmad. As Muhammad Nu'man says, the San'anis and the Imam's officials long shared a view of the tribes summed up in the phrase 'the fang of a cur in a cur's head'.[12]

Law and Order: the Place of Tribal Custom

Although the Zaidi Imams always depended on the tribes for support and never attempted to abolish tribalism, their view of tribesmen was consistently hostile. The tribes scarcely appear in the Zaidi chronicles except as 'warriors in the cause of God', when they happen to be with the Imam of the day, or as virtually infidels, 'evil ones' and 'followers of the *taghut*',[13] when their support for the Imam is less than whole-hearted. There is no account given of tribal affairs in tribal terms. Although by reading between the lines we can be sure tribal structure and practice alike have changed very little, the tribes are displaced from centre-stage in a millennium of historiography which begins with the first Imam's *sira*.

The Imams claimed to provide order on the basis of the Holy Book and the Prophet's *sunna*. The tribes often accepted this claim in that they made sayyid families hijra (that is, they took them in as protected persons), and the idea of the 'holy family' intervening as respected arbitrators in tribal conflicts is as attractive to the sayyids or the tribesmen themselves as it is to Arabists and anthropologists. However, with a few notable exceptions, Yemen was in fact no more orderly with Imams than without them. The tribes' own means of preserving themselves were constantly needed and survived vigorously for all that references to them in the Zaidi histories are fragmented.

In the absence of state intervention tribesmen resort to arbitration. Those who have committed an offence may give right of judgement to the victim's people, or the disputing parties may agree on an arbitrator, usually a noted shaikh or 'committee' (*lajna*) of shaikhs. If they fail to agree they may be 'driven' (*al-musawaqa*) by others to accept arbitration.[14] Once an arbitrator is agreed on, he conventionally appoints, or has those at odds choose, 'guarantors' (*kufala'*) who are then responsible for both the good conduct and the debts of the disputing parties. Relations between the disputing parties are 'cut off' (*fakk al-qata'*) and they communicate only through their guarantors. If either party to the dispute now breaks the peace by a fresh offence against the other, he insults his guarantor and thus owes the guarantor amends. These may be set in advance at a high level, but in the absence of such agreement the guarantor is entitled to amends of the same amount as the damage done, and in a serious case he has the right of *kharab wa-turab*, that is laying waste the offender's property. In a potentially difficult dispute the guarantors may be supported by 'secondary guarantors' (*kufala' al-radm, rudama'*). Within each of the groups at odds a 'bondsman' (*sawan*) may be held responsible to the guarantors for the conduct of those particularly involved in the dispute. A complex web of relations is thus built up to contain further violence. These relations are always between named individuals, who need to be carefully chosen for their probity and influence, but behind them are their tribesmen who should, ideally, support them if the need arises.

In a major dispute these involvements will span a number of tribes. Let us say, for example, that Kharif (Hashid) and Sufyan (Bakil) are set somehow at odds. The arbitrators might be drawn from Dhu Muhammad and Dhu Husain (both Bakil, but the sympathies of their leading shaikhs differ greatly), the guarantors for Kharif's behaviour might come from Bani Suraim (Hashid) and for Sufyan from Arhab (Bakil), and so on until most of the major tribes are in some way committed. The structure of containment may simply not work or, worse still, may unravel so that the relations intended to contain conflict in fact lead to further disputes. On the whole, though, at the present day the system works remarkably well. Even where a conflict between tribes is greatly exacerbated by party politics (and, it must be said, sometimes by gross interference from outside Yemen) large-scale violence is usually smothered in a matter of days. It is probably not all that common for the nominal cause of a dispute to be dealt with definitively, but disputes are contained none the less. The structures of containment set up to do this may last for some time. Much of the detail of tribal politics turns out to depend on these structures, which may lie dormant for years until a truce is breached which the outsider until then knew nothing of.

The rules of procedure which govern attempts to contain disputes and bring them to arbitration are all part of *'urf* or 'custom'. Most tribesmen hold that 'urf also specifies exactly the amends due for any offence.[15] In fact settlements of what seem to be comparable cases differ widely. A certain uniformity in the terms used is very noticeable, which is often taken to show how definitive custom is, but their application to particular cases can be highly ambiguous. For example, it may be agreed that a certain class of offence is to be paid for *bil-marbu'* or *bil-muhaddash*, but quite what the sum is that one multiplies 'by four' or 'by eleven' may be open to debate. 'Custom' provides primarily a language in terms of which settlements can be attempted, rather than a set of prescriptions. There are genuine regularities none the less: a standard *'aib* (amends for a 'disgraceful' act) is recognised as 88 silver thalers and a bull, with a corresponding 'half-'aib' of 44 thalers and a ram, and a killing in disgraceful circumstances is always to be paid for by a multiple of the standard blood-money. There is little disagreement, at least in the abstract, about what counts as an offence. It is a 'disgrace' or 'aib, and amends are thus due in addition to blood-money or material damages, if one kills a man from behind or mutilates the corpse, if one takes a man's weapons or attacks him when he is unarmed, if one offers violence of any sort to women or to 'weak' non-tribal people, if one breaks the market-peace or the peace attaching to another man's house, if one breaks a truce, and so on.

The detailed differences between custom and Islamic law are best left to a scholar of the latter, but the two are by no means opposed in their entirety. The great bulk of custom consists in local understandings about water-rights, rights to pasture and so forth, which, so long as they did not conflict with shari'a, were accepted by Zaidi scholars as a valid source of law. Much of the rest comprises rules of procedure recognised by Imams as much as by tribesmen. Even the scales of compensation laid down by custom are not incompatible with those of Islamic law, although many of the offences for which custom demands compensation would not be recognised everywhere in the Islamic world. The Imams, though, often condemned customary law as taghut.[16] The rhetorical opposition between taghut and shari'a seems in fact to have rested largely on a radical difference in the way they are administered and in the political conceptions which underlie them.

From the time of the first Imam to that of the last, and even now that the Imams are gone, tribes have been constantly accused of 'cutting the roads', an offence for which the *hadd* is amputation of a hand and a foot. In custom a tribe has every right to deny access to its territory and detain outsiders found there, provided always that the 'cutting' is announced in advance. What is at stake is something akin to sovereignty. Again, it is the essence of 'urf that settlement depends largely on the disputing parties themselves and that they choose their own arbitrator. It is of the essence of shari'a, as administered by a state, that the judge is specified by the government, not by those involved. It might be noted that one of Imam Yahya's main demands in the treaty of Da''an (1911, with the Ottoman Turks) was that in areas ruled by him he was to appoint judges to administer the shari'a.[17] The law they administered may in particular cases not have differed enormously from custom, or indeed from the Turkish *qanun*, but the apparatus they made up was to be his; a prime means of control over his part of the population. Once the Turks left a policy of centralisation set in whereby the previous loose web of arbitrators (sayyids, qadis and shaikhs) in a given area was replaced with a single *hakim*, responsible to the Imam's *'amil* or district governor. As part of the process, markets where arbitration had previously been pursued were sometimes closed down and new ones encouraged where the Imam's functionaries had the monopoly of justice.[18] All of this was presented as 'establishing the true shari'a'.

The tribes' own methods were not dismantled but made use of. Very often the structures of containment outlined above were built up as the tribes had always done, with the whole apparatus of guarantors, secondary guarantors and even arbitrators 'topped off', as it were, by the Imam's officials, who would then add an *i'timad* or 'confirmation' before forwarding the papers to the 'noble presence' of the Imam himself. Urf and shari'a were in practice very much entangled. The rhetorical opposition between them, however, was maintained by the Imams to the last. Tribal custom was condemned as taghut, whose servants, of course, 'receive a worse recompense from God than those whom he has cursed, on whom his wrath has fallen and whom he turns into apes and swine'.[19]

At the level of detailed politics, relations between Imams and tribes were very complex. At the level of political rhetoric and of historiography they were very simple. The Imams claimed to produce order in accordance with Holy Writ, and the tribes were the formless but recalcitrant matter they worked with to do so. A powerful stereotype was built up. Whatever was good was identified with learned men and whatever was bad with the tribes. The tribesmen's faults were repeatedly dwelt on and their virtues were all but ignored, to the point that if for once their actions were approved of they were characterised as good Muslims, not good tribesmen, as if the two were somehow incompatible. In a situation like this no contrary evidence can make an impression. Even now, the tribesmen themselves show a certain reticence in talking about customary law, often speaking of what in fact is contemporary practice as if it were what their grandfathers did and it had all but died out. There is always the fear among the less educated that what they do will be thought disgraceful by more educated outsiders. Tribal law remains politically very important, but in a rhetorical confrontation tribalism is always liable to cede place to any claim vigorously put which invokes ideas of the state or religion.

The Tribes and the Revolution

The image of the tribes as opposed to both piety and order accompanied them into the modern period. It is not, then, altogether surprising that, as the rhetoric of a more equitable statecraft was worked out by the liberal movement, tribalism was at first conspicuous by its absence from liberal writings. From the outset, liberal thinking contained ideas which were not incompatible with tribalism, notably that of *la-markaziya* or 'decentralised government' (as opposed to the personal and arbitrary rule of the later Imams, *hukm fardi*). Tribalism itself, however, was not addressed as either an asset or a liability.

One of the first to so much as mention the tribes explicitly was Muhsin al-Aini, at that time a very junior member of the movement. As an image of future Yemeni unity he invokes the perhaps mythical unity of pre-Islamic Yemen where Bilqis, Queen of Sheba, consulted her chiefs on all points of policy, and he goes on to say that a ruler of Yemen should derive his authority from the people, including the tribes.[20] The problem that Imam Ahmad already did derive his authority, and certainly his power, from a tribal base is not really tackled. Two years later (in 1959) al-Zubairi, by far the most widely respected figure in the present-day ideology of the revolution, mentioned the tribes as enslaved to the Imam by the 'spiritual poisons' they had imbibed.[21] In al-Zubairi's last great prose work (in 1961), however, the tribes are suddenly accorded the hero's role in the struggle against Imam Ahmad: 'And in their vanguard Husain bin Nasir al-Ahmar and Abd al-Latif Rajih, who represent the honour of all Hamdan, both Hashid and Bakil, and represent behind them the whole of the people.'[22] In the timeless dream-world of the book the same image is used as was earlier used by al-Aini; as supposedly happened in pre-Islamic Yemen, the tribes would now all take part in the government. Even the defeat of al-Wazir's revolt, which was crushed by a tribal army that then sacked San'a', is included to the tribes' advantage:

> the defeat of the 1948 revolution was the strange but effective means whereby the idea of revolution spread to a wider circle. It filtered down from the upper, ruling strata to the popular base just as did Islam among the Tartars, who smashed the Islamic empire only to suffer a spiritual collapse of their tyranny. They thus embraced Islam and became its greatest power.[23]

The whole book makes it abundantly plain that the Tartars in this case are 'greater Hamdan, to which belong the two mightiest tribes in our country, in our history, and indeed in the history of Arabism and Islam'.[24] In other words, Hashid and Bakil, who until now have been inimical to the rightly ordered state, are to be the means by which that state is set up and defended.

The 1959 revolt which prompted these ideas remains little studied.[25] When Ahmad returned from Rome, though, his wrath largely fell on a number of shaikhly families: Husain and Hamid al-Ahmar and Abd al-Latif Rajih were executed; Abdullah al-Ahmar, Ali al-Sha'if, Abdullah Daris and Hamid Abu Ra's were imprisoned;[26] and many of those fortunate enough to avoid capture fled to Aden by way of Baihan. The call to defend tribal inviolability, and at the same time to change the form of government, was overridden by the Imam's 'summons' or da'wa to 'promote what is right and prohibit what is evil'; precisely the terms used by Imams for a millennium. Once Ahmad was dead, however, the experience of those tribes whose shaikhs had particularly suffered in the revolt was sufficient to rally many tribesmen to their shaikhs' support against Ahmad's son, al-Badr. At the time of the 1959 revolt many shaikhly families had been in touch for some time with liberal political thinkers. It was only through that revolt, though, that the tribes themselves, who might make or break any attempt to depose the imamate, secured the liberals' attention at the eleventh hour before the 1962 revolution.

On the night of the 1962 *coup* a number of men from the tribes were actively involved. What is more important for the present purpose, however, is the role certain tribal leaders and tribalism itself played in the ensuing civil war. In the first months of the war a political stalemate developed. San'a' became dominated by the Egyptians and their adherents, at the expense of the revolutionary officers and the older liberal politicians alike, whose own attempts to settle Yemen's affairs were stifled.[27] As early as April 1963 these latter groups put forward a provisional constitution (in which, among other things, a council of shaikhs was suggested), but the only result was that al-Iryani, al-Zubairi and Abd al-Salam Sabrah were packed off to the disputed areas and thus removed from the centre of events. A second attempt was made in September 1963, this time at Amran.

Amran is a nominally Hashid site surrounded by Bakil and readily accessible to tribes of both major confederations. It has often been the venue for tribal conclaves. The conference of September 1963 was convened by republican shaikhs (notably al-Ahmar and Abu Ra's) acting in a largely tribal capacity, and the fact that the meeting could be held at all was due more to tribal forms of politics than to methods drawn from a supposedly more 'modern' system. The latter had by then jammed almost completely as the dispute between republicans and royalists became assimilated to that between Egypt and Saudi Arabia. So far as tribal forms are concerned, it was only to be expected that royalist and republican shaikhs could meet under truce. When Iyal Yazid's delegation walked out it was Iyal Suraih who brought them back, although Iyal Suraih by then had complaints of their own against the Egyptians and President al-Sallal. They demanded that two shaikhs from Hashid and two from Bakil be sent to demand an account from Nasser of his role in Yemen. A series of resolutions was passed which concerned tribal affairs: that a committee of shaikhs be set up to resolve disputes between tribes, that a further committee be charged with ending foreign intervention in tribal territory, that the council of shaikhs suggested earlier in the year be convened as a 'consultative council', and so on. Another provisional constitution was drawn up. The attempt to resolve Yemen's national problems from a tribal basis only broke down when the proposals were taken back to San'a'.

The histories of the war pay more attention to the Khamir conference of two years later. On 30 March 1965 al-Zubairi was murdered, having been moving among the tribes in search of a truce, and under threat of massive tribal secession al-Sallal asked Nu'man to form a government. As Minister of the Interior, Abdullah al-Ahmar, the paramount shaikh of Hashid, convened a conference at Khamir, which is virtually Hashid's 'capital'. By this time dissatisfaction had reached the point where many royalists refused to attend and even some staunch republicans attended only under pressure. A new constitution was again drawn up but the initiative was again crushed in San'a'.[28] Nu'man resigned, and delegations of Khamir participants who went to argue their case in Cairo were detained at Nasser's pleasure. Those who remained, including a large number of important republican shaikhs, finally took matters into their own hands and in July slipped out of Yemen to pursue negotiations elsewhere. Again an axis of tribal leaders and the forms of tribalism had provided the basis for an attempt to solve national problems which was suppressed by the supposedly national government.

In the following year, 1966, certain tribal areas provided a refuge for a number of 'Septemberists' and older liberals of the sort who were eventually to form Yemen's government when the war ended. After the British suddenly announced that they would leave Aden, the Egyptians decided on retrenchment, 'the strategy of the long breath'. As part of this retrenchment, after an abortive conference with the Saudis they brought back al-Sallal, who had been absent for almost nine months, and carried out a thoroughgoing purge in San'a'. Many of the republicans who escaped fled to the north. By the end of the year something very like a republican government in exile was to be found in the north of Hashid's territory under the protection of that confederation's paramount shaikh.

Throughout the period, of course, it was tribesmen who did much of the fighting. However, the tribes' own means of containing disputes proved remarkably resilient in the face of modern weapons, extreme political rhetoric and foreign intervention alike. From the outset, tribes which were opposed as republican and royalist arranged truces between themselves, and some of these agreements, whereby each tribe guaranteed the integrity of the other's borders, access to its markets and the security of its roads, in fact remain in force even now. Some idea of what might have happened had purely Yemeni initiatives been allowed to succeed is given by what in fact happened during the 'long breath' period. The Egyptians withdrew from the north, the royalist tribesmen harried the retreat and a pitched battle was fought near San'a'. However, royalist and republican tribes did not then descend on each other's territory to decide the issue. Instead they relapsed into a series of purely local conflicts and truces of the sort which had always been familiar to them. This does not mean that the allegiance of those involved, whether to the Imam or the Republic, was necessarily insincere or weakly held. One tribe, though, can contain one faction and a second tribe another, and, although the factions may be irreconcilably opposed, a decision between them is prevented by the 'inviolability' of the respective tribes' territory. Outside tribal territory these considerations do not apply. Much of the heaviest fighting between tribal levies thus took place in the Western Mountains, while on the plateau what would otherwise have been war *à outrance* was consistently checked by the forms of tribalism.

In the national reconciliation at the end of the war an alignment of political figures which had formed at the start of the war, if not earlier, emerged in government. Many of the ideas they had promoted at last took practical form. In particular, the council of shaikhs which al-Zubairi had written of a decade earlier, and which had been attempted more than once in the war, became a reality with the formation of a national 'consultative council' in which the representatives of Upper Yemen were shaikhs almost to a man. This was not without its problems.[29] However, the tribes were now spoken for in central government, and although the consultative council was dissolved in 1974, in large part to exclude the shaikhs, the idea it represented has since surfaced again in a number of forms. Since the war certain shaikhly families, not all of them basing their influence on a tribal following, have been prominent in affairs of state and have held important governmental positions. More generally, the tribes themselves emerged from the civil war far stronger than they had ever been. The tide of money and guns which flowed into the north from all sides has never receded, and in the post-war period such patronage, on an enormous scale, has often been important. At the same time the ability of tribal forms to englobe political differences has remained at least as marked as it was in the war.

The Tribes at the Present Day

Despite the role of the republican tribes in defending the revolution, and despite the more contentious role of tribalism in moderating the effects of the civil war, the tribes in general remain the object of suspicion in many quarters. If tribesmen are no longer condemned as *ahl al-taghut*, tribalism is now often perceived as a threat to 'unity' (*wahda*), as fertile ground for 'factionalism' (*ta'ifiya*) and as an obstacle to the country's development. The language of statecraft still excludes that of tribalism, and tribalism is still seen by many as the antithesis of government; 'the fang of a cur in a cur's head' as ever was.

Since the war the tribes' propensity to harbour opposing factions and at the same time contain their antagonism has often been in evidence. Even the most sanguine observer would have to admit that governments in San'a' have repeatedly come under serious pressure, sometimes bedevilled by a violent antagonism between North Yemen's neighbours which others have exploited for their own ends.[30] The tribes have been subject to the same strains. 'Inviolability of territory' remains important, however, and tribes still do not invade one another to decide a political point, although groups within one may bring whatever other pressure they can on groups in another tribe. The methods of containing disputes outlined earlier are applied to all sorts of conflicts, and the resulting patchwork of mutually incompatible tendencies can be confusing if viewed through the usual categories of national or international politics.

During the late 1970s, when the National Democratic Front was a major feature of Yemeni affairs, those tribes which in the main expressed sympathy with the Front, and whose members declared themselves Nasserist or socialist, were precisely the tribes which a few years before had been thought staunchly royalist. The routes over which rifles had come from British-occupied Baihan were precisely those over which mines, ammunition and even ground-to-air missiles now come in support of a movement which seemed quite the opposite of royalism. What has happened is that a core of tribes which supported the republic in the war (the three Hashid tribes of al-Usaimat, Kharif and Bani Suraim, but also, for example, Dhu Muhammad) have remained on good terms with each other and their shaikhs have pursued a fairly consistent line. Certain other shaikhs and tribes (mainly from Bakil, such as Iyal Yazid, Dhu Husain and Sufyan) have tended, as it were, to swing around this core with the changing winds of regional politics. It is not a question of all of Bakil against all of Hashid. On the Bakil side we have already mentioned Dhu Muhammad. We might also mention Murhiba, a tiny tribe of about ten villages which enjoys excellent relations with its Hashid neighbours, and Bani Matar, west of San'a', whose shaikh has often been a mediator between different tribes and between tribes and government. On the other hand, Udhar are unequivocally a Hashid tribe but most of them refuse to co-operate with the core of Hashid tribes we mentioned earlier or with the confederation's paramount shaikh. The details are complex, and when one considers differences of opinion within tribes they become more complex still.

Tribes, as we have said, are not solidary blocs. However, the power of tribal names to mobilise large numbers of men in certain circumstances remains perfectly real, and the oppositions between these names may be assimilated to the rhetoric of non-tribal politics. The name of one confederation, for example, may for some men be a synonym for the party of 'reaction' and the name of the other for the party of 'progress'. There is no reason why the tags should not swap around fairly readily. Political alignments depend to a great extent on the allegiance of influential shaikhly families within tribes, but the tribal divisions remain almost fixed and may be used as the board for very different political games, while the 'inviolability' of each tribe's territory sets strict limits to the likely outcome. In some circumstances tribal considerations often come first. If, for example, one tribe is imposed on within its territory by a particular government administration, its 'brothers' in the confederation may rally to its support even if they agree with the political line of the administration and disagree with that of their fellow tribesmen. Let us be clear, though, that this is not at all automatic. Tribalism is not a mechanism like so much clockwork but a way of perceiving the world, and as such it is far from dead.

Writing at the end of the civil war, al-Wazir noted two main threats to the future of tribalism: first, that economic changes might undermine the tribesmen's interest in honourable combat and perhaps make the shaikhs into a bourgeoisie, and, second, that a powerful army might subdue the tribes more directly.[31] Both are live issues.

The northern tribes, like the rest of Yemen, have sent large numbers of men to work in Saudi Arabia and the Gulf in recent years, and the flood of remittances has brought trucks, water-pumps and imported goods of all sorts, which have improved the material standard of living immeasurably. Tribesmen are now caught up in an entrepreneurial cash economy. The monstrous urban sprawl around San'a' and elsewhere has already covered land which would previously have been subject to tribal rights of pre-emption. In the countryside few households now depend only on what they can produce, but tribalism has not yet melted in the face of prosperity. Customary procedures englobe disputes arising from the new ways of life much as they did those arising from the old. If major economic changes continue, then of course tribesmen may simply cease to be tribesmen. The qat trade and long-distance trucking both give rise to the kind of disputes which keep tribalism very much alive. Working in a factory would not. Given the extraordinary vulnerability of the Yemeni economy, it would be rash to guess what will happen, and, if a slump occurred, the present tendencies could reverse very quickly. A great deal of land in rural areas has gone out of production because men are working outside Yemen, but the territorial bounds which contain that land are still known and enforced. In some areas, too, almost as much land now seems to be idle because men have been posted elsewhere within Yemen on government service, a phenomenon connected more with the second of al-Wazir's points than with the first.

The army is already numerous and powerful, remarkably so for a country like Yemen. It is not, though, a question of adding up numbers on two distinct sides: a great many men are both tribesmen and regular soldiers and may therefore be counted as either. The very distinction between government and tribes, which underlies that between tribes and army, is in some ways misleading. It is true that on occasion certain tribes have been at odds with the government of the day and a border has thus existed between the territory of each,[32] but those who for the moment dissent from a particular administration do not consider themselves somehow outside the Republic. They are as much Yemenis and republicans as anyone else.[33] Within a few weeks or months they may be again with the government, and their leading men may hold high governmental rank, while those who were previously with the government might now be against it. Even when a given tribe is, as it were, within the governmental pale one is constantly surprised by men struggling out of their kilts or *futas* and into army uniform for occasions which have for the moment been deemed governmental, or out of their uniforms and into futas for occasions deemed tribal. A shaikh who holds colonel's rank or is a government Minister does not thereby cease being a shaikh. Much of the detail of Yemeni politics cannot be grasped without some knowledge of tribal affairs, but relations between tribes and state are not a matter of two forces facing each other on a common border. That is only an occasional symptom. What is at stake are two views of the world and two sets of loyalties which are opposed, if anywhere, in the understanding of those involved.

A somewhat muted debate on the 'problem of tribalism' has done little to collapse that opposition. The emphasis in contemporary Yemen on 'unity' (and now even 'unity of thought') tends to leave tribalism as its antithesis much as a partisan religious da'wa did historically. In case of conflict, a tribe responds only with a da'wa of its own (its ancestral name), which is the focus of *'asabiya* and thus, to the hostile observer, of 'factionalism'. Until a language is evolved that includes statecraft and tribalism together this remains a dilemma, and progress is always liable to be impaled on the horns. Tribalism, of course, appears to many as less modern and progressive than, let us say, a cult of the army. In the short term it may wither away for no better reason than that. We should be aware, though, that the exclusion of tribalism from political debate by an appeal to 'modernity' is in large part a mere transformation of the way in which tribalism has long been excluded by an appeal to quite different terms.

Notes

The author would like to acknowledge the generous support of the Social Science Research Council, which has made possible extended field-work in Yemen.

1. A sketch-map showing the locations of the major tribes is provided at Figure 11.1.
2. See for example the figures quoted in R. Tutwiler and S. Carapico, *Yemeni Agriculture and Economic Change* (American Institute for Yemeni Studies, San'a', 1981), pp. 61-2.
3. Abdullah al-Shamahi, *Al-Yaman: Al-insan wal-hadara* (Alam al-Kutub, Cairo, 1972), p. 173.
4. Abd al-Wasi' al-Wasi'i, *Ta'rikh al-Yaman* (Matba'at al-Hijazi, Cairo, 1948); Abdullah al-Jarafi, *Al-Muqtataf min Ta'rikh al-Yaman* (Isa al-Babi al-Halabi, Cairo, 1951); Husain al-Sayaghi, *Safahat Majhula min Ta'rikh al-Yaman* (Markaz al-Dirasat al-Yamaniya, San'a', 1978); Abdullah al-Hibshi (ed.), *Hawliyat Yamaniya* (Wizarat al-I'lam wal-Thaqafa, San'a', 1980).
5. Muhammad Nu'man, *Al-Atraf al-Ma'niya fil-Yaman* (Mu'assasat al-Dabban, Beirut, 1965), pp. 22, 25-6.
6. Zaid bin Ali al-Wazir, *Muhawala li Fahm al-Mushkila al-Yamaniya* (Mu'assasat al-Risala, Beirut, 1971), p. 149.
7. For a more extended discussion see P. Dresch, 'The Several Peaces of Yemeni Tribes', *Journal of the Anthropological Society of Oxford*, vol. XII, no. 2 (1981).
8. For an account of the different estates of Yemeni society and their inter-relations see R. B. Serjeant, 'South Arabia' in C. Van Nieuwenhuijze (ed.), *Commoners, Climbers and Notables* (Brill, Leiden, 1977).
9. A good account of this market's place in the region, from a purely economic point of view, is given in Tutwiler and Carapico, *Yemeni Agriculture*, pp. 77-98.
10. See P. Dresch, 'The Position of Shaykhs among the Northern Tribes of Yemen', *Man* (forthcoming).
11. See the references provided in note 4 above, and especially al-Sayaghi, *Safahat*, pp. 125-6.
12. Nu'man, *Al-Atraf*, p. 33.
13. 'We have sent to every nation a prophet to say: Serve God and spurn the taghut' (Qur'an XVI, 36). A term of violent condemnation often translated or mis-translated as 'idol' or 'devil', but in Yemen usually applied by 'ulama' to customary law among the tribes.
14. It is at this point that sayyids and other members of the hijra now usually intervene. They separate the combatants, often by slaughtering beasts for them (*'aqa'ir*), but arbitration then devolves upon shaikhs. This would seem to have been the case during the last century as well, before the rise of powerful Imams; Hayyim Habshush, *Travels in Yemen*, ed. S. D. Goitein (Hebrew University Press, Jerusalem, 1941), p. 40.
15. For accounts of 'urf see E. Glaser, 'Meine Reise durch Arhab und Haschid', *Petermanns Mitteilungen*, no. 30 (1884), and E. Rossi, 'Il diritto consuetudinario delle tribù arabe del Yemen', *Rivista degli Studi Orientali*, vol. XXIII (1948).
16. C. Rathjens, 'Taghut gegen Scheri'ah' in *Jahrbuch des Museums für Länder- und Völkerkunde* (Linden-Museum, Stuttgart, 1951).
17. Sayyid Mustafa Salim, *Takwin al-Yaman al-Hadith* (Ma'had al-Buhuth wal-Dirasat al-Arabiya, Cairo, 1971), pp. 516-9.
18. The suq at Raida is a case in point. Kharif's markets were closed down and Raida became the administrative centre for one part of the tribe's territory, Dhibin the centre for another part. The establishment of the 'new suq' at Bait Harash a few years ago is thus in part an attempt to restore the *status quo ante* Imam Yahya.
19. Qur'an V, 60.

20. Muhsin al-Aini, *Ma'arik wa Mu'amarat didd Qadiyat al-Yaman* (n.p., 1957), pp. 60 and 143.

21. *Al-Imama wa Khataruha*, quoted Serjeant, 'The Yemeni Poet al-Zubayri and his Polemic against the Zaydi Imams', *Arabian Studies* (Middle East Centre, Cambridge, 1979), vol. V, p. 102.

22. Muhammad al-Zubairi, *Ma'sat Waq al-Waq* (no publisher, Cairo, 1961), p. 244.

23. Ibid., p. 63.

24. Ibid., p. 148.

25. For fragmentary accounts see al-Shamahi, *Al-Yaman*, pp. 312-14; *Thawrat 26 September* (Markaz al-Dirasat wal-Buhuth al-Yamani, San'a', 1981), p. 143; and scattered references throughout al-Zubairi, *Waq al-Waq*.

26. Bait al-Ahmar, of course, are the paramount shaikhs of Hashid; Bait Rajih are from Bani Shaddad of Khawlan al-Tiyal but in fact are based largely in Lower Yemen; Bait al-Sha'if are from Dhu Husain; Bait Daris and Bait Abu Ra's are from Dhu Muhammad.

27. The best account of the first year of the war is Abd al-Ilah bin Abdullah (Abd al-Malik al-Tayyib), *Naksat al-Thawra fil-Yaman* (n.p., n.d., but probably 1964).

28. See Zaid bin Ali al-Wazir, *Mu'tamar Khamir* (n.p., n.d.), a tract in support of Ibrahim bin Ali al-Wazir's 'Union of Popular Forces' which is as interesting for what it omits as for what it includes.

29. Ahmad Nu'man resigned his post as Prime Minister, complaining among other things at the enormous cash subsidies paid to northern shaikhs. See R. Stookey, *Yemen: The Politics of the Yemen Arab Republic* (Westview Press, Boulder, Colorado, 1978), p. 262. At present (1982/3) something of the order of 30 million riyals a month are probably being paid to the northern tribes under the rubric of the popular army alone, quite apart from development projects and personal gifts.

30. See Stookey, *Yemen*, and J. Peterson, *Conflict in the Yemens and Superpower Involvement* (Georgetown University Centre for Contemporary Arab Studies, Washington, DC, Occasional Paper, 1981).

31. Al-Wazir, *Muhawala*, p. 152.

32. Between 1975 and 1977, for instance, a border existed between al-Hamdi's government and an alliance of mainly Hashid tribes. See Stookey, *Yemen*, pp. 278-80.

33. The royalist card is still occasionally played in local politics (one hears that Shaikh so-and-so has been talking with Prince Muhammad Husain in Jeddah, for instance), but there is no royalist movement worth mention. Although they may disagree violently, most factions are now strongly attached to the idea of the Republic and conduct their debates in the language of republicanism.

12 THE JUDICIAL SYSTEM IN DEMOCRATIC YEMEN

Naguib A. R. Shamiry

In this chapter I shall endeavour to state the general principles and the main features of the judicial system, and also to give a sketch of the provisions governing the working of the courts in the People's Democratic Republic of Yemen (commonly referred to as South Yemen). To achieve accuracy in a necessarily incomplete discussion of any legal subject is an impossible task. Furthermore, to go minutely into detail would defeat the object I have in view and would confuse, rather than help in acquiring a general notion of the subject.

The territory with which this chapter is concerned (South Yemen) seized its independence on 30 November 1967. Before that date the territory had been partly governed and partly protected by Britain, and consisted of Aden Colony, the Protectorates of South Arabia and many small islands. In all, there were more than twenty states,[1] each of which had its own form of government, more or less developed according to circumstances, and each of which had its own legal system. The Colony of Aden was occupied by the British on 19 January 1839, and was the first colonial acquisition of Queen Victoria's reign. The rest of the territory was tied to Britain by many treaties of protection and friendship until February 1959, when a Federation was inaugurated as an autonomous entity subject to British advice, and guaranteed by a British defence treaty. The whole country was taken over by the National Liberation Front on 30 November 1967, thus ending 128 years of British rule. The territory became one united republic, Aden being the capital. The new Republic has an area of 130,000 square miles, and the population, according to the official census of 1973, is little more than one and a half million. The Republic is divided into six regions, each known as a governorate, each of which is further divided into several districts. This new administrative or local government organisation forms the basis for the judicial system.

The Republic is a member of the United Nations and the League of Arab States. It has a constitution which came into force on 30 November 1970,[2] the third anniversary of independence, and was amended on 31 October 1978, after the first conference of the Yemeni Socialist Party, the leader and guide for both society and state. It consists of 139 articles, in six parts: the political, economic, social and cultural, and national-defence foundations of the national democratic regime; rights and duties of the citizens and their organisations (such as trade union, youth union, women's union, peasants' union, etc.); the organisation of the powers of the state (which cover the People's Supreme Council (Parliament), the Presidium of the People's Supreme Council, the Council of Ministers and Local Councils, i.e. local authorities); democratic legality — the judiciary and Attorney-General's chambers; the Republic's ensign, flag, capital and national anthem; operation of the constitution and principles for its amendment.

According to the constitution there is no separation of powers in the sense described by Montesquieu, but there is only one state power which is vested in the 'sovereignty of the working people'.[3] The power of the state is exercised through elected councils or by organs which these councils form in accordance with the aims and tasks of the constitution. The highest organ of state power is the People's Supreme Council, which approves the political principles of the state, guarantees its coherent implementation through all the governmental and social bodies, enacts laws and discusses the basic issues concerning the internal and external policy of the state. The Presidium of the People's Supreme Council, the Council of Ministers and the People's Local Councils are organs of the People's Supreme Council, and they all implement the general policy of the state as laid down by the People's Supreme Council. The judiciary is an organ of state power and its function is to guarantee the implementation of all the laws, which must agree with the contents and spirit of the constitution. It protects the peaceful life, liberty and rights of the citizens. That function of the judiciary is exercised through the courts, which are formed in accordance with the law. Justice is administered by the Supreme Court, the Provincial Courts, Divisional Courts and Military Courts, while the constitution of extraordinary courts is not permitted.[4]

Just before independence on 30 November 1967 there were more than twenty states, as pointed out earlier. The state of the courts and the laws then was as follows:

(1) A complete legal and judicial system in what used to be called

Aden Colony. The laws of Aden are to be found in five volumes known as the *1955 Revised Edition of the Laws of Aden*, which were supplemented by annual volumes of ordinances and of subsidiary legislation. The Indian Companies Act, 1913, and the Indian Life Assurance Companies Act, 1913, continued to apply to Aden, despite the fact that Aden ceased to be ruled from India in 1937. There were four magistrates' courts (known as Divisional Courts), a Chief Magistrate's Court and the Supreme Court of Aden. The judiciary in Aden was headed by the Chief Justice who, according to the Courts Ordinance (No. 7) of 1961, was appointed by the Governor. There were Puisne Judges in the Supreme Court, a Chief Magistrate and Divisional Magistrates, all appointed by the Governor on the advice of the Chief Justice. The chief administrator in the courts was the Registrar of the Supreme Court, also appointed by the Governor, on the advice of the Chief Justice. There were also 'honorary magistrates' appointed from the Justices of the Peace for a period not exceeding six months.

The magistrates' courts, including the Chief Magistrate's Court, dealt with petty offences, traffic offences, small claims, affiliation and maintenance orders and workmen's compensation cases, and acted as coroners, in addition to having committal jurisdiction. Their jurisdiction was limited to two years' imprisonment or £100 fine, or both (with the powers of the Chief Magistrate extending to four years' imprisonment, or £200 in civil cases). The same courts dealt with juvenile cases. Magistrates, whether full-time (which is equivalent to stipendiary magistrates) or otherwise, sat alone.

The Supreme Court Judges, including the Chief Justice, had equal powers. All the serious crimes such as murder, manslaughter, rape, offences under the Official Secrets Ordinances and any other offence which carried the death penalty under any ordinance, came within the criminal jurisdiction of the Supreme Court. So also did habeas corpus applications. The civil jurisdiction of the court covered cases where the claims exceeded £200, injunctions and declarations, divorce, custody, adoption and guardianship, inheritance, admiralty jurisdiction and appeals against the income-tax authorities. The above jurisdiction covered the work of the court when acting as a first-instance court. The court had appellate jurisdiction as well, and that involved looking into appeals and applications for revision from the judgements and orders of magistrates' courts, including the Chief Magistrate's Court, in civil as well as criminal matters. The court also exercised supervisory jurisdiction over inferior courts and other tribunals, such as the rent tribunals, and that was done by the power to revise all proceedings and the legality of any orders made, and exercised through judicial circulars issued by the Chief Justice within his powers under the Courts Ordinance (No. 7) of 1961. Appeals from the Supreme Court, Aden, in all matters used to be sent to the High Court in Bombay, India, until 1947, and thereafter to the Court of Appeal for Eastern Africa, established under the constitution of the East African Common Services Organisation, with an ultimate right of appeal to the Judicial Committee of the Privy Council. All trials in the Supreme Court in Aden were by common or special jury of seven persons. All questions of fact were decided by the jury and of law by the judge. The judge was bound by the verdict returned by the jury, whatever that may be, if reached unanimously, otherwise a majority verdict of at least five to two was binding upon the judge if it was in favour of the accused.

(2) Outside Aden there were courts and a certain amount of local legislation (in Arabic) based on the Muslim religion — which mainly adhered to the Shafi'i school of jurisprudence — and on customary law (known as 'urfi law). Judges and magistrates were appointed by the local rulers (shaikhs or sultans or amirs) and were chosen from those persons who were acquainted with the Muslim religion. The ruler was, in all circumstances, the highest judicial authority within his state. Hadramawt and Lahej in particular were more advanced in this local field.

(3) The official language in the courts in Aden was English, though Arabic was also used. Outside Aden, the official language was Arabic.

(4) In Aden there were advocates (doing the job of both solicitors and barristers), but outside Aden hardly any existed. In Aden itself the advocates were members of the Council of Legal Practitioners set up by a law passed in 1954, though the profession started as far back as 1926. The Chief Justice granted licences for all those legally qualified persons to become advocates, and that function of the Chief Justice was provided for under the Courts' Ordinance, 1961.

(5) In Aden the Attorney-General's chambers and the police were in charge of prosecutions, while in other parts of the territory the job was done by the police alone.

On Independence Day the above state of affairs existed and a Republican Decree (No. 5 of 1967) was passed which provided, *inter alia*, that all laws, resolutions, regulations, by-laws, etc. which were in force were to remain effective in the same way as they had always been, unless they were repugnant to the sovereignty of the state or contrary to the aims of the revolution. That decree meant, in practice and as far as the judiciary was concerned, that there were different laws and legal systems in the country and that the right of appeals to the Court of Appeal for Eastern Africa and to the Judicial Committee of the Privy Council was abolished. And things remained unchanged for the period from November 1967 until November 1970, except that all proceedings in all courts of law were in Arabic.[5] The government began to take effective steps aimed at developing the judicial structure and its relationship with society, especially after the 'Corrective Move' of 22 June 1969. The government embarked on a process of law reform, based on the theory that if law reform is to be done properly, it must be done patiently and thoroughly.

The first step towards setting up a complete legal system came with the constitution in 1970. Article 119 provided that

> the State shall guarantee the unity of the judiciary and shall issue gradually a democratic civil law, a law of employment, a family law and a criminal law in accordance with the principles of the constitution. The State shall provide the conditions which help to resolve the problems of the citizens speedily, justly and in a democratic procedure, through the restoration of a democratic reorganisation of the Judiciary and the laying down of democratic measures.

In addition, Article 124 of the constitution speaks about the Attorney-General, and provides for the regulation of his jurisdiction by law relating to public prosecution.

To give effect to these measures the following steps were taken during the last thirteen years.

(1) A number of laws were promulgated, and these laws are:

(i) Law No. 1 of 1973 in connection with prosecution was passed on 10 January 1973 (I shall refer to the prosecution process later).
(ii) Law No. 1 of 1974 in connection with the family was promulgated on 5 January 1974.
(iii) Law No. 3 of 1976, the Penal Code, was passed on 9 March 1976.

180   *The Judicial System in Democratic Yemen*

(iv)   Law No. 11 of 1978, the Labour Law, was passed on 30 April 1978.
(v)   Law No. 1 of 1980, the Social Security Law, was passed on 28 April 1980.
(vi)   Law No. 7 of 1980, the Courts Law, was passed on 1 September 1980.
(vii) Law No. 5 of 1981, the Court Fees Law, was passed on 1 February 1981.
(viii) Law No. 12 of 1982, the Legal Profession Law, was passed on 21 February 1982.
(xi)   The Civil Code, consisting of 1,930 sections, was passed by the People's Supreme Council in April 1983.
(x)   Criminal Procedure and Civil Procedure are expected in 1983, though they are in force as rules issued by the Ministry of Justice under powers conferred on the Minister of Justice by the Penal Code and civil courts.

(2) An Institute of Law was set up, attached to the Ministry of Justice, with a view to arranging courses in order to have legally qualified personnel. And in 1978 a Faculty of Law was established, as part of the University of Aden. That is in addition to those graduating from universities abroad.

(3) Many small courts throughout the country were abolished, and a gradual process of relocating courts in order to correspond with the new administrative organisation in the Republic took place between 1969 and 1977. The result has been a complete and new legal system, simplified and able to cope with the problems of the people, speedily and justly, and the state has guaranteed the unity of the judiciary.

The hierachy of courts at present, which is the result of gradual reforms, the constitution and the Courts Law is as follows:

(1) In every district there is one or more 'divisional magistrates' court, depending on the number of people living there.
(2) In every region, or 'governorate', there is a 'provincial court' with regional judges sitting.
(3) In the capital, Aden, there is a Supreme Court of the Republic, consisting of the Chief Justice and the Puisne Judge of the Supreme Court.
(4) The Ministry of Justice is the administrative organ, with super-

visory jurisdiction in relation to administration and financial matters as well as courts' buildings. The judges of the Supreme Court of the Republic, provincial courts judges and magistrates are elected by the People's Councils concerned.

The jurisdiction of the magistrates' courts in the districts is as follows:

(1) In criminal matters they deal with all crimes in the Penal Code except those serious crimes which come within the jurisdiction of the regional courts or the Supreme Court; all traffic offences under the Traffic Law No. 30 of 1974 and its amendments; all offences relating to the control of civil supplies and many offences under the local authorities' by-laws. They also deal with juvenile cases.
(2) In civil matters they deal with all cases where the claim does not exceed 1,000 Yemeni dinars and also workmen's compensation matters, housing, land and irrigation disputes.
(3) In family matters their jurisdiction covers divorce cases — whether contested or by consent, maintenance and affiliation orders, custody and access applications, family property matters and disputes concerning the matrimonial home.

The jurisdiction of the provincial courts:

(1) In criminal matters they deal with all the serious crimes under the Penal Code — which include murder, manslaughter, rape, gross indecency, arson, sabotage of communications, etc. They also deal with any offence under any other law which carries the death penalty or long-term prison sentence. The courts have jurisdiction to try any case which comes within the jurisdiction of magistrates' courts, if public interest warrants that, or if the Attorney-General decides so.
(2) In civil matters any claim which exceeds 1,000 Yemeni dinars (no matter what the amount) comes within their jurisdiction, as do appeals against the Commissioner of Income Tax and cases involving ships and aeroplanes.
(3) All inheritance cases come within the jurisdiction of these courts, in accordance with the Muslim Law of Inheritance for Muslims and an enacted Law of Succession for non-Muslims.

(4) All appeals from the magistrates' courts within the governorates, in civil, family and criminal matters. Appeals are by way of re-hearing.
(5) Supervisory jurisdiction over all inferior courts.[6]

The jurisdiction of the Supreme Court is threefold: appeals from the provincial courts in all matters;[7] interpreting the constitution and all the fundamental laws and issuing the interpretations in the form of judicial circulars and directions binding upon all the inferior courts in the Republic;[8] as the highest judicial tribunal in the land, it exercises supervisory jurisdiction over all the other courts.[9]

The Prosecution Process

Prosecution is at the instance of the Attorney-General of the Republic.[10] Before 1967 there were three bodies with some legal powers in this respect; the Attorney-General's chambers in the Colony of Aden, the Attorney-General's office in the Federation (for all Federal matters, and exclusively concerned with drafting all laws in the Federation) and the Legal Department at the office of the British High Commissioner (for all legal matters). The first two merged and became part of the Ministry of Justice after 1967,[11] while the third one was abolished. In 1970 Article 124 of the constitution dealt with the Attorney-General and stated, *inter alia*, that the Attorney-General directs the prevention of crime and ensures that those who commit crimes or any offences account for their deeds in the courts; he also supervises the adherence to the law in detention and prevention centres. The article also provided for the jurisdiction of the Attorney-General to be regulated by a law relating to public prosecutions. On 10 January 1973 Law No. 1 of 1973, in connection with prosecution, was promulgated, and the problem of the management of prosecutions — controversial in many countries — has been solved once and for all.

The 1978 constitution stated that the Attorney-General and his subordinates shall exercise supreme supervision over the implementation of the laws.[12] The prosecution is composed of the following persons and offices:

(1) the Attorney-General of the Republic;
(2) the representatives of the Attorney-General;

(3) the Crimes and Civil Office;
(4) the Supervision Office;
(5) the Documents and Library Office.

The Attorney-General presides over the prosecutions of the Republic, and he exercises his responsibilities according to the Law (that is to say Law No. 1 of 1973), with a view to ensuring the correctness of the application of laws, the defence of the interests of the community and public ownership, and the legitimate rights of the citizens.

The principal tasks of the prosecution are:

(1) To defend public ownership and political power, and to exert every effort to abide by the constitution and all laws and resolutions issued by the People's Supreme Council, the Presidium of the Council and the Council of Ministers.
(2) To work, in the field of law, to protect the national democratic revolution and to ensure the fulfilment of democratic legitimation.
(3) To undertake supervision over the accurate application and execution of laws by Ministers, organisations and public corporations, and their abidance by all citizens of the Republic.
(4) To undertake the fight against crime and the submission of persons suspected of having committed one, or any other legal contravention, to the courts concerned.
(5) To supervise the inquiries and investigations departments.
(6) To ensure the execution according to the law of the judgements passed.
(7) To file criminal and civil suits, in which the state or any organisation or public corporation is a party, according to the law.
(8) To conduct the ways of challenging criminal and civil judgements before the courts concerned.
(9) To suspend or stay proceedings in any criminal or civil suit in which the state or any organisation or public corporation is a party, and at any stage of the suit, before giving judgement, whenever deemed necessary for the fulfilment of public interest.
(10) To submit written application for staying the execution of a challenged judgement when deemed necessary.
(11) To undertake supervision over inquiries and investigations departments, penal and reformatory organisations, and

suspension and detention centres, and the issue of the necessary instructions.
(12) To name, suspend and transfer individuals of the prosecution.
(13) To require any ministry, organisation or public corporation to submit any document or instrument to be seen by the Attorney-General's chambers, provided that it has relation with the law.
(14) To undertake informative campaigns, with the assistance of the various information organs, for explaining the various legislations, spreading legal consciousness and explaining the concepts of democratic legitimation.

The representatives of the Attorney-General are those persons named by the Attorney-General himself to assist him in carrying out his activities. They must be in possession of recognised degrees or certificates of law, or be police officers, or other inspectors in connection with law enforcement (such as those of the Ministry of Commerce and Supply, whose job is to see that retailers adhere to the prices system fixed by the government). They are found in the courts, police stations, government departments, organisations and public corporations. All the representatives act in the name of the Attorney-General, and in accordance with his instructions. The Attorney-General, as a matter of practice, represents the state in the big trials.

Procedure in Criminal Cases

Until 31 December 1976 trials in the magistrates' courts and the Supreme Court were in accordance with the Criminal Procedure Ordinance of 1955. Summary trials were common in the magistrates' courts, with committal procedure adopted for the offences which were within the jurisdiction of the Supreme Court, and there the powers of the courts were limited to deciding whether or not there was a *prima facie* case to commit the accused for trial to the Supreme Court. There was, too, a special procedure for inquests, where the magistrates acted as coroners in situations where the cause or causes of the death of a person were not clear; the duty of the coroners would be to decide where, when, how and by whom the death was caused. Appeals against the decisions of the magistrates' courts were to the Supreme Court, and appeals could be against conviction (unless the plea of the accused was one of guilty) and also against sentence. The Supreme Court had power to reduce or increase the sentence, but in the latter case that could not be done except after giving the accused the chance of appearing before the court. There was a special procedure for juveniles.

In the Supreme Court trials — all trials — were by jury, special or common, of seven persons. Special jury trials were very rare. Any male or female over the age of twenty-one was eligible to serve, but there were exceptions, which included members of the legal profession, police officers, prison officers, etc. The prosecution or defence had the right to challenge the names of the persons to serve on a jury, and that right extended to four challenges for each party without cause, and to any number with sufficient cause. The trial started with reading and explaining the charge to the accused, then taking down his plea, which could be one of 'not guilty' or 'guilty' or 'guilty but . . .'; the accused might refuse to plead at all, which was taken to mean 'not guilty'. In practice, the trial would proceed even if the accused pleaded guilty, knowing the court had the power to convict him because of his plea. The prosecution would open its case, followed by the witnesses, whose depositions in the lower court (magistrates' court) during the committal procedures (or preliminary inquiry) could be read in certain circumstances, such as the death of the witness during the period between committal and trial. They were followed by the accused, who had three rights: to give evidence in his defence, on oath, where he could be cross-examined by the prosecution; to give evidence not on oath; and to remain silent. The accused would be called upon to exercise his rights, unless the evidence tendered so far was such that the jury could not convict, in which situation the judge was bound to direct the jury to return a verdict of not guilty. If the trial continued, the defence would be allowed to bring witnesses. That would be followed by the prosecution and defence addressing the jury, the last word being for the defence. The judge would sum up the case for the jury, and the jury would retire and then return their verdict.

The above-mentioned procedure was only applied in Aden, because the Criminal Procedure Ordinance was in force from 1955, i.e. before independence in 1967, and continued to be effective by virtue of Republican Decree No. 5 of 1967. Outside Aden the trials were by a legally qualified magistrate sitting with two assessors (or lay magistrates), and decisions were taken by a majority. The procedure for inquests was made to apply to the rest of the country.

However all court trials were in public, as a general rule.

Since 1 January 1977 a new Criminal Procedure Law has been in force. The main steps, or principles, are as follows:

(1) The courts are under an obligation to examine and investigate the case from all aspects, including the personalities of the accused and victim.[13]
(2) The courts are also under an obligation to ensure that all citizens are equal in the eyes of the law,[14] irrespective of their race, ethnic origin, religion, faith, language, level of education or social status.
(3) That personal freedom is guaranteed, in that arrest is not permitted except in connection with deeds which are punishable by law and according to the law, and that no person shall be subjected to torture during investigations, nor shall he be forced to confess or be treated in an inhuman way.
(4) That corporal punishment is prohibited, and that criminal responsibility is personal.
(5) That no punishment shall be inflicted for actions committed before the enactment of the law prohibiting such acts, nor shall there be inflicted any punishment not provided for by the law, and that self-defence is guaranteed.
(6) That dwellings are entitled to privacy sanctioned by the law, and this privacy shall not be interfered with except in connection with deeds affecting security and with due regard to the law.
(7) That the courts adjudicate and pronounce judgements in the name of the people.
(8) That trials are public,[15] except where the nature of the dispute necessitates privacy, or if state security or public morality is otherwise in jeopardy.
(9) That the accused is innocent until the contrary is proved, that the burden of proof is on the prosecution to prove the guilt of the accused beyond all reasonable doubt, and that the benefit of any reasonable doubt should go to the accused.[16]
(10) That no punishment shall be inflicted except by a competent court.[17]

The new Criminal Procedure Law consists of 581 sections and is made up of the following chapters:

Chapter I deals with the general principles. The jurisdictions of the different degrees of courts; the parties (prosecution, accused, the victim, representatives of mass associations, etc.); evidence in criminal cases (where all principles of evidence are included, for example witnesses, experts, accused's evidence including confession, exhibits and presumptions). The most important rule is that there shall be no conviction unless based on evidence, and that conviction should be in accordance with the satisfaction of the trial court based on the evidence tendered. It deals also with the procedure for juveniles and mentally sick persons, and the contribution of the people in the administration of justice.[18] This takes three main forms; first, by assessors or lay magistrates,[19] where two should be present in every case, and their presence is for two years at the rate of two to three weeks every year, with compulsory training in the beginning; second, by the presence of representatives of mass associations, such as trade unions, local councils and women's unions, in trials where the accused is a member of that body; and third, by setting up voluntary bodies called 'Social Justice Organisations'[20] in the residential areas or estates to deal with petty offences, such as affray, simple grievous bodily harm and causing damage (not serious) to private, personal or public property. The idea is to re-educate the public. The power of the organisations is stated in sections 41 to 47 of the Penal Code 1976.

Chapter II deals with arrest, custody and search (which have to be on the orders of the courts or the Attorney-General), and investigations — which are under the supervision of the Attorney-General through his representatives.

Chapter III deals with trials. These have to be in open court, with the public having the right to be there; this is as a general rule, the exceptions being on grounds of public morality, state security, etc., and as an exception, too, juvenile cases should be *in camera* where only the juvenile or juveniles, their parents and other close relatives, prosecution, witnesses, defence, social and probation workers, and educational supervisors are allowed to be present. Even where the trial is not public, the judgement should be pronounced in open court. The procedure for trial is that the accused, as a general rule, must be present throughout his trial, in addition to victim, defence, prosecution and mass associations' representatives. The court should hold continuous sittings (except for adjournments for lunch or because of the end of the working day) until it pronounces judgement, and should not conduct another trial unless judgement is pronounced in the first case. The courts' role is very active, or positive, in the conduct of the trial. A secretary records the proceedings. The charge is read and explained, and — no matter what the plea of the accused is — the trial must proceed. The accused is the first person to give evidence, but not on oath, and he is examined by the court, followed by the prosecution, victim, defence, representatives of mass organisations (in defence of the accused), the other accused (if any) and his or their defence. There is re-examination if necessary. The victim is the second person to give evidence (if still alive) and he is examined by the court, the prosecution, the accused, the defence, the other accused (and his defence), and there may be re-examination in the same order. Then come the witnesses, beginning with those for the prosecution. All witnesses have to wait outside the court-room while one of them is giving evidence. The examination of every witness, whether for the prosecution or for the defence, is started by the court, then the prosecution, victim, accused and the defence thereof. Re-examination is permitted in the same order. As a rule, re-examination of accused, victim and every witness is in order to clarify certain things which appear ambiguous in the evidence of that party. The victim and all witnesses give evidence on oath or by affirmation. The last stage in the trial, before judgement, is the address by the mass association's representative, then the prosecution, accused, defence, etc., with a right of reply in the same order, and the last word is reserved for the accused personally. Following that is pronouncement of judgement in open court, in all circumstances, immediately after the parties have addressed the court, or shortly afterwards. If need be, the court has the right to adjourn pronouncement of judgement for a maximum period of three days.

The chapter also deals with appeals, which should be lodged by the prosecution or defence within thirty days with effect from pronouncement of judgement. Appeal may be against sentence or conviction, even if the plea of the accused in the court below was one of guilty, and on grounds of both facts or law, or mixed facts and law. The appellate court has the power to order stay of execution of sentence pending the disposal of the appeal. The powers of the appellate court are wide-ranging, from dismissal of the appeal to amendment of the nature of the sentence (but on condition that sentence should not be increased under any circumstances if it was the defence which made the appeal), to quashing the conviction and sentence, to ordering a new trial in the court below before another panel. Appeals are, however, by way of re-hearing. Finally, the chapter deals with the execution of sentences by different organs of the state.

Civil Procedure

In civil cases the procedure is governed by ordinances and rules of courts effective throughout the Republic. The parties can appear in person, or by retained attorneys or advocates. There are laws concerned with evidence, limitation, fees, advocates, contract, tort, family and so on, which apply in courts when they are exercising their civil jurisdiction. One of the main safeguards, where it is essential that justice must not only be done but must also be seen to be done, is that trials are public except when the dispute necessitates privacy (especially in domestic cases), or if state security or public morality is otherwise in jeopardy. Lastly, the composition of the court is similar to that in criminal cases.

The Legal Profession

Mention was made earlier of the legal profession, which has existed in Aden since 1926. Outside Aden there was no legal profession at all, and parties used to appear personally or with attorneys who were usually their close relatives. Things have changed a great deal. A law was passed in 1981 which concerns the legal profession[21] and which means that advocates can work anywhere in the Republic and have the right of audience before all the courts. They have to obtain licences in order to be enrolled on the register of advocates: licences are granted by the Minister of Justice, and are renewed every year on payment of a fixed fee. There are rules of court governing appearance of the advocates, their rights and duties, their relationship with their clients, the fees that they can charge in all types of cases and applications, their dismissal (which is by striking the name of the advocate off the register) or their suspension if there is any breach of the rules governing their rights and duties. The disciplinary regulations are applied, on the application of the aggrieved party or any court, by a committee. The presence on it of a representative of the

Council of Advocates is essential. The committee submits its findings and recommendations to the Minister of Justice.

There has recently been a reorganisation of the profession to cover the whole Republic. Under the reorganisation plan, the profession consists of three main branches:

(1) Advocates who can do all sorts of legal work, who are legally qualified, and have the right of audience before all courts.
(2) Attorneys, carrying powers of attorney, who have the right of audience only before magistrates' courts, and even there only in civil cases. They have no legal qualifications, but have some knowledge of procedure and evidence, or some experience as ex-police or army officers or civil servants.
(3) Petition-writers, who have no legal qualifications, but have some knowledge of procedure and evidence, and some experience in drafting. Their main job is to draft petitions and suits, powers of attorney, applications, etc., where the claims do not exceed 50 Yemeni dinars, otherwise the drafting should be done by advocates.

Legal Aid

Before 1977 legal aid in criminal cases was confined to having a right to the defence counsel appointed by the court in jury trials in the Supreme Court. In civil cases there was a system of assistance in drafting and in exemption from court fees. The system is still in force and it is by means of pauper applications. A social inquiry report is prepared by the social and probation services of the local authority concerned, on the order of the court to whom the application is made, before exemption and/or any other legal assistance may be rendered. The law has changed with the coming into force of the Criminal Procedure Law on 1 January 1977. According to the constitution, every citizen may resort to the judicature to protect his lawful rights and interests: self-defence is guaranteed. The state shall facilitate the people's resort to the judicature and the means of defence. The Criminal Procedure, and Civil Procedure and Court Fees laws, have given effect to that provision in the constitution. Provision is made for legal aid in criminal cases, right from the moment the accused is charged in the police station. Legal aid is compulsory in cases involving juveniles and persons physically or mentally handicapped, and in all cases coming within the jurisdiction of the provincial courts and the Supreme Court, as well as in all cases where the accused does not understand Arabic. The Attorney-General or his representatives, in the pre-trial stage and the trial court, all have a duty to ensure there is legal representation as provided by the law. The state shoulders all financial responsibility in this respect. Moreover, provision is made for legal aid in civil suits, especially compensation cases.

Modern Trends in the Legal System

(1) The constitution provides that 'the state shall guarantee the contribution of the citizens to the exercise of judicial authority in an increasing way'. The Criminal Procedure and Civil Procedure, the Penal Code and the Courts Law have given effect to the provision in the constitution in this respect.

(2) The functions of the judges and magistrates have changed a great deal. They have to play a leading role, that is to say they have to play an active or positive part in every case, and it may be true to say that we are moving towards a kind of inquisitorial attitude in trials. Moreover, judges and magistrates have to write reports on the wave of crime as seen by them, to give lectures in departments, public corporations and mass associations, and to the police force (at stations or training schools and colleges), to explain the important laws on radio and television and to take part in different committees concerned with law reform.

Yet, one important safeguard is an article in the constitution concerning the independence of judges in general, which includes both judges as such and magistrates. Article 125 provides that 'judges are independent in their powers and bound by the constitution and the law in the realisation of democratic legality'.

(3) Symposia are playing an important part in developing the legal system. During 1977 symposia were held in every governorate, and there was a national symposium to discuss the role played by the judiciary in the first ten years of independence and, further, to see to what extent the administration of justice needs reform and what the proper machinery is for the purpose. One of the main resolutions was that judicial personnel should expand their knowledge in order to march with the spirit of the age. They could do this by informing themselves of judicial references and courses linked with their work;

by linking theoretical studies with realities of life, which could be achieved by becoming acquainted with the masses and living with them in urban as well as rural areas, and by field exercises and visits. The symposia discussed documents submitted by the Ministry of Justice on the judiciary at the stage of national democratic revolution, on prosecution, advocacy and the first few years' experience of the Family Law and Penal Code. The judges played a leading role in the local symposia, as well as in the national symposia.

(4) Bail: this system has been reformed in many respects. An accused can be released, on the order of a magistrate, on personal surety by a friend or relative; on personal recognisance; on a promise by the accused himself to stay within the boundary of a certain town; by a promise from one of the mass organisations to bring him before the court when required or asked so to do; by initial deposit of certain amounts in court; or on an order to the accused to appear daily or weekly at the police station nearest to his place of work or residence. All these changes in the law concerning the conditional release of an accused make the law more humane in this respect than is the case with many developing countries.

(5) The courts have to cope with changes, some drastic, in Family Law, the Penal Code and the Civil Code. In Family Law, bigamy is not permitted; divorce has to be effected with the leave of the magistrate's court concerned; both spouses share in the upkeep of the matrimonial home and in maintenance; both parents share in the maintenance of their children; both spouses are equal in all rights and duties; custody of children revolves round the principle of the interest of the children being the paramount consideration. As far as the Penal Code is concerned, the courts deal with suspended and deferred sentences, community service, probation orders, conditional discharge and compensation in lieu of punishment. And as far as the Civil Code is concerned, almost everything is now guided by new principles; a concept such as 'urf is no longer a source in this respect. All these matters are new as far as many developing countries or Muslim countries are concerned, and are in conformity with changing circumstances in the second half of the twentieth century. The task that has faced the courts, as a result of those changes, is enormous.

I hope that I have succeeded in trying to give a clear outline of the judicial system in Democratic Yemen. It is, however, only an outline and a thorough study of the subject requires a deeper and more detailed approach.

Notes

1. Sir Bernard Reilly stated that there were 25 states as follows:

(a) 20 in the Western Protectorate;
(b) 4 in the Eastern Protectorate;
(c) Aden.

See *Aden and the Yemen* (HMSO, London, 1960), pp. 5-6.

2. The Constitution of 1970 consisted of 135 articles, in six parts. Articles 116 to 124 deal with the judiciary and the Attorney-General.
3. Article 68 of the constitution and 62 in the 1970 constitution.
4. Article 121 of the constitution.
5. Law No. 4 of 1969 which stated that Arabic shall be the official language.
6. Courts Law No. 7 of 1980, sections 13 (8) and 23.
7. This is provided for in the Criminal and Civil Procedure, and sections 13 (1) and 14 of the Courts Law.
8. Article 82 of the constitution states that the Supreme Court is the highest judicial organ and it exercises supervision over all the courts in the Republic.
9. Ibid., and sections 13 (2) and (3), 19 (3) and (4) of the Courts Law. There is also the General Society of the Supreme Court, presided over by the Chief Justice, which meets four times a year.
10. The Attorney-General is appointed by the People's Supreme Council: Article 83 of the constitution.
11. Republican Decree No. 11 of 1967.
12. Articles 130 to 132 of the constitution run as follows:

(a) With the aim of realising democratic legality, protecting the national democratic regime and defending the public property, the Republic's Attorney-General, his deputies, and representatives subordinate to him, shall exercise supreme supervision over the precise and unified implementation of the laws by all the ministers, the other central departments, the organisations, corporations, the executive bureaus of the People's Local Councils, the social organisations, the co-operative societies, all the administrative superior officers and the citizens.

The Attorney-General shall appoint his civil and military deputies and they are responsible and accountable for their functions to him.

(b) The People's Supreme Council shall appoint the Republic's Attorney-General.

The Attorney-General is responsible and accountable for his functions to the People's Supreme Council and to the Presidium in the intervals between the sessions of the People's Supreme Council.

The Attorney-General's chambers shall be reorganised in a lineal manner throughout the Republic. They are independent of all the local organs and are subordinate only to the Republic's Attorney-General.

The law shall regulate the functions and powers of the Attorney-General's chambers.

(c) The Attorney-General shall direct the combating of crimes, and ensure that persons who commit crimes or any other breaches shall be called to account for their deeds before the courts. He shall also supervise adherence to the law in the detention and prevention centres.

13. Sections 13 and 14 of the Criminal Procedure.
14. Article 35 of the constitution and section 8 of the Criminal Procedure.
15. Article 126 of the constitution; sections 19-20 and 328 to 332 of the Criminal

Procedure; sections of the Civil Procedure.

16. Sections 9 and 100 of the Criminal Procedure.

17. Article 48 of the constitution.

18. Article 124 of the constitution; Criminal and Civil Procedure; Courts Law, sections 34 to 37.

19. Ibid.

20. Ibid. Penal Code, sections 41 and 42. There are Social Justice Organisations in Aden and Abyan governorates at present. There are similar bodies in the Soviet Union and East Germany (called Comrades' Courts and Social Courts, respectively).

21. Article 127 of the constitution requires that the legal profession be regulated by law 'with the aim of submitting legal aid to the citizens and Judicial persons'.

13 ASPECTS OF NORTH YEMEN'S RELATIONS WITH SAUDI ARABIA

M. S. El Azhary

Although North Yemen was one of the early members of the Arab League, it was not until the resolution of the civil war and the reconciliation between the republicans and royalists in 1970 that the Yemen Arab Republic (YAR) ended her traditional isolation and developed multifaceted relations — including cultural, economic, political and military ties — with the other Arab states. Since then the YAR has played a significant role in most Arab councils and participated in Arab decision-making in all major regional issues.

Being the most densely populated country in the Arabian Peninsula (7.039 million in 1980; annual growth rate 3 per cent) and strategically located at Saudi Arabia's back door, North Yemen occupies a key position that affects the safety of Saudi Arabia, the Gulf states and the oilfields. It is this strategic reality that makes YAR-Saudi relations — as I will show in the following pages — loom so large for the YAR that her relations with any of the other Arab states pale by comparison and, to a very large extent, Riyadh sets the parameters as to how far San'a' can steer an independent foreign policy. This is not to say that San'a' has not sought independence from Riyadh. Indeed it has done so on several occasions in the past, and continues to do so, by reaching out and developing close relationships with other states in the Arab world and beyond, to create a balance against its more powerful neighbours to the north.

Saudi Fears

The relationship between the Yemen Arab Republic and Saudi Arabia is perhaps the closest in the Arab world linking two countries economically, politically and militarily. Since the oil boom of the 1970s over half a million Yemenis have been working regularly in Saudi Arabia. The majority do menial tasks, but their remittance of about $1 billion annually has helped to ease the YAR balance of payments deficit.[1] This situation is bound to continue for years to come, not only to keep the Saudi economy functioning but also to implement Saudi Arabia's ambitious development plans. Yet because the Yemenis form the largest group of aliens in the Kingdom, they represent a security threat and can be said to constitute — at least theoretically — a Yemeni 'fifth column'. The Saudis also worry about the dispute over their undefined borders with North Yemen. Intermittent skirmishes remind the Saudis that the North Yemenis have never given up their claim to the fertile Asir region, whose loss to Saudi Arabia in the war of 1934 was confirmed by the Treaty of Taif of the same year. It is interesting to note that on many occasions these skirmishes result in serious fighting causing casualties, but one never hears of them because both sides prefer to keep them quiet.

To allay Saudi fears YAR leaders have found it necessary — every time there is a change in leadership in San'a' — to rush to Riyadh and reaffirm the continuation of 'eternal' and 'historical' relations between the two countries that are based on 'good neighbourliness and blood ties'. These are code-words that reassure the Saudis that the YAR will continue to respect the 1934 treaty. Moreover, in 1974 Saudi Arabia obliged the Yemeni Prime Minister Abd al-Rahman al-Hajri to sign an agreement renewing the 1934 treaty but this agreement was never ratified because of the strong opposition it engendered from all political strata in North Yemen. According to a Yemeni politician, this issue has been so sensitive that previous governments have not been able to resolve it without provoking a revolt. He concluded that the current President Ali Abdullah Salih 'wants it to be ratified by an elected [consultative assembly], and not by an appointed one; no government would take this responsibility'.[2] Be that as it may, it is not inconceivable that this issue might cause serious problems in the future.

What the Saudis have feared most, however, has been the instability and unreliability of the central government in San'a', particularly in the face of pressures from the Marxists in Aden since they gained power in 1967. From the beginning the latter have not only espoused Marxist-Leninist principles but have also maintained as one of their aims the spread of socialist revolution throughout the Arabian Peninsula. Moreover, it may be recalled that in the early 1970s the South Yemeni leaders began recruiting opposition elements and radical followers inside North Yemeni territory, and these anti-regime rebels in turn began a sporadic guerrilla war and carried out acts of terrorism. It will also be recalled that Saudi Arabia, supported by the other conservative regimes in the area, spurred on the YAR regime, led then by President Abd al-Rahman al-Iryani, to respond in kind, which it did, but only half-heartedly. The Saudis financed, organised and armed the South Yemeni exiles in North Yemen who stepped up their guerrilla attacks across the border into South Yemen with the intent of overthrowing the Marxist regime in Aden.[3] The Saudis also encouraged Sultan Qabus to start, with Iranian help, an all-out military drive to crush the Dhofari guerrilla movement in western Oman. After two or three years all of these Saudi-sponsored subversive activities came to nothing. Their failure stemmed partly from divisions among the Southern exiles and partly from the clumsiness and antiquated attitudes of the Saudis themselves. Perhaps the only thing the Saudis achieved by these military ventures was that they intentionally so heightened the tensions in the area that, in early 1972, border clashes between North and South Yemen escalated into a full-blown war. But the Saudi plan misfired, and, instead of the Marxist regime in Aden being overthrown, events moved with such bewildering speed that the two Yemens, within a few short weeks, moved from a fully fledged war to unification talks which produced a merger agreement signed by the two countries in Tripoli, Libya, later the same year.[4]

Whether or not this merger agreement was serious, the Saudis opposed it in principle, and since then they have opposed every similar effort towards this goal, including the second merger agreement that followed the border war of March 1979. Saudi opposition to the unification of the two Yemens stems from the simple reason that if the conservative republican regime in San'a' were to unite with the Marxist regime in Aden, Saudi Arabia would be confronted with a hostile state with a population twice the size of that of the Kingdom. Even if a compromise could be agreed upon between the two ideologically opposite regimes, as proposed in the draft constitution completed in early 1982 which stated that Islam would be the religion, and socialism the creed, of a United Yemen,[5] the Saudis would still consider such a regime inimical to their interests. After all, the Saudis' experience in the 1960s, during the Egyptian intervention in North Yemen, convinced them that their security, and that of the Red Sea, would be threatened if San'a' were controlled by an unfriendly regime. It is this perception that makes Saudi leaders consider North Yemen a security corridor against danger from South Yemen.

Financing a Security Corridor

Having failed to overthrow the Marxist regime in Aden, the Saudi leaders had no choice but to bolster the regime in North Yemen against its southern neighbour. But the Saudis, fearing for their own security, have been reluctant to make North Yemen too strong. A strong regime in San'a' might also become too independent, something which is likely to be at odds with Saudi policies elsewhere in the Peninsula and beyond. Therefore, in order to keep North Yemen in line with Saudi Arabia's security requirements, the Saudi leaders combined their policy of strengthening the YAR regime with a policy of making it financially dependent on Riyadh. That course allowed them to apply political and military pressure on San'a', thus interfering in Yemeni affairs. As early as 1971 King Faisal began what have become two permanent features of Riyadh's financial assistance to North Yemen: first, annual budget support to maintain the central government by paying its functionaries and armed forces personnel; second, direct subsidies to the tribes, thus aiding the three most important groups for the political and physical survival of the regime in the YAR.[6]

Soon this policy of financial dependence was institutionalised and in 1975 a joint Saudi-YAR council was created to review periodically (every six months) the relations between the two countries in all fields. In the same year it was announced that Saudi Arabia provided North Yemen with aid worth £100 million plus 50,000 tons of petroleum.[7] Through this joint council, hundreds of millions of dollars have been channelled to numerous development projects making up nearly one-third of the total of $3.7 billion for the last five-year plan (1977-81).[8] More recent reports put Saudi annual direct aid at about $1 billion,[9] but whether the under-developed YAR has the ability to absorb the artificial economic boom created by these relatively large sums of money is another matter.

Hand-in-hand with their financial assistance to the government in San'a', the Saudis have also continued over the years to subsidise the tribes, to an extent perhaps equivalent to the amount of funding provided to the YAR government. These subsidies are viewed by Saudi officials as an essential effort to establish 'a buffer zone of

Aspects of North Yemen's Relations with Saudi Arabia   199

Saudi influence against some future central government in North Yemen which may seek to adopt anti-Saudi policies'.[10] The Saudi leadership believes that, so far, the power of the tribes as a counter force to the central government has served them well and, accordingly, Riyadh will most probably maintain this policy, at least in the short term. Whether the Saudis may be over-estimating the power of some of these tribes in relation to the central government and the extent of the Saudis' influence over them is difficult to say. However, it would seem on the whole that Saudi Arabia, through her two-tier policy of making North Yemen financially dependent on her, has strengthened her influence in North Yemeni affairs. Indeed, several analysts see the Saudis as having been responsible for the overthrow of several YAR leaders who became too independent or moved closer to Aden; for example, the removal of Abd al-Rahman al-Iryani from the presidency in 1974, the dismissal of Muhsin al-Aini from the premiership in 1975, and the murder of President Ibrahim al-Hamdi in 1977.[11]

Balance between Riyadh and Aden

The Saudis might have influence with the different political strata in North Yemen, but what so far has eluded their control is the unreliability of the regime in San'a', which has been plagued by chronic instability since the reconciliation in 1970. There have been frequent governmental changes and reorganisations, and several political assassinations. When President Salih took over in July 1978 everybody in the country, remembering the violent death of his two predecessors, believed that he would not last for more than a few weeks. More than five years have passed and he is still there, which is quite an achievement, considering the military threat he has been facing from the South-Yemeni-supported rebels of the National Democratic Front (NDF), a collection of the main left-wing elements, Communists, Ba'thists and Nasserites, all of whom are anti-Saudi, anti-United States and pro-Soviet. After staging an abortive *coup* in October of the same year, the NDF started prolonged border clashes which escalated into the border war between the two Yemens in February 1979, mentioned earlier. The Saudis tried to help the YAR militarily but they were so hopelessly disorganised that this help never materialised; they even interfered with the American military help which the Saudis themselves had originally requested.

This point will be discussed further below. In the end it was the Arab mediation efforts which saved the YAR from utter defeat.

Defeated, Salih had no choice but to sign a new unification agreement with South Yemen. He began a 'dialogue' with the NDF which was then in control of many villages covering wide areas in the southern and central YAR, and turned to the Soviet Union for arms supplies. In response Riyadh cut off its budgetary assistance and suspended economic aid.[12] The negotiations with the NDF opened the way, in January 1980, for the signing of an agreement between Salih and the rebel leader, Sultan Omar, to give the NDF a greater role in the North Yemen government by including some of its members in a new Cabinet, and to hold a national election for a new, more democratic consultative assembly, as well as to release political prisoners. To help reach these goals Salih urged Aden to cease offering military aid to the NDF. But by mid-1980 the negotiations between the government and the NDF broke down, and with Aden's encouragement the NDF resumed its military activities against the regime. Worse still, South Yemen moved closer to Libya and Ethiopia, and a defence agreement was signed with the latter.[13] Libya, which, as we will see below, is an enthusiastic supporter of the NDF, extended a generous aid package to Aden.

San'a' perceived this co-operation between the three states as a threat and Salih quickly patched up his differences with Riyadh, which resumed its financial assistance. He also reshuffled the Cabinet and appointed essentially unpolitical technocrats, as well as demoting and evicting any progressives who were acceptable to the NDF. The North Yemeni President learned his lesson from the 1979 débâcle, and since then has been determined to keep a balance between Saudi Arabia and South Yemen. He needs the economic help he receives from Riyadh, but he cannot afford to lend credence to the South Yemeni (and the NDF) accusation that he is a Saudi stooge. This policy of balance can be seen also in the removal of several pro-Saudi politicians from positions of power.[14] Moreover, Salih has been equally determined to avoid open war with South Yemen. He seems convinced that, without South Yemen's support, the NDF cannot win. Therefore he appears to be playing a dual political game by keeping the unification talks and related schemes going with South Yemen while simultaneously maintaining a military stalemate against the NDF.[15]

US-Saudi-YAR Triangle

An important part of the Saudi design to ensure the safety of the Kingdom's southern border is its goal of supplanting a long-established arms supply relationship between the YAR and the Soviet Union. In 1970-2 a rift developed in YAR-Soviet relations because the Soviets dramatically increased quantitatively and upgraded qualitatively their arms supplies to South Yemen while reducing their military aid to North Yemen. This provided the Saudis with an opportunity to prod San'a' to switch to the West for arms. But because the Saudis are never sure of how strong they want the YAR to be, it took them three years to make up their minds, and it was probably President Hamdi who forced their hands when he turned to the United States and France for arms deals.[16] With Saudi Arabia financing, the United States and France agreed, in January 1976, to their first sales of military equipment to the YAR worth $139.5 million and $80 million respectively. The French purchase consisted of armoured cars and communication equipment.[17] The American deal, however, was envisaged as the first stage (3-5 years) of a more comprehensive 10-year modernisation plan for the YAR armed forces. It was also hoped that, once this modernisation plan was completed, the re-equipped YAR armed forces would be modelled on the Saudi force structure in equipment and training.

Once the implementation of the modernisation plan began, however, the Saudis showed their ambivalence about strengthening the armed forces of their more populous neighbour to the south. Firstly, they delayed making a firm commitment on which arms would be purchased; secondly, equipment had to be delivered through the Saudi military mission in San'a' which phased the release of equipment to the Yemenis only after the Saudis were 'satisfied that training and reorganisation schedules had been met'; thirdly, the Saudis insisted on administering the training of the YAR armed personnel. In this way the Saudi authorities were able to exclude from training any YAR officers who had previously received training in the Soviet Union. It should be mentioned here that YAR policy has been to exclude Soviet-trained personnel from important positions.[18] In short, the whole experience was very frustrating to both the Yemenis and the Americans, and no doubt the former resented the Saudis' heavy-handedness throughout the whole affair.

From a US perspective, this trilateral relationship with the YAR and Saudi Arabia, although it proved cumbersome, was hoped to be the beginning of a regional military arrangement which would leave the United States in the background assisting Arab allies who would take a larger military role. Moreover, building on this assumption, the Carter administration, in September 1978, followed its predecessor's policy towards North Yemen and approved an additional arms sale of approximately $400 million, which was also financed by Saudi Arabia. This additional equipment included a squadron of F-5E jet fighters, several C-130 transport planes, 64 M-60 tanks, 100 armoured personnel carriers and Vulcan anti-aircraft guns. The first consignment of this equipment had to be rushed to the YAR when the border war of February 1979 broke out between the two Yemens. The Carter administration even waived the customary 30 days of Congressional review in order to get the arms to North Yemen. In a show of force, the United States also sent two AWACS (Airborne Warning and Control Systems) reconnaissance planes to Saudi Arabia, and ordered the aircraft-carrier *Constellation* to proceed to the Gulf of Aden.[19] The United States seemed to be overreacting but, according to US officials, this show of force was intended to 'draw the line' against Soviet-backed 'destabilisation' efforts — in this case by South Yemen — against governments friendly to the West, Saudi Arabia in particular.[20] Furthermore, the American response was also dictated by the circumstances then prevailing which included the overthrow of the Shah's regime in Iran, as well as steady Soviet expansion in the Horn of Africa and Afghanistan.

    The Saudis were relieved and impressed by the US show of force, but the border war was short-lived and once a ceasefire was arranged (before the American equipment reached North Yemen) the Saudis were again ambivalent about building up the YAR military capacity, reverted to delaying tactics, and withheld the delivery of the military equipment.[21] The North Yemenis were disappointed with Saudi Arabia's attitude towards extending military aid to their country, and realising that it was not possible for them to deal directly with the United States, the leadership in San'a' became convinced of the soundness of the earlier YAR policy over the past two decades of relying on the Soviet Union for military aid. Within a few months of the ceasefire with South Yemen, President Salih renewed his country's long-standing military relationship with the Soviet Union. Moscow's response was equally swift and generous, as indicated by the large amount of arms provided to the YAR since then. Between 1979 and 1981 alone, the Soviet Union provided the YAR — on

Aspects of North Yemen's Relations with Saudi Arabia

easy credit terms — with some $600 million worth of major military equipment including advanced Sukhoi bombers, Mig-21 fighters, helicopters, T-55 tanks, ground-to-air missiles and armoured carriers. Furthermore, several thousand military and civilian Yemenis have travelled to the Soviet Union for training since then.[22] It should be added that, after twenty years of experience with the Soviet Union, North Yemen's military personnel had become familiar with Soviet equipment and therefore had little or no difficulty in switching back to it. Moreover, YAR leaders have always felt that, while the Soviet Union has provided considerable military assistance, it has not tried to dominate their country. They also view YAR relations with the Soviet Union as a counterbalance to Saudi influence in their country.

The shock to Washington from this renewed YAR-Soviet accord resulted in the Carter administration cooling its earlier enthusiam for expanding its military relationship with San'a', and this also might have blocked the development of a major economic assistance programme to North Yemen. The same can be said about the Reagan administration, which gives very low priority to its relations with North Yemen. At present the United States is providing the YAR annually with $25 million to $30 million in economic assistance, and about $11 million in military aid; the latter consists mainly of providing the training and maintenance necessary to absorb the US equipment sold to the YAR through the Saudis, as mentioned earlier. It would seem that, for now, the United States is resigned to dealing with North Yemen through Saudi Arabia even though this has, on occasion, operated to 'the detriment of the United States' interests'.[23]

Reaching out to Other Arabs

In seeking to maintain its independence from Riyadh, the YAR has been careful to develop closer bilateral relationships with its other Arab brethren. It has cultivated friendships with the Gulf states and it has sought aid from them to lessen its financial reliance on Saudi Arabia. It has now become a yearly ritual for the North Yemeni Head of State and Prime Minister to tour the Gulf countries (including Iran under the Shah) and ask for aid. In recent years the aid provided from the Gulf states has increased significantly to an extent equalling what the YAR receives from Saudi Arabia, amounting to another $1 billion.[24] The Gulf countries have also accorded North Yemen special treatment in relation to oil.[25]

From the North Yemeni perspective, Iraq has proved valuable, not only financially but also politically to counter Saudi influence. Even in the early 1970s when Baghdad had close relations with Aden, YAR leaders pragmatically ignored the frequent allegations that Iraqi Ba'thists were behind several *coup* attempts and other subversive activities in North Yemen. Relations between the two countries were not affected by these allegations because the YAR benefited from Iraq's openly anti-Saudi political posture in those days when Baghdad was in competition with Riyadh for leadership in the Gulf region. Moreover, YAR leaders have relied on Iraq on several occasions to bring pressure to bear on South Yemen to lessen its support of anti-regime insurgents. It was Iraq, in concert with Syria and Jordan, which saved the present regime of President Salih from collapse during the 1979 border war by putting enough pressure on Aden to stop the fighting.[26] Salih is repaying the favour by his unequivocal support of Iraq in her war against Iran, and the sale to Iraq of Soviet weapons from North Yemeni arsenals.[27]

Although Egypt cannot afford financial aid to the YAR, relations between the two countries are substantial. Egyptian technicians, advisers and teachers in North Yemen are in the thousands, working at all levels to implement YAR development plans.[28] Moreover, Egypt has supported the YAR's repeated calls for regional security arrangements among countries overlooking the Red Sea.[29] This is the most important regional issue that concerns the YAR, as it relates to the security of the strategic strait of Bab al-Mandab which has frequently been a cause for concern to both countries.[30] On one of these occasions (April 1976), Egypt and Saudi Arabia encouraged the YAR to host a conference which was attended by the Heads of State of South Yemen, Sudan and Somalia. Nothing came of the meeting; perhaps its failure was due to South Yemen having already moved closer to Ethiopia, with the latter objecting to making the Red Sea an 'Arab lake'.

Egypt and North Yemen were on good terms even after Sadat went to Jerusalem. Salih praised Sadat's position on the Arab-Israeli conflict and the Camp David agreement saying that the Egyptian President was taking these measures 'for the higher interests of the Arab nation and to achieve peace based on justice in the area'.[31] Bowing to criticism, however, Salih recanted his earlier opinion and severed diplomatic relations with Cairo in accordance with the Baghdad summit resolution.[32] Since then the YAR, by and large, has been following the Saudi line on the Egyptian-Israeli peace treaty, and supporting the Fahd plan and the Fes summit resolutions. In recent years, Yasser Arafat and other Palestinian leaders have included San'a' in their tours of Arab capitals, particularly if Aden has been included in the itinerary. On these occasions YAR leaders reiterate their support for the Palestinian cause but their rhetoric has also increased in tone.[33]

Reaching out beyond the Peninsula and the Gulf region, the YAR has repeatedly tried to cultivate its relations with Libya in the hope of obtaining financial assistance, but the results have been disappointing for San'a'. The Libyan leader, Mu'ammar Qaddafi, finds the YAR too close to the conservative Arab regimes and too friendly to the West. Qaddafi has, moreover, always blamed San'a' for the failure of the unity agreements between the two Yemens. It may be recalled that he himself was instrumental in bringing together the leaders of San'a' and Aden to sign the first unification agreement following their border war of 1972. Since then YAR-Libyan relations cooled considerably, reaching their lowest ebb in November 1978, when it was alleged that Tripoli was behind the abortive *coup* against President Salih, and that the NDF had received financial assistance from Libya (and Syria).[34] Consequently, relations between the two countries were 'frozen' until they resumed in early 1980. Since then Libya, however, has moved closer to South Yemen and Ethiopia, and the three countries formed a pact in August 1981. This pact is perceived as a threat in San'a' because of its military overtones, and Salih has expressed his opposition, saying that the YAR is opposed to the formation of any 'foreign axis' in the region, and that security of the Red Sea is part of the security of the Gulf region.[35] These are code-words meaning that Salih supports the Saudi-sponsored Gulf Co-operation Council. But the irony here is that Libya, which accuses the YAR of being too close to the conservative Saudis, by joining a pact with South Yemen and Ethiopia, is pushing North Yemen further towards the 'Saudi big brother' instead of helping San'a' to maintain its independence from Riyadh.[36]

Notes

1. In 1972, the year before oil prices were quadrupled, remittances from Yemenis working in Saudi Arabia totalled $55 million; *Financial Times*, 15 Dec. 1972. Seven

years later remittances increased dramatically. According to the YAR Minister of Economy and Industry, Muhammad al-Shohati, remittances from the 1 million Yemenis working abroad reached a peak of $1.7 billion in 1979 but have declined since then; *Focus on Yemen Arab Republic* (Arab-British Chamber of Commerce, London, 1982), p. 18.

2. Quoted in *The Middle East* (Jan. 1981).

3. Chief among these groups which were plotting the downfall of the Aden regime were the 'Army of National Unity' led by Abd al-Qawi al-Makkawi, who, with Abdullah al-Asnag, was the leader of the Front for the Liberation of Occupied South Yemen (FLOSY), and the 'Salvation Army of the Hadramawt', led by Brig. Nasir Buraik, a former senior officer in the South Arabian Federation Army; *Daily Telegraph*, 17 Oct. 1972.

4. Throughout 1972 David Hirst wrote several excellent articles covering the tensions between the two Yemens; among these see the *Guardian*, 10 Mar. and 16 Oct. 1972; *Daily Star*, 11 Oct. 1972.

5. Beside emphasising Islam as the religion of the new state, the head of the North Yemeni team to the constitutional talks, Mr Husain al-Hubaishi, said that the name of the country will be 'the Yemen Republic and Sanaa its capital'. His South Yemeni counterpart, Mr Abdullah Ghanem, said that the draft would seek 'a comprehensive development of society to be based on Socialist relations and guided by the circumstances and heritage of the Yemeni society'. *Guardian*, 14 Jan. 1982.

6. Robin Bidwell, *The Two Yemens* (Longman, London, 1983), pp. 243-4.

7. *Daily Star*, 1 Aug. 1975.

8. *Middle East News*, 7 Apr. 1978.

9. *The Economist*, 16 Jan. 1982. Another report puts Saudi aid to the YAR through the joint council at SR 5.7 billion but it does not indicate the year or years which the amount is earmarked for; *Arab News*, 4 May 1982.

10. Saudi leaders confirmed this view to a US congressional delegation during a visit to Riyadh in October 1980. See House of Representatives Committee on Foreign Affairs, *US Security Interests in the Persian Gulf* (Washington, DC, 1981), p. 36.

11. For example, see Bidwell, *The Two Yemens*, p. 296.

12. *The Middle East* (Jan. 1981).

13. Earlier, Aden signed a Treaty of Friendship with the Soviet Union in October 1979.

14. Interior Minister and head of national security Muhammad Khamis was removed in the 1980 reshuffle to become Minister of Local Affairs, and Foreign Affairs Minister Abdullah al-Asnag was removed in March 1981. *Arabia: The Islamic World Review* (Jan. 1982).

15. For more details on Salih's parallel juggling act in the internal politics of the YAR, see J. E. Peterson, *Yemen: The Search for a Modern State* (Croom Helm, London, 1982), pp. 124-6. See also his 'The Yemen Arab Republic and the Politics of Balance', *Asian Affairs*, vol. LXXXVIII, pt. 3 (Oct. 1981).

16. *International Herald Tribune*, 4 Aug. 1975.

17. US House of Representatives Committee on International Relations, *United States Arms Policies in the Persian Gulf and Red Sea Areas: Past, Present and Future* (Washington, DC, 1977), pp. 76-7.

18. Ahmad al-Ghashmi, then Chief of Staff, in a rather candid interview admitted that this was the policy until 'the corrective revolution of June 1974' which he claimed 'changed this policy'; *Al-Nahar*, 21 Aug. 1975.

19. US House of Representatives Committee on Foreign Affairs, Subcommittee on Europe and the Middle East, *Proposed Arms Transfers to the Yemen Arab Republic: Hearing March 12, 1979* (Washington, DC, 1979), pp. 10-11.

20. *Washington Post*, 14 June 1979.

21. US official figures for arms sales in 1980 show that the total the YAR received was only $316.4 million out of the approved total for the combined two deals of $540

million. US House of Representatives, *US Security Interests in the Persian Gulf*, p. 41.

22. The Soviet Union has also increased its presence in the YAR by several hundred, including more than 250 military advisers; ibid., pp. 37-8.

23. *International Herald Tribune*, 24 Apr. 1982.

24. *The Economist*, 16 Jan. 1982.

25. This policy goes back to 1975 when the then President Hamdi asked for and got 'special treatment' from Kuwait; *Gulf Mirror*, 7 July 1977. The most recent of such deals, also from Kuwait, amounted to $222 million worth of refined oil products; *Al-Siyasah*, 12 Jan. 1982.

26. *Arab Times*, 1 Mar. 1979.

27. *Christian Science Monitor*, 1 Apr. 1982.

28. *Akhbar al-Yaum*, 10 June 1977.

29. *Egyptian Gazette*, 16 June 1977.

30. In April 1976 Israel was accused of violating the airspace of the YAR, and it was alleged Israeli forces occupied several small islands in the vicinity.

31. BBC, *Summary of World Broadcasts*, 8 Nov. 1978.

32. *Al-Siyasah*, 22 Aug. 1979.

33. Following the Israeli invasion of Lebanon in the summer of 1982, Salih and the President of South Yemen, Ali Nasir Muhammad, embarked on a tour of several Arab countries including Saudi Arabia and Syria 'in search of a united Arab stand' to face the Israeli invasion; *Arab News*, 5 Aug. 1982.

34. *Jordan News*, 16 Nov. 1978.

35. An interview with President Salih, *Arab Times*, 15 Feb. 1982.

36. A more explicit support to the GCC is indicated in the following statement by the North Yemeni Prime Minister Abd al-Karim al-Iryani: 'The GCC functions within the framework of the Arab League Charter, which encourages bilateral and collective cooperation, which is why we support it.' *Foreign Broadcast Information Service*, Arabian Peninsula, 20 Oct. 1982, col. 9.

This article also appeared in *Asian Affairs* (London), vol. XV (old series vol. 71) part III, October 1984.

14 SOVIET RELATIONS WITH SOUTH YEMEN

Fred Halliday

Introduction

South Yemen occupies a special place in the Soviet view of the Arab world, and in the West's view of Soviet strategy in the region. Since gaining independence from Britain in 1967, the PDRY has pursued a radical path in both internal and international policies and has established close relations with the Soviet Union. These relations are closer than those established by any other Arab state, a comparison reflected in the degree of internal social and political transformation and in the degree of alignment on foreign policy issues. For their part, the Russians have provided South Yemen with substantial military aid, and some economic assistance, and have considered it as one of those states following a programme of 'Socialist Orientation'. Within the general category of such states, South Yemen occupies a favoured place, along with Ethiopia, Angola and Afghanistan, and it is often cited as an example of what such states can achieve.[1] Those opposed to the PDRY seem to share a comparable estimation of its character. Conservative Arab states frequently criticise the PDRY as being a Soviet 'colony', as having 'abandoned Arabism' and as being disqualified from the right to participate in Arab regional consultation.[2] The United States echoes these concerns: the threat from South Yemen is cited as one of the main reasons for supplying arms, such as F–15s and AWACS planes, to Saudi Arabia, and South Yemen is conventionally listed with Libya, Iraq and Syria as a country which provides support to what is, on a loose definition, categorised as 'terrorism'.[3]

The analogy with Cuba is frequently drawn by Arab and Western critics of the PDRY. It is a comparison with some, albeit limited, relevance. First, South Yemen is a country in which the ruling party came to power through guerrilla action but without having adopted an orthodox 'Marxist-Leninist' character. It was only after the establishment of a new regime that this transition occurred, under the pressure of internal and external conflicts, and with the absorption into the dominant radical nationalist party of a smaller, previously separate and hostile, pro-Soviet communist grouping. The evolution of the NLF of South Yemen is comparable to that of the 26 July Movement in Cuba, as is the process of incorporation agreed by the small communist groups, the Popular Democratic Union in the PDRY and the Partido Socialista Popular in Cuba.[4] Such a process is distinct both from cases in which orthodox communist parties themselves direct the guerrilla movement (China, Vietnam) and those cases, frequent in the Arab world, where nationalist groupings or parties acquire power but fail to develop into 'Marxist-Leninist' regimes (Nasserite Egypt, Ba'thist Syria and Iraq, FLN Algeria, the Libyan Jamahariya). In both South Yemen and Cuba this process involved several internal conflicts in which factions of the radical nationalist movement sought to defend unorthodox political and social policies, as well as to maintain some equilibrium between Soviet and Chinese orientations. Yet it also involved the removal from positions of influence of those who embraced the Soviet Union too uncritically and in so doing alarmed other sections of the party.[5] Secondly, South Yemen has come to occupy a strategic position in some ways analogous to Cuba. Both have been isolated cases of post-revolutionary consolidation, exposed to blockade, military clashes with intervening forces and persistent economic difficulties. Both are located in areas where the force of revolutionary example might at some point in the future exert attraction upon other states in the region, and where the West feels at least uncomfortable about the presence of such a state because of the importance of the region to its long-run interests, strategic as well as economic. In both cases the attractions of consumption at markedly higher levels in neighbouring regions have posed difficulties for the ruling parties (attractions of North Yemen and the Arabian oil-states, and of Miami). Both have had disappointments in their policy of encouraging revolutionary forces in other states of the region (Oman, the YAR, and Bolivia, Brazil and Venezuela) but both have also received some support from the development, at a later stage, of revolutions in the neighbouring region (Ethiopia, Nicaragua). From the Soviet Union's point of view, South Yemen and Cuba also have a certain military potential. They can be used for naval support, in an era where the Soviet Union now has a world-wide capacity. They can serve as secure over-flying and air-refuelling bases, as stages to continental areas further afield (Africa, Latin America). They can provide, albeit at restricted levels, facilities of communication and conventional military support that would be of use in the event of a full-scale confrontation. The opportunities they provide for reconnaissance, storage and training must be welcome to Soviet military planners.

Yet the comparison of South Yemen with Cuba also has its limits. As in all its dealings with the Third World, Soviet policy towards South Yemen is marked by a strong dose of realism and restraint. The Soviet Union has shown considerable reserve about the evolution of the ruling party in South Yemen and has been unable to ensure that those most well disposed towards it have remained in power. The Soviet Union has taken the opposite decision on economic policy to that taken in Cuba: whereas it has been forthcoming to the latter, providing up to 25 per cent of Cuba's GNP in various forms of aid, it has been markedly restricted in its aid to South Yemen.[6] In the military field, the Soviet Union is aware of the fact that the forward position of South Yemen is, by the same token, a factor leading to that country's isolation. South Yemen, unlike Cuba, has land frontiers along which dangerous conflicts can erupt, and the Soviet Union has been keen to limit the degree of confrontation between Aden and its neighbours. Whereas in domestic policy the Soviet Union has been disturbed by what it considers to be right-wing or nationalist trends within the party, it has been monitoring international policy for what are seen as ultra-left or adventurist policies which might lead South Yemen into uneven conflict with its Arabian neighbours. The Soviet Union has other interests in Arabia, interests that find no analogue in the Caribbean and Central America. In particular, the Soviet Union has since 1962 maintained a working relationship with North Yemen, one it has not been willing to abandon. Hence, whilst the Soviet Union has supported South Yemen and guaranteed its security, it has at the same time sought to temper South Yemeni foreign policy and to encourage it to seek accomodations that might contribute to its longer-run security. Whilst the Soviet Union supports South Yemen, in both its domestic and international orientation, it offsets this support with a realistic view of what South Yemen itself is capable of, politically and economically, and of what the Soviet Union's military and economic capabilities towards a country like the PDRY still are.

The Arab Context

The first Soviet diplomatic relations with the Arab world were with Arabian states: with Saudi Arabia, and with the imamate of Yemen, in the middle 1920s. The Soviet Union was in fact the first country in the world to recognise the Saudi Kingdom.[7] These relations were allowed to wither in the 1930s and henceforward Soviet attention was focused on other Middle Eastern states, either because of the growth of significant state-to-state relations, or because these countries had active communist parties. In the 1940s and early 1950s attention was focused on the northern tier of Afghanistan, Iran and Turkey, countries in which the Soviet Union had a natural security interest, as it still does.[8] From the mid-1950s until the mid-1970s, Soviet attention was devoted to the radical nationalist states ruled by 'anti-imperialist' military regimes — Sudan, Egypt, Syria, Iraq, Libya, Algeria and, accepting its dubious claim to be an Arab country at all, Somalia. Yet as a by-product of its alliance with Nasser's Egypt, the Soviet Union also became involved once again in North Yemen, first in support of the Imam, who was deemed to be waging an 'anti-imperialist' campaign against the British in South Yemen, and then in support of the Republic which came into being in 1962 and which was embroiled, with Egyptian military support, in a conflict with Saudi-backed royalist rebels.

The history of this Soviet involvement with the radical Arab states is not one that can have brought the Russians much satisfaction.[9] First, although substantial communist parties have existed in some of these states — Iraq, Syria, Sudan — and smaller influential groupings in others — Egypt, Algeria — in none of these was Soviet strategic influence converted into domestic policy in such a way as to consolidate a 'non-capitalist' or 'socialist-oriented' regime. The communists were never given substantial authority, especially in matters of security, and on several occasions they were imprisoned or even executed by military regimes that were officially favoured by the Soviet Union (e.g. Egypt 1958-60; Iraq 1963, 1978; Sudan 1971). Although what the Russians saw as 'progressive' economic reforms were carried out, and foreign interests nationalised, such changes tended to consolidate new systems of inequality within these countries rather than to pave the way for further transformations. The case of Egypt is paradigmatic: Nasserite reforms did effect wide-ranging land reforms and nationalisations, but this period of etatist rule (1956-70) only paved the way for the later reopening of Egypt to capitalist markets and investors in the 1970s. The uncertain political character of these regimes was compounded by two other factors: (a) their espousal of Arab nationalist ideologies — with all their variations, these were anti-communist, indulgent towards religion and resistant to concepts of class struggle; (b) the availability of large quantities of money from the Arab oil-states which were able, from 1971 onwards, to use this money to detach more radical Arab states from their alliances with the Soviet Union. As a result, these Arab states developed strong military ties with the Soviet Union, and up to two-thirds of all Soviet military exports in the post-1945 period have gone to Middle East countries. In the 1967–76 period 9 of the 21 Arab countries received 60 per cent or more of their military supplies from the Soviet Union. The Soviet Union provided the Arab states confronting Israel with the means to continue this conflict. But this military relationship was not matched by comparable economic or diplomatic reliance. Soviet economic interests in the Middle East have been concentrated in the non-Arab states of the northern tier: Iran was, prior to the Shah's downfall, the Soviet Union's main Third World trading partner; Turkey is the largest recipient of Soviet aid in the non-communist world; Afghanistan was, even under Zahir Shah, carrying out most of its trade with its northern neighbour. But, with the temporary exception of Egypt which did export 60 per cent of its goods to the centrally planned economies in the first half of the 1970s, the Arab states that had close military links with Moscow did not reflect this in their trade. One obvious reason was that the Soviet Union did not need to import oil. Another was that the consumer goods being increasingly demanded in these countries were more readily available in the West. In the diplomatic field, there was of course convergence on international issues, not least on the Arab-Israeli question. But this convergence never led to unanimity, since the Soviet Union has always insisted on the right of an Israeli state to exist side-by-side with a Palestinian one.

By the latter half of the 1970s, the Soviet Union was facing increasing difficulties with its Arab allies.[10] Egypt had expelled Soviet military forces and advisers, had abrogated the existing treaties and had cancelled existing debts and trading agreements: all this occurred despite the fact that it was Soviet arms which enabled the Egyptian army to regain its honour in the 1973 war. Egypt had been the prime example in the late 1950s and 1960s of a country taking the 'non-capitalist road'. Now, without any overt counter-revolution or drastic shift in personnel beyond the death of Nasser in 1970, it had rejected socialism and the alliance with the Soviet Union. Somalia did the same thing in 1977 — as had earlier been the case with Egypt, Somalia's switch owed not a little to the financial inducements of Saudi Arabia. Iraq, although maintaining outwardly friendly relations with Moscow, also began to improve its relations with the West and to criticise Soviet policy on such issues as the Horn of Africa and Afghanistan. Three substantial countries were still allied to the Soviet Union but each presented difficulties. In Algeria, the Chadli Ben Jadid government was less closed to Western influence than had been that of Houari Boumedienne: although 90 per cent reliant on the Soviet Union for arms supplies, Algeria began to explore diversification in 1980 and its role as mediator in the Iran hostages crisis was not to Moscow's liking. Syria remained militarily dependent on Moscow and had little room for manoeuvre given the pressures to which it was subjected in Lebanon: but although the Soviet Union signed a Friendship Treaty in October 1980, this was to reassure the Syrians and prevent a deterioration in the situation, rather than an index of increased influence. The Syrian assault on Yasser Arafat in 1983 greatly displeased the Russians. Moscow's other significant ally was Qaddafi: he had begun his rule as a strong critic of Soviet policy, and even during his visit to Moscow in 1981 there were signs of stress over Afghanistan, Palestine and the Spanish Sahara. The incident in August 1981, when US planes shot down two Libyan jets over the Gulf of Sirte, may have reconciled Qaddafi to Moscow for the time being: but the Libyan leader has shown himself to be a resentful and unpredictable ally, a far cry from the kind of steady but cautious leaders most favoured in the Kremlin. Libyan requests for increased arms supplies from the Soviet Union in early 1983 were refused.

The lessons which the Russians would appear to have drawn from this experience suggest that they have developed a cooler, in their view more 'realistic', assessment of the Middle East, and of the Arab countries in particular.

(1) They have a more cautious view of how far radical nationalist organisations can convert themselves to socialist or communist parties. The experiences of Iraq, Syria, Egypt, Sudan and Algeria in this respect have all been negative. The non-communist forces have maintained power, facing the weaker communist groups with the alternative of submission or repression.

(2) They also have a more realistic view of the obstacles faced in states on the 'non-capitalist path'. The original theory, evolved in the 1950s implied that the transition to socialist development could be a relatively smooth one, depending on the weight of the demo-

cratic forces.[11] What this ignored was the manner in which, under 'non-capitalist' states, new class relations could develop which could open the door not to socialism but to capitalism. Beyond such an evolution, dependent upon social change, lay the possibility of *coups* which would abruptly change the orientation of the regime.

(3) The Soviet experience with the ideology of Arab nationalism has led them to reassess how far such an outlook can be radicalised. Russian writings tend to skirt round the irreducible difference between Arab and Soviet views of the Palestine question, and to focus instead on the class character, or apparent lack thereof, within Arab nationalism. But in the fields of both diplomacy and political theory, this conflict remains a strong one, however much both sides seek to minimise such differences at particular junctures.

(4) The Soviet experience has made them more cautious about the military relations they could develop with the region, about how far to provide arms on easy credit terms, and how far to build up military facilities in the region. Given the Egyptian and Somali repudiations, the Russians must be wary of supplying arms for anything but cash payment. Their loss of facilities in Egypt and Somalia in the 1970s has made them wary of entering into such visible but vulnerable commitments. At the same time, developments in satellite technology may have reduced the need for airfields from which to deploy reconnaissance planes.

(5) The changes in the Arab world as a whole have not been encouraging to the Soviet Union. The rising power of the conservative oil-states, most of whom refuse to have even diplomatic relations with the Soviet Union; the increasing dominance of Islamic radicalism which is anti-Soviet as well as anti-American; and the rightward shift of supposedly 'non-capitalist' allies have all contributed to making Soviet diplomacy proceed carefully. No better illustration of this can be found than the consequences of the Camp David agreement: while many Arab states condemned this treaty, and the US role in it, most of them did not match this critique of Washington with any closer alliance with the Soviet Union.

The experience of relations with the Arab world has therefore led to a reassessment. As one author has written:

> Some Soviet scholars argue that in most Third World countries there are powerful forces working against continued socialistic development over the medium term . . . officials in the governmental sector have an opportunity to accumulate funds through

bribery and other forms of corruption and to funnel them into the private sector, perhaps through relatives. Soon, the Soviet scholars fear, the officials stop supporting socialism and begin to form a capitalist class, with all its characteristic attitudes.[12]

Three results of this caution are relevant to the case of South Yemen.

(1) From the mid-1970s onwards Soviet writers began to advance a new theory of Third World development, the theory of 'States of Socialist Orientation'.[13] Whilst not rejecting the earlier theory of the 'Non-Capitalist Road', it marked a change in certain significant respects: (a) it laid much greater stress on the obstacles which socialism encounters — in class terms, in the survival of tribal and religious ideologies, in the possibility of right-wing *coups*; (b) it stressed the gap between superstructure and base, i.e. between leadership and mass, abandoning the pretence of a common front earlier emphasised; the conclusion was that the masses cannot immediately exercise power, but must be educated before this becomes possible; (c) it selected and identified a group of countries that were potentially more advanced than merely national democratic ones, i.e. where the process towards socialism had gone further. The two paradigmatic cases where such a transition had occurred were Mongolia and Cuba, i.e. where non-communist movements did succeed in so transforming themselves that they started to construct socialism. In much of the literature South Yemen is seen as a possible case of such a 'socialist-oriented' state: but, as will be shown, South Yemen also embodies some of the limitations to which the theory draws attention.

(2) With growing difficulties in the core of the Arab world, Soviet attention shifted more towards the periphery. Indeed, the countries where Soviet advances have been greatest in recent years have been around the edge of the Middle East — Ethiopia, South Yemen, Afghanistan and, initially, Iran. There is no reason to suppose that this corresponds to any preconceived Soviet grand design, but it reflects the difficulties which the Soviet Union has encountered at the centre, and the maturing of social conflicts elsewhere in the region. But some connections do exist. Thus, the decision to support Ethiopia decisively in its 1977-8 confrontation with Somalia would probably not have been taken, had relations with Egypt not deteriorated in previous years: in this sense, there was some conscious connection between the two sets of events. The result has, however,

been to give Soviet policy a new focus of political and strategic interest, within which South Yemen finds a place. Earlier losses confirm Soviet determination to maintain those interests it now has in recompense for those that it has lost as a result of the growth of US and Saudi influence.

(3) Developments in Soviet naval theory and capability have also brought South Yemen more into Soviet view. The loss of naval facilities in Egypt and Somalia has confirmed the importance of Aden and other South Yemen facilities, and the Soviet view of its naval role in the Indian Ocean has been affected by what is seen as an increased US naval and military presence there: by the build-ups of the Diego Garcia base in 1973 and again in 1979, following the Iranian revolution; by the increased US attention to the Persian Gulf and the surrounding states: and by the possible deployment of US Poseidon and Trident submarines. Soviet naval access to the Indian Ocean is, however, difficult: unless its ships can pass through the Suez Canal, the Ocean is far from Soviet naval bases in the Black Sea, Far East and Baltic. Moreover, lacking a base infrastructure in the countries surrounding the Ocean, Soviet naval forces in the region would be exposed in the event of an all-out conflict. The Soviet navy has, however, been expanding its surface and submarine long-range fleet since the early 1960s, and Admiral Gorshkov has enunciated a clear theory of the multiple functions of the navy in peacetime as a diplomatic instrument, as a means of assisting and defending liberation movements, and as a component of Soviet maritime strategy. The first substantial Soviet naval deployments began in the Indian Ocean in 1968, and the first Soviet ships visited Aden in June 1968, as part of a tour of the ports of the region. Subsequent visits have occurred at frequent intervals, especially from 1978 onwards, and Aden plays a significant part in the facility structure of the Soviet forces in the Ocean. Yet Soviet naval activity in the Ocean is far less than that of the United States, let alone that of the Western countries combined: in April 1981 the Soviet Union had 21 ships in the Ocean, compared to the United States' 32, but only 5 of these were combat ships, the rest being support vessels, compared to the United States' 17 combat ships and 15 support ships.[14]

The combination of these factors has therefore produced a situation in which South Yemen has become a more significant factor in Soviet Middle East policy. It is within this strategic context, as much as in the nature of the internal evolution of South Yemeni politics and economics, that the growth of ties between Moscow and Aden may be seen, in each of the four main dimensions.

Party-building: the Yemeni Socialist Party

Soviet theory lays great emphasis on the need for 'party-building' in revolutionary states, and the emergence of an orthodox party in South Yemen has been an important goal of Soviet encouragement since independence. The National Liberation Front of South Yemen was founded in 1963 and in the ensuing four years it waged a guerrilla campaign in both the mountains north and north-east of Aden and in Aden city itself. By the time of the British withdrawal in November 1967 the NLF had defeated not only the planned South Arabian Federation, composed of local rulers loyal to Britain but also a rival, Egyptian-supported, group, the Front for the Liberation of Occupied South Yemen. In its origins, the NLF was a nationalist group, influenced by Nasserism. But within the four years of the pre-independence period, it underwent a radicalisation with the emergence within it of a faction committed to 'Marxism-Leninism'. This radicalisation had several causes: a conflict with Egypt, which tried to curb the NLF and in so doing provoked hostility to Nasserism as a whole; the political conflict within South Yemen itself, which acquired a certain if vaguely formulated social character, directed as it was against the landowners and merchants supporting the Federation; and the radicalisation of Nasserism in Lebanon and amongst the Palestinians, where a 'Marxist-Leninist' current emerged and, with superior intellectual resources, had its effects upon the NLF. At the time of independence the NLF contained both 'right' and 'left' factions but the centre of gravity had shifted noticeably to the left in the preceding years.[15]

There is no evidence of direct Soviet involvement with the NLF prior to independence. The 'Marxism-Leninism' of the radicals was, if anything, as sympathetic to China as to the Soviet Union, and the mood amongst Arab left-wing groups at this period was critical of the Soviet Union, for what were felt to be Moscow's failings in the 1967 Arab-Israeli war. Given the Soviet Union's alliance with Egypt, it is also unlikely that the Russians would have risked antagonising Nasser by establishing contact with the group that had rejected his leadership. Soviet coverage of independence welcomed the new Republic, but was cautious in its characterisation of the

NLF and called for reconciliation between the NLF and FLOSY.[16] This call was quite unrealistic: the two groups had been fighting up to the moment of the British withdrawal, and FLOSY leaders had then to flee to exile in North Yemen and Saudi Arabia. In the post-independence period, direct relations were established with the NLF and its 'left' faction, and the ensuing decade was one in which the Soviet Union welcomed the triumph of this left, and its consolidation. At the Fourth Congress of the NLF, in March 1968, the 'left' won on votes and called for South Yemen to follow the 'non-capitalist road'. It attacked the 'petty bourgeois' policies of Egypt, Syria and Algeria and propounded what appeared to be an orthodox Soviet programme for such a country.[17] But the right forces within the NLF, deriving support from the army and with encouragement from Egypt, were able to impose their control and the leaders of the left went into exile. It would seem that at this point closer relations were established by NLF members who stayed in Eastern Europe and will have had time for theoretical and political discussions.

The NLF left returned to power as a result of an internal conflict in June 1969, a date later celebrated as an important occasion, 'The Corrective Move'. The left's programme was put through in various fields of social policy: all banks and insurance companies were nationalised in October 1969; the country was renamed the People's Democratic Republic of Yemen; in 1970 a land reform limited holdings to 20 acres of irrigated land, or 40 of unirrigated, and laid the basis for a system of co-operatives and state farms that was to encompass most of the countryside by the late 1970s; most industry was nationalised; foreign trade was brought under state control; the free-port status of Aden was abolished. In party affairs, the Fifth Congress of May 1972 confirmed the victory of the left, with a new orthodox structure of Central Committee and Politburo, and orthodox 'non-capitalist' policies. A number of innovations derived from the Cuban experience were introduced: a militia, local Popular Defence Committees, a literacy campaign.

The NLF was by this time receiving substantial ideological assistance from the Soviet Union and party delegations were visiting each other's countries.[18] Soviet text-books were provided in education and party programmes, and a School of Higher Socialist Studies was set up in the former palace of the Sultan of Lahej in Aden. Instructors were brought from the Soviet Union, who lectured in English, through Arabic translators; other instructors wre provided by Arab communists driven from their own countries — from

Egypt, Iraq and Sudan. This growth of relations with the CPSU was accompanied by an alliance with two smaller groups that had remained apart from the guerrilla movement, the Popular Democratic Union, a pro-Soviet communist party of around fifty members, and the Vanguard Party, a Ba'thist faction loyal to the left Ba'th leadership of Nureddin al-Atassi, in power in Syria from 1966 to 1970. PDU and Vanguard leaders were given Ministerial posts and in October 1975 the three groups united to form the United Political Organisation of the NLF, UPONF.[19] This process then paved the way for the construction of what was proclaimed as 'Hizb Min Tiraz Jadid' — the 'party of the New Type', in the Leninist style. In October 1978 the process of transformation was formally completed: the NLF dissolved and became instead the Yemeni Socialist Party, with a structure and programme of the conventional Soviet type.[20] A parallel process of transformation was taking place in the institutions of state. In 1977 elections were held for local Majalis Sha'biya, Popular Councils, which functioned in each of the six governorates very much as the Regional Assemblies in Cuba do, discussing a limited range of economic issues and ratifying decisions submitted to them. In 1978 elections were held for the Supreme People's Council, the national legislative body, which itself had statutes derived from those of the Supreme Soviet.

This process of consolidation encountered considerable resistance, however.[21] For the radicals of the guerrilla NLF were not all convinced of the necessity of adopting Soviet models of organisation, or of the need for a complete party and state alliance with the Soviet Union. The eviction of the right in June 1969 paved the way for a protracted struggle between two factions, the orthodox pro-Soviet one led by Secretary-General Abdul-Fattah Isma'il, and a more independently minded one led by President Salim Rubai'a Ali. Salim Rubai'a was sympathetic to China and to Chinese models of mobilisation: in the aftermath of the Fifth Congress he launched his own version of the cultural revolution, bringing thousands of peasants and workers into the streets of Aden to demonstrate against bureaucratic tendencies and in favour of mass *intifadat*, or uprisings. The evolution of Chinese foreign policy and China's inability to provide substantial military aid and protection did, however, lessen Peking's appeal and in November 1972 Salim Rubai'a Ali paid a visit to Moscow during which Soviet economic, cultural and military aid agreements were signed.[22] The President then tried to secure aid from another source, namely Saudi Arabia, and he used Saudi aid to fund his own economic projects in which he relied on politically sound, but untrained, cadres, in preference to what he saw as the 'bureaucratic' elements favoured by the party leadership. The economic failure of his favourite ventures, combined with the growing crisis in the region attendant upon the war in the Horn of Africa, closed the political space in which Salim Rubai'a Ali could operate. In June 1978 he attemted to stage a *coup*, using his personal guard and party elements loyal to him; but he was defeated and executed along with several of his followers.[23] The issues surrounding the fall of Salim Rubai'a Ali are comparable to those which have rent other post-revolutionary regimes — in China and Cuba. Although not of a theoretical bent, the late President was seeking some model of social and economic mobilisation that relied on moral rather than material incentives, which stressed the 'red' above the 'expert' and which sought to involve mass initiative as much as central control. Foreign policy issues played their part, but it seems that it was the internal factors, the dispute over the model of social and party policy, which were most significant.

The victory of the orthodox pro-Soviet faction in June 1978 might have been expected to end the divisions within the NLF-YSP. But this was not to be. For other issues then came to the fore: security personnel responsible for arbitrary initiatives in the earlier years were now called to account; conflicts between North and South Yemenis within the party came to the fore — as in Korea and Germany, personnel from both regions of the divided country were present in the party; above all, the victory of the more pro-Soviet faction exposed them to the criticism that Soviet support was not as substantial as it might be. This accounts for the fact that over the next two years South Yemen began to move in a somewhat different direction. In 1979 the PDRY became an observer of Comecon and in October 1979 Abdul-Fattah Isma'il visited Moscow to sign a Twenty-Year Treaty of Friendship and Co-operation, similar to those signed with Ethiopia, Syria, Egypt, Iraq and other 'non-capitalist' states.[24] But in April 1980 Abdul-Fattah Isma'il was ousted as Secretary-General and as President, positions he had combined since the fall of Salim Rubai'a Ali. His place was taken by Ali Nasir Muhammad, formerly Prime Minister, who, while continuing the alliance with the Soviet Union, nevertheless sought to present a more nationalist image and to loosen party and state controls at home.

The fall of Abdul-Fattah Isma'il can be attributed to three factors.

The most important is that the economic problems faced by South Yemen were, by the late 1970s, being increasingly blamed on the limited economic support provided by the Soviet Union, and the refusal of Arab states to aid South Yemen was blamed on the country's excessive identification with Moscow. Secondly, the very success of the Soviet Union in supporting Abdul-Fattah Isma'il concealed the fact that he was an unrepresentative leader, an intellectual given to theorising who had little popular base and little feel for popular problems: he was known derisively as *al-faqih*, a term designed to suggest that he concerned himself only with abstractions. Thirdly, despite its apparently successful transition to orthodoxy, the NLF-YSP contained many who were not convinced of the wisdom of such a process. Factionalism along personal and tribal lines continued. The transformation of the party was therefore much less successful than surface appearance suggested. For their part, the Russians knew this. In dealings with the NLF-YSP they tended to rely on certain trusted individuals — such as Abdul-Fattah himself. They were suspicious of other members, such as Salim Rubai'a, and a number of Ministers known to retain nationalist loyalties. There is no evidence that the Russians intervened directly in any of the party conflicts: the events of June 1978 were directed by Yemenis, and the Soviet Ambassador's attempts to save Abdul-Fattah Isma'il in April 1980 were unsuccessful. But the Russians did have an interest in the outcome and made this clear.

The result of the 1980 changes has not been to breach the previous alliance. Ali Nasir Muhammad visited Moscow a month after the fall of Abdul-Fattah although his visit was preceded by some hard bargaining on both sides. In November 1982 Ali Nasir was one of the six leaders of 'socialist-oriented' states given special prominence at Brezhnev's funeral. Inter-state and inter-party exchanges continue at the same high level; but controls on trade have been loosened internally, relations with Arab states have improved, and the leadership is more attentive to popular concerns. In sum, the evolution of the South Yemeni party has illustrated the difficulties of transforming a radical nationalist grouping into an orthodox pro-Soviet party, the internal resistance this may generate and the need for the Soviet Union to prove itself able to supply more than military and political support if it is to consolidate its influence in such states. On the other hand, it has shown the degree to which the underlying process of transformation can continue, despite sharp leadership changes.

Economic Changes

Under the pressure of necessity and of socialist theory alike, the PDRY has established preponderant state control over all sectors of the economy since independence. In no domain is the difference more palpable than between Aden's path and that pursued as 'Arab Socialism' in Cairo, Baghdad and Damascus. Central to this process has been the introduction of a planning mechanism covering the first three-year plan (1972-4) and the two subsequent five-year plans (1974-8, 1981-5). Yet South Yemen has remained an extremely poor country, among the most indigent in the Arab world. *Per capita* income in 1978 stood at $420; the country has a large balance of trade deficit, covered by foreign aid and emigrants' remittances. The longer-run prospects are also meagre, given the lack of any substantial productive forces which could be developed. Only if oil or some other export-earning mineral resources are discovered can this situation be resolved.[25]

The Soviet Union has supported the policies of the PDRY government, and has provided some aid. But it is noticeable that Moscow has not done what it did in Cuba — it has not provided massive aid of a kind that would noticeably buoy the economy up, and it has not reoriented South Yemen's trade away from the capitalist world. Soviet economic aid at the end of 1980 stood at $153 million, compared to $127 million from diverse Arab sources, multilateral and bilateral, $84 million from China and $35 million from the IDA. Other Eastern European countries provided $56 million in bilateral aid.[26] The volume of Soviet-Yemeni trade has increased substantially since independence, but, given the inflation in import and export prices, this has not greatly altered the proportion of Soviet trade in the total. Soviet goods represented 1 per cent of the PDRY's imports in 1968, and 3.2 per cent in 1977, totalling $17.5 million in that year. South Yemeni exports to the Soviet Union at $527,000 in 1976 were a negligible proportion of the total. Most of South Yemen's exports — fish, cotton, processed oil — went to the West, or south-east Asia and Japan.

Soviet economic aid has involved assistance with irrigation projects, a joint fishing fleet, constructing a thermal plant in Aden, and the training of personnel. It has, however, been limited, in comparison with the Cuban case or South Yemen's needs. Several reasons for this suggest themselves. First, the Russians have limited resources for foreign aid programmes: they have neither the foreign exchange, nor the technology nor the personnel to be able to meet all the requirements of their poorer allies. Cuba is a special case, as is Vietnam; South Yemen does not fall in this category, above all because of remaining political doubts. Secondly, the Russians consider that the PDRY should try to get aid from a more forthcoming source, namely the Arab world. The Russians, far from opposing such ties, have in fact encouraged them, provided the political cost is not too high. They have also encouraged South Yemen to seek support from the UN and particularly from the IDA, the World Bank fund devoted to the world's poorest nations. Thirdly, the Russians must have a pessimistic view of what South Yemen's long-run economic potentiality is. Cuba, Vietnam, Afghanistan — all these countries could, after some time, become self-sufficient and even profitable economies: this is not the case in South Yemen. The British, who ruled parts of South Arabia for 129 years, were reluctant to invest money there for the same reason. Both the Russians and the South Yemenis have criticisms of the economic policies pursued by the other.[27] A Soviet article published in 1980 talks of the problems faced:

> There are also subjective difficulties, such as the attempts (contradicting the party line and censured by it) at solving economic problems by 'volitional' decisions, as, for example, establishing higher-type co-operatives when conditions were not ripe for it, efforts to have retail trade completely controlled by the state, etc. Sometimes individual failures caused setbacks; such was the case with the fishing co-operative in Province Six, where it was demanded that the means of production, expropriated under the agrarian reform law, be returned to the former owners. The recent YSP Congress stated that it was the opportunist, left-extremist elements in the party who were to blame for the slow growth of production in agriculture. Cases of insufficient attention being paid to economic progress in out-of-the-way places were also criticised.[28]

This criticism was directed at the policies of Salim Rubai'a Ali; but it is unlikely that all disagreements will have disappeared with his departure.

The South Yemeni criticisms include the low level of Soviet aid, and the low quality. The fishing fleet is a source of muted criticism: as in other cases of joint Soviet fishing companies, there are allegations that the Russians are fishing in protected waters, or are endangering stocks. Great friction was caused in 1980 by the incidence of power failures in Aden which were blamed on the failure of the Russians to construct a power station originally agreed to in 1972. The Minister of Fisheries, Mahmud Akkush, was reportedly dismissed by Abdul-Fattah Isma'il after criticising Soviet officials during a visit to the Soviet Union. South Yemeni officials alleged that the Russians had offered to build a 100 kW plant in 1972 for 65 million roubles, and that the one they offered in 1980 was for 110 million roubles, with half the capacity. Bulgarian aid has also been criticised: Bulgarian officials working on a major agrarian project in the Third Governorate east of Aden abandoned the project after three years. While it is difficult to evaluate these criticisms, some dissatisfaction is certainly there and formed an important component of the fall from power of Abdul-Fattah Isma'il in 1980.

Military Relations

The Soviet Union has two military interests in South Yemen: to train and equip the PDRY's forces, so that they are best able to defend themselves — 'to strengthen the PDRY's defensive capability' in the official Soviet idiom — and to acquire facilities in the PDRY that can be of use for the Soviet Union's global strategy. The first military agreement between the two countries was reached in February 1968 and since that time the South Yemeni armed forces have been reorganised and almost completely re-equipped along Soviet lines. There has been a wide-ranging replacement of the officer corps of the British-trained South Arabian Army by new guerrilla and party personnel. Figures for 1980-1 give total armed forces of 23,800 of which 22,000 are in the army, and defence expenditure of $56 million, or 11 per cent of GNP. The army has 375 Soviet tanks (T-62s and inferior types); the navy is equipped with Soviet ships; the air force relies on Mig-21 fighters and 11-28 light bombers.[29] Western sources give the number of Soviet advisers as 600.[30] Of equal importance to this technical restructuring has been the political change: the imposition on the armed forces of party control, through the introduction of commissars and the appointment of the top military commanders from among former organisers of the guerrilla movement.

The Soviet Union has also given South Yemen a defensive

capacity in the event of air attack: since the acquisition by Saudi Arabia of the F-15 fighters, the Soviet Union has been constructing a missile system to protect Aden. These defensive systems are also of use for protecting the facilities which the Russians have for their own purposes in Aden, of which by far the most important are their naval ones. The Soviet Union does not have a base, in the proper sense of that word, in Aden, but it does use the port for refuelling, changing crews, and repair work. Aden therefore performs an important function in the Soviet Union's whole Indian Ocean strategy. It is also used for some air facilities as well: as a staging post on flights to Ethiopia and further destinations in Africa, and as the base for some reconnaissance flights. The Russians must, however, be aware that in the event of a world conflict there is very little they could do to protect the PDRY and that in such circumstances the PDRY would have to fend for itself.

Foreign Relations

The alliance with the Soviet Union is a guarantee of the South Yemeni regime's survival, both through the provision of aid to the Yemeni armed forces, and through the fact that the Soviet Union would seek to a limited degree to protect the PDRY in the event of an all-out attack. By the same token, the Soviet Union has given more attention to the military than to the economic support programmes, because this is, in its view, the priority area; and, whilst giving support to the most prominent features of South Yemen's foreign policy, the Soviet Union has also sought to temper what it considers to be the PDRY's more adventurist foreign policy initiatives.

In the years immediately following independence, the PDRY government saw itself as the base area for a set of revolutionary movements in the surrounding region: in North Yemen, in Oman, in the Arab countries of the Gulf, in Eritrea, Palestine and, intermittently, Iran. South Yemen had no relations with Saudi Arabia and none with the United States, the former because of a Saudi refusal to recognise a communist regime in Arabia, the latter because the PDRY broke links in October 1969 as a protest against US citizens with dual nationality serving in the Israeli Army. South Yemen was also involved in military conflict with all three of its land neighbours: North Yemen, in the border war of September 1972; Saudi Arabia, involving both the Saudi forces and the 5,000-strong Army of Deliverance, comprising South Yemeni exiles financed in Saudi Arabia; and Oman, in whose Dhofar province, bordering South Yemen, a guerrilla war was being waged with South Yemeni assistance.

The Soviet Union was cautious about these South Yemeni initiatives. Moscow had had relations with North Yemen both before and after the revolution of 1962 there; the North Yemeni armed forces remained reliant on Soviet equipment through the civil war of the 1960s, and in the period after the Egyptian withdrawal of late 1967 Soviet pilots flew combat missions in defence of San'a', when it was besieged by royalist tribes. The Soviet Union also began to supply arms to the YAR directly at this time, whereas hitherto Egypt had insisted that all arms were to be channelled through its forces in the country. After the establishment of the coalition government in North Yemen in 1970 Soviet arms supplies ceased, and the Soviet military mission declined to a handful of experts, who were not allowed to perform any functions by the YAR authorities. Soviet support for the South in the 1972 and 1979 wars greatly disturbed the North Yemenis. Yet neither side wanted a complete break — the Russians because they hoped to keep some influence in an important country, the North Yemenis because they were trained on Soviet equipment and did not want to switch suddenly to the West's supplies. Both Egypt under Sadat and Saudi Arabia planned to replace Soviet with Western supplies, and in February 1979 it seemed that this long-delayed transfer was about to occur, as Carter promised to send $400 million worth of arms to San'a' as emergency aid to face the South. But, just as the Egyptians had long controlled Soviet aid in the 1960s, so the Saudis now sought to control the flow of US aid in the 1970s, and to exact political concessions from San'a' in return for agreeing to allow the arms to flow. The result was that the long-latent Soviet commitment to San'a' bore fruit: the Soviet Union agreed to supply up to $600 million worth of equipment on better terms, including Mig-21 planes, helicopters and T-55 tanks, and by 1981 the Soviet military mission had risen to 600 men, with another 1,500 North Yemenis being trained in the Soviet Union itself. In October 1981 President Ali Abdullah Salih visited Moscow and both sides agreed that a considerable measure of agreement on security in the Red Sea and on Middle Eastern policy had been reached.[31]

This curious history of military links reflected a deeper Soviet assessment. For despite an increase in Saudi and US influence in the

North during the 1970s, the Soviet Union maintained its foothold. When war broke out between North and South Yemen, in 1972 and again in 1979, Moscow adopted a relatively neutral stance, blaming the war on Saudi and US interference in North Yemen, rather than on the North Yemeni government. In private, the Russians urged restraint upon Aden and advised against increased support for left-wing guerrillas operating in North Yemen. Although the radical republican opposition groups in the YAR were supporters of the PDRY and of Soviet foreign policy generally, the Soviet Union refused to recognise them or alter their diplomatic positions to take account of the civil war that continued sporadically until June 1982; the irony was that the 1982 defeat of the National Democratic Front guerrillas in the YAR was carried out by an army equipped with Soviet weapons. The Russians would favour Yemeni unity if (a) this could be achieved without creating an international crisis and alarming Saudi Arabia; and (b) the PDRY personnel would be able to control such a state. Since neither prospect appears likely, they have laid more stress upon reconciliation between the two states than upon the unity about which Yemeni leaders speak. Soviet attitudes to Saudi Arabia, although hostile, were along similar lines: the Soviet Union welcomed the establishment of diplomatic links between Aden and Riyadh in 1976, and encouraged the South Yemenis to tone down their anti-royalist propaganda. The Russians were also cool about the guerrilla movement in Dhofar, partly because they considered it had little chance of success, and partly because of the movement's earlier espousal of a Chinese policy. They did supply some arms to the guerrillas after 1971, but these were not at the technical level required, and propaganda support was directed more against the presence of foreign troops in Oman than in favour of the revolutionary movement.[32]

Two areas where Soviet and PDRY policy converged were the Horn of Africa and Palestine. Moscow never supported the Eritrean guerrilla movement to which the South Yemenis, up to 1974, supplied large quantities of arms. But with the emergence of a left-wing government in Somalia after 1969 both Moscow and Aden saw the possibility of the latter acquiring a regional ally for the first time, and so breaking its isolation. During the mid-1970s South Yemeni officials said that Somalia was the country with which their relations were closest. The Ethiopian revolution of 1974 altered these relations. South Yemen now accepted the view that the Eritreans should accept the unity of Ethiopia and acquire regional rights within a single socialist entity. Relations with Somalia deteriorated as Somali forces began, in 1977, to operate in the Ogaden region of Ethiopia and as Somalia's relations with Saudi Arabia and the West improved. By 1978 South Yemen's closest ally was Ethiopia. South Yemeni forces fought in both the Ogaden and Eritrean theatres, and Abdul-Fattah Isma'il went to Addis Ababa on several visits to 'advise' the Ethiopians on party formation. In August 1980 South Yemen joined Libya and Ethiopia in signing a defence treaty that gave Aden a substantial military guarantee in the event of renewed clashes with its three Arabian neighbours. On Palestine, the South Yemenis and the Russians have common ground, but not identical positions. In the early post-independence years the Soviet Union was willing to endorse the Palestinian movement, but not the PLO: Soviet official recognition of the PLO came only in October 1981. The two sides repeated calls for Israeli withdrawal from occupied territories and condemned the Camp David agreement. But disagreements remained on aims and tactics. On aims, the PDRY supported the call for a 'secular democratic Palestine', a unitary state that would have denied the Israeli population their own state: the Russians had never accepted this, and continue to argue for a two-state solution. The South Yemenis have also given training facilities to elements of the PFLP guerrilla group who have been responsible for terrorist acts; the Russians do not endorse these and have criticised a number of such Palestinian actions. The old problem of Soviet divergence from Arab nationalism therefore remains, albeit this time in a 'left' rather than a 'right' way.[33]

These regional issues aside, the PDRY and the Soviet Union have a common view of international issues and the PDRY has supported most Soviet positions in the UN. For years the South Yemenis denied that they were going to sign a Friendship and Co-operation Treaty with the Soviet Union, on the grounds that such a formal agreement was not needed and that the previous example of states which had signed such treaties, such as Egypt, was not a positive one. The decision to sign a treaty in 1979 was taken, so it was later said, on the personal initiative of Abdul-Fattah Isma'il and without the collective consent of the YSP leadership. The *rapprochement* of the two countries none the less illustrates the working out of pressures that are evident in a variety of other Third World countries, i.e. they illustrate the factors encouraging the Cuban model. These can be summarised here, by way of conclusion.

Conclusions

(1) Despite initial intentions, it proved impossible for the NLF to pursue a model of political and socio-economic development distinct from the orthodox 'non-capitalist' one. Once it broke with the patterns of Nasserism and the Ba'th, and after some years of uncertainty, the NLF accepted the path suggested to it by the Soviet Union. A similar process of increasing realism could be detected in Cuba after the Guevarist experiment of the 1960s, and in China with the 'four modernisations' of the late 1970s, despite China's foreign policy disagreements with Moscow.

(2) The alliance with the Soviet Union has been imperative for reasons of military survival. Similar concerns also operated in Cuba, as they increasingly do in Angola, Mozambique and Nicaragua. China cannot offer either the sophisticated weapons or the naval protection which the Soviet Union can provide. This elementary strategic reality would have operated even without the alliances established by China with such opponents of South Yemen as the Shah, Numeri, Haile Selassie and Sultan Qabus of Oman.

(3) While seeking to protect and influence radical Third World allies, the Soviet Union remains cautious about its own ability to support them economically and about the underlying pattern of social and political change in these states. In the Soviet view, South Yemen has not yet entered the category of such states as Cuba, Vietnam or, in earlier times, Mongolia. It is neither ruled by a communist party nor by a party that is yet transforming itself into such a party: the internal transformation process is by no means complete and may, as the case of Abdul-Fattah Isma'il showed, even suffer setbacks. The history of Soviet relations with Egypt and other nationalist states, as well as with South Yemen, suggests that it is above all else the evaluation of the party and its leadership which determine Soviet views of the country as a whole. Yet the Soviet Union-PDRY alliance has stood the test of over ten years of collaboration and both states have considerable confidence in each other. If the degree of advance along the 'Cuban' path is still partial, the underlying 'orientation' has, to date, been consistent.

Notes

1. At the funeral of Leonid Brezhnev in November 1982, the Heads of State of six leading 'socialist-oriented' states were placed immediately after the core-members of

the Soviet bloc in the official list of mourners: these states were Afghanistan, Ethiopia, South Yemen, Angola, Mozambique, Nicaragua; *Soviet News*, 17 Nov. 1982.

2. The PDRY's membership of the Arab League was suspended, at Saudi instigation, after the twin crises in North and South Yemen in June 1978. The PDRY was readmitted after the signing of the Egyptian-Israeli peace treaty.

3. For a characteristic official US view of the PDRY see Central Intelligence Agency, National Foreign Assessment Center, *Patterns of International Terrorism: 1980* (Washington, DC, 1981).

4. On the Cuban process see Andrés Suárez, *Cuba: Castroism and Communism 1959-1966* (MIT Press, Cambridge, Massachusetts, 1967); K. S. Karol, *Guerrillas in Power* (Cape, London, 1971); Carmelo Mesa-Lago, *Cuba in the 1970s* (University of New Mexico, Albuquerque, 1976).

5. Thus the '*microfracción*' of Anibal Escalante was removed from the Cuban leadership in 1965, while Abdul-Fattah Isma'il fell from the PDRY Presidency in 1980.

6. Soviet aid to the PDRY up to 1981 of just over $200 million is small compared to amounts given to Iran ($1,165 million), Iraq ($705 million) or Syria ($770 million): figures from US State Department, *Soviet and East European Aid to the Third World, 1981* (Feb. 1983).

7. On Soviet relations with the Arabian Peninsula see Stephen Page, *The USSR and Arabia* (Central Asian Research, London, 1971), and Aryeh Yodfat, *The Soviet Union and the Arabian Peninsula* (Croom Helm, London, 1983).

8. Soviet nomenclature distinguishes between *sredni vostok*, 'central east', comprising Turkey, Iran and Afghanistan, and *blizhni vostok*, or 'near east', comprising the Arab world. The former is more vital for Soviet strategic and economic interests.

9. Among many studies on Soviet-Arab relations see especially Karen Dawisha, *Soviet Policy toward Egypt* (Macmillan, London, 1979), and Hélène Carrère d'Encausse, *La Politique Soviétique au Moyen Orient, 1955-1975* (Fondation Nationale des Sciences Politiques, Paris, 1975).

10. I have discussed this at greater length in *Threat from the East? Soviet Policy from Afghanistan and Iran to the Horn of Africa* (Penguin, Harmondsworth, 1982).

11. For the earlier formulations see Hélène Carrère d'Encausse and Stuart Schram, *Marxism and Asia* (Penguin, Harmondsworth, 1969).

12. Jerry Hough, *Soviet Leadership in Transition* (Brookings, Washington, DC, 1980), p. 165.

13. V. Chirkin and Y. Yudin, *A Socialist-oriented State, Instrument of Revolutionary Change* (Progress, Moscow, 1978); Anatoly Dinkevich, 'Principles and Problems of Socialist Orientation in the Countries of Asia and Africa', *Soviet News*, 16 Oct. 1979; Sylvia Edgington, 'The State of Socialist Orientation', *Soviet Union/Union Soviétique* (Oct. 1981).

14. *International Herald Tribune*, 21 Apr. 1981. For more general background see Michael MccGwire and John McDonnell (eds.) *Soviet Naval Influence* (Praeger, New York, 1977).

15. On the background history of the NLF see Joseph Kostiner, 'Arab Radical Politics: The Qaumiyyun al-Arab and Marxists in South Yemen's Turmoil, 1963-1967', *Middle East Studies* (Oct. 1982); and my *Arabia without Sultans* (Penguin, Harmondsworth, 1974), Chapters 6-8.

16. *Current Digest of the Soviet Press* (hereafter *Current Digest*), vol. XIX, no. 48.

17. Commentary and documents of the Fourth Congress in Naif Hawatma, *Azmat al-Thawra fi Yaman al-Junub* (Al-Tali'a, Beirut, 1968).

18. The first official agreements on Soviet party assistance to the National Front were signed in 1970. BBC, *Summary of World Broadcasts*, ME/3396/A/11.

19. Documents in 'Al-Jabha al-Qawmiya: Al-Tandhim al-Siasi al-Muwahhad', *Al-Mu'tamar al-Tawhidi, Oktobr 1975* (Beirut, 1976).
20. *Barnamaj al-Hizb al-Ishtiraki al-Yamani* (Aden, 1978).
21. For further analysis see my 'The People's Democratic Republic of Yemen' in G. White, R. Murray and C. White (eds.), *Revolutionary Socialist Development in the Third World* (Wheatsheaf, Brighton, 1983).
22. *Current Digest*, vol. XXIV, no. 47.
23. For a contemporary account by an Arab journalist see Nabil Hadi, *18 Sa'at Ta'rikhiya 'ind Bab al-Mandab* (Beirut, 1978).
24. Text in *Soviet News*, 13 Nov. 1979, and *Current Digest*, vol. XXXI, no. 43.
25. Detailed analysis of the South Yemeni economy is given in World Bank, *People's Democratic Republic of Yemen. A Review of Economic and Social Development* (Washington, DC, 1979) and in Moshe Efrat, 'The People's Democratic Republic of Yemen: Scientific Socialism on Trial in an Arab Country' in Peter Wiles (ed.), *The New Communist Third World* (Croom Helm, London, 1982). See also Maxine Molyneux, *State Policies and the Position of Women Workers in the PDRY* (ILO, Geneva, 1982).
26. These are figures for *disbursed* aid as at 31 December 1980. Source: UN, *PDRY-Agricultural Sector Memorandum*, Report no. 4006-YDR, p. 30.
27. For Soviet assessments of the PDRY economy see the article by Naumkin in *Economy, Society and Culture in Contemporary Yemen* (Croom Helm, forthcoming).
28. Alexei Chistyakov, 'PDRY: Towards Consolidation of Economy', *Asia and Africa Today*, no. 1 (1980).
29. International Institute for Strategic Studies, London, *The Military Balance 1980-81*.
30. *The Times*, 18 Nov. 1981. In the late 1970s some increase in the number of Soviet military personnel was brought about by transferring of training programmes from the Soviet Union back to the PDRY. Higher figures of Soviet 'personnel' include families and civilian advisers.
31. *New Times*, no. 45 (1981), and Yodfat, *The Soviet Union and the Arabian Peninsula*.
32. Soviet support for the Omani guerrillas came to a peak in 1975, by which time the situation on the ground was overwhelmingly in the government's favour.
33. Other areas of divergence during the 1970s were Cambodia and the Western Sahara: South Yemen recognised the guerrilla forces in both cases as the legitimate government. The Soviet Union did not.

15 THE COMMUNIST PARTY OF THE PEOPLE'S DEMOCRATIC REPUBLIC OF YEMEN: AN ANALYSIS OF ITS STRENGTHS AND WEAKNESSES

John Duke Anthony

The People's Democratic Republic of Yemen (PDRY) has been governed by a militant, Marxist-oriented regime since June 1969. Although a local communist party, the People's Democratic Union (PDU), has existed for two decades, the party has never been the dominant power in South Yemeni (PDRY) politics. Throughout the past decade the PDU's status and role in national affairs have been highly circumscribed by the practical necessity, both legal and political, for it to operate in close association with a substantially larger organisation.

In 1983, the party enjoyed official status in the prevailing larger organisation — the Yemen Socialist Party (YSP). Communist party members hold one of five posts in the YSP's Politburo — which is both the YSP's and the government's highest policy-making body — and several seats on the YSP's 47-member Central Committee. In addition, party representatives sit in the non-party 111-member Supreme People's Council, which serves as a consultative body and debating forum for the government. These positions, in addition to other, less formal ones within the national power structure, accord the party a degree of influence in PDRY politics far beyond what its limited membership (estimated at less than five hundred) would suggest.

Evolution of the Communist Party

The party's headquarters, both before and since national independence in late 1967, have always been in the South Yemen capital of Aden. It has always been led by one of three sons of the Ba Dhib family, which comes from the Hadramawt region in eastern PDRY. The party's rank-and-file membership, moreover, has long been identified with support for the poorest and most disenfranchised among the country's working-class elements. Yet many of these elements have their roots not so much in Aden or in the tribal-oriented regions of the country's interior as in the villages of the neighbouring Yemen Arab Republic (North Yemen). These distinguishing characteristics of the party are from time to time the cause of difficulties between the party and some of the more nationally oriented, indigenous organisations. Similarly, the party's perenially close identification with youth and student groups has been at times a source of strength, certainly in terms of the social importance accorded those two constituencies, just as, at the level of real power, it is often a source of weakness.

The party was officially founded in October 1961 under the name of the People's Democratic Union (PDU) by Abdallah bin Abd al-Razzaq Ba Dhib — the first communist in Aden and eventually the foremost communist in all Arabia. Regarded from the outset as a communist organisation, the PDU supported a variety of groups that sought to cater to the needs of labourers and students. Given the severe restrictions placed on trade union organisations by British colonial authorities a year prior to the PDU's establishment, the party chose to establish a youth group instead: the Shabiba (Youth).

In October 1975, the ruling National Front Party (NF), in a major reform, aligned itself with both the PDU and al-Tali'a (the Vanguard), a comparatively small, pro-Syrian, Ba'thist group. With the NF retaining its position as the predominant group, they formed a new, much larger party, the United Political Organisation of the National Front (UPONF). The Shabiba retained, as it had since its merger with the NF in 1970, its official status, accorded in the 1970 constitution, in the 111-member Supreme People's Council. In addition, its members were permitted to retain previously held Ministerial posts — the Ministry of Education, the Ministry of Information and/or the Ministry of Culture and Tourism — in the government's Council of Ministers. Shabiba had been allotted portfolios after the 'Corrective Movement' of June 1969 and Abdallah Ba Dhib held such posts at different times in the 1970s, providing the Shabiba a degree of visibility and respectability that was highly valued by PDU members. As PDU leader, and as journalist, poet, administrator and teacher, his numerous cultural and educational contributions would leave their mark on other PDRY citizens as well. After his untimely death on 16 August 1976, the PDU leadership passed, in accordance with a previous agreement, to his younger brother and party co-founder, Ali Ba Dhib. Involved in PDU affairs from the beginning, and long identified with the

Shabiba, Ali Ba Dhib brought his own impressive credentials to the post of party leader. He was, in addition, a high-ranking PDRY government official in his own right.

During the next four years Ali Ba Dhib headed the PDU in a period of deepening Soviet influence in the country. The period was one when, largely because of that influence, a temporary *rapprochement* with Saudi Arabia, which had begun in 1976, lost momentum; when UPONF Secretary-General Abd al-Fattah Isma'il increased the frequency of contacts between the Communist Party of the Soviet Union (CPSU) and the UPONF; and when a Treaty of Friendship and Co-operation between the Soviet Union and PDRY was signed on 25 October 1979 at the end of an official visit by Isma'il to Moscow.

Of even greater significance, however, were events on the domestic front. In October 1978, for example, Isma'il and his supporters oriented the UPONF more directly along the path of 'scientific socialism'. At its First Congress, the UPONF changed its name to Yemen Socialist Party (YSP) and reorganised itself along the lines of Soviet-style Marxist-Leninist organisations found elsewhere. Moreover, the YSP constitution adopted at the congress accorded PDU members official status in the YSP's Politburo and Central Committee.

A significant PDU achievement was the election of its new Secretary-General, Ali Ba Dhib, to the YSP's powerful, eight-man Politburo. In addition, Ba Dhib was appointed to two other important posts: Secretary of the Ideology Department of the Secretariat of the YSP's 47-member Central Committee, and Deputy Prime Minister (one of three) in the government's Council of Ministers. These achievements, the high point of official communist influence in PDRY politics, were short-lived however. Indeed, they lasted only until April 1980, when Isma'il, long-time collaborator with the PDU/Shabiba on ideological, cultural and foreign policy matters, was ousted from his positions as YSP Secretary-General and Head of State, and replaced by Prime Minister Ali Nasir Muhammad al-Hasani.

The Post-Isma'il Balance of Power

The transition from the Isma'il era to that of Ali Nasir has been swift, far-reaching and, in mid-1983, on-going. The process itself was facilitated by Ali Nasir's use of his posts as *de facto* Head of State, Prime Minister, Member and Chairman of the YSP's Politburo and Central Committee, and Chairman of the Supreme People's Council eleven-man Presidium to convene an extraordinary congress of the YSP in October 1980. Elections for a new Presidium confirmed Ali Nasir in the YSP positions he had assumed upon the ouster of Isma'il.

One other revelation of the 1980 election was a substantial decline in popularity for Ba Dhib and other PDU/Shabiba stalwarts, largely due to their previous close association with Isma'il. Ali Ba Dhib has since remained active as a senior government official, YSP member and lecturer at the PDU-dominated Higher Institute for Scientific Socialism in Aden (also known as the Party School), but in recognition of the electoral results he was dropped from the YSP Politburo.

Abu Bakr Ba Dhib, Ali Ba Dhib's younger brother and an adviser to Ali Nasir, was appointed in his place. Some observers viewed this shake-up among the PDRY's political elites as a major setback for the pro-Soviet and pro-North Yemen factions in PDRY politics. Others, however, viewed the departure of the pro-Isma'il faction as having been offset by the appointment to what would henceforth be only a five-man YSP Politburo of two other (non-PDU) Marxists — one as a full member, the other as an alternate. Hence, depending on the issue before the Politburo and on which members were present, it remained theoretically possible that positions originating with the PDU representative could become government policy. Balanced against such a potential combination, however, were other Politburo members who placed less emphasis on ideological or pro-Soviet considerations than on personal, regional and factional variables. Nevertheless, although the two founding members of the PDU were no longer in the forefront, members of the PDU and a number of other prominent leftists previously unassociated with Isma'il retain an important measure of influence within the state's ruling councils.

The Role of the Communist Party

Besides the several reasons already mentioned, three other attributes explain the party's limited role in the PDRY: the party's less than fully nationalist credentials owing to its consistently pro-Soviet orientation; its exceptionally small membership; and its geographic base, which, being centred mainly on Aden, compares poorly with the country-wide breadth and depth of the YSP. In 1983, these characteristics continued to constrain the PDU in terms of its overall acceptance and effectiveness in PDRY society.

Another factor dates from the pre-independence period. Many YSP members have remarked that it is difficult for them, in policy matters, to accord PDU leaders and members the kind of respect that others receive for the roles they played in liberating Aden from colonial rule. Many PDU members, to be sure, are too young to have participated in the independence movement. Others, however, are considered to have deliberately avoided the armed struggle that, from 1963 to 1967, was waged against the British and other groups in Aden and against the traditional, tribal-oriented rulers in the interior. Although local and Arab nationalist leaders urged Yemenis to side with one or another of the several guerrilla groups, the vast majority of PDU members remained in urban Aden and refused to join forces, either there or in the more rugged regions of the interior, with anyone. The PDU leadership, although never eschewing violence as an appropriate revolutionary tactic, thus produced few practitioners of violence within its own ranks and, in comparison with most other groups, suffered few casualties. In their defence, PDU leaders have explained that the revolutionary situation in the early to mid-1960s was one that called for tactical flexibility and a division of labour. Their strength, they emphasise, has never been in their numbers but, rather, in their organisational and journalistic skills, in their role as liaison with kindred organisations abroad, and in their proven ability to provide an ideological orientation for a given objective. It has been primarily these attributes, among others, that have earned the PDU its official status, its relative autonomy and its influence over policy matters and government activities.

In education and culture, as in national political life, the PDU has wielded a degree of influence far in excess of its numbers. As an example, PDU lecturers at the Higher Institute for Scientific Socialism in Aden have provided doctrinal and organisational training in accordance with Marxist-Leninist principles for many YSP members. In an effort to limit the role of Soviet-bloc instructors at the Institute, they have used their connections with other communist parties in Lebanon, Sudan and Iraq to recruit lecturers who are Arabs.

Not the least of the PDU's roles, however, have been those of obtaining scholarships for South Yemeni students seeking further training abroad and in obtaining medical help from socialist-bloc countries for government and other PDRY leaders, The PDU, in short, has played the role of agent and broker — material, ideological, cultural, educational, political — for both the Soviet Union and an important segment of the South Yemeni people.

Whether the PDU's new leader, Abu Bakr Ba Dhib, can match, let alone surpass, the influence and political longevity of his two older brothers is impossible to predict. It is significant, however, that he, like his predecessors, has become the leading communist in both the NF/YSP and government. Even so, the nature and extent of his role in the period ahead will depend, just as much as his brothers' did, on the personal relationships he and the PDU as a group can establish with the far more numerous, and at times quite differently oriented, members of the YSP mainstream.

Whether, also, the PDU would be able to maintain, let alone increase, its previous influence over national policy questions had, by 1983, come to depend on whether changes in the international environment would diminish its influence generally. Certainly, a less visibly prominent role seemed necessary if the regime's efforts to improve relations with Saudi Arabia and the Gulf states — and, towards that end, with North Yemen and Oman — were to succeed.

During 1982, efforts to effect a *rapprochement* with San'a' and Muscat were more numerous and successful than any since the short-lived reconciliation with Saudi Arabia in 1976. An agreement between the PDRY and Oman concluded on 27 October signalled an end to nearly fifteen years of mutual enmity. A joint draft constitution calling for unity between the two Yemens, which pointedly made no reference either to 'socialism' or to the kind of economic system which might be adopted, was completed and submitted to their respective governments for discussion, debate and amendment prior to a referendum in each of the countries. And the YSP, during its sixth annual meeting in May, went to greater lengths than in previous years to stress peaceful co-existence with the PDRY's neighbours.

The pragmatic tone to YSP and PDRY government policy that these initiatives implied was evidence of a national need for financial assistance from the country's more economically endowed neighbours to the north. It was indicative, as well, of the force of two other factors: (1) an awareness, even among YSP and PDU stalwarts, of the relatively limited political and diplomatic dividends produced by their more doctrinaire approach to international relations during the previous half-decade; and (2) Soviet encouragement of such overtures to the PDRY's wealthier Arab neighbours. Behind the latter phenomenon was Moscow's preference for avoiding the necessity of providing the level of additional financial assistance needed from its own funds and, also, a hope that Soviet Union-Gulf states relations might improve as a consequence.

In the PDRY's relationships with countries outside the Arabian Peninsula, however, a substantially different foreign policy tactic was pursued. Both the YSP and the PDU, as cases in point, not only retained but broadened and deepened their links with a dozen or more Arab, African and Asian communist parties, as well as European and Latin American parties. During the course of the year, YSP Chairman Ali Nasir Muhammad al-Hasani completed an extensive tour of the Soviet Union and several other Eastern-bloc countries, signing new agreements and solidifying bilateral party and governmental links at each stop along the way. He devoted special personal attention to increasing YSP co-operation with kindred political groupings in Syria, Lebanon, Algeria, Ethiopia, France and Cuba. In February 1982, on behalf of the World Peace Council, he hosted a major international conference in Aden devoted to 'the Middle East and the dangers of the imperialist military build-up'.

At the intra-regional level, the nucleus around which many of these activities revolved was the alliance, established in August 1981, which grouped the PDRY, Libya and Ethiopia as joint signatories to a Treaty of Friendship and Co-operation. The first meeting of the Tripartite Supreme Council, the highest organ of the alliance, was held in Aden in May 1982 and presided over by Ali Nasir Muhammad. In the discussions that ensued the parties reiterated the essentially strategic nature of the alliance, signifying that its specific purposes remained their joint opposition to the Camp David agreements, imperialism, reactionary regimes and Zionist designs on Arab lands, on one hand, and, on the other, the more general goal of making it difficult for their adversaries to attack or undermine them in isolation.

The YSP and PDU, as in previous years, were simultaneously active in developing bilateral relations with the CPSU. The frequency of visits between the two countries' party officials, functionaries of their supreme organs of state power, and representatives of their respective parliamentary bodies reached an all-time high. At a less visible level, there occurred an equally impressive exchange of working visits between their respective youth groups, *World Marxist Review* journalists, and officials of their Ministries of Interior, Planning and Justice.

The event of most tangible relevance to the PDRY's pressing economic needs, however, was the third annual meeting in Aden on 6 April 1982 of the Soviet-PDRY Standing Committee on Economic Co-operation. The Committee, established at the time of the 1979 Treaty of Friendship and Co-operation, reached an agreement on launching a range of new activities aimed at strengthening industrial and agricultural development in the PDRY, as well as planning and technical training. The level of mutual interest and involvement that these visits manifested demonstrated how little in the PDRY's general foreign policy orientation had changed in terms of its relationship with Moscow. Some 1,500 Soviet military and technical personnel remained in the country alongside a similar number of East Germans in the state security apparatus and a comparable contingent of Cubans working as advisers in the popular militias and as physicians and paramedics at health centres throughout the country. The nature and extent of such a foreign presence provided ample testimony to the Eastern bloc's continuing stake in the PDRY's stability, security and development. It was an indication as well that the interests at stake for the bloc remained as strategic and ideological as before and — notwithstanding the changes in the PDRY's relationships with neighbouring countries — of how minimal were the immediate prospects for their lessening in any fundamental way.

16 THE GENESIS OF THE CALL FOR YEMENI UNITY

Sultan Nagi

After his 1911 agreement with the Turks which gave him mediatised status, Imam Yahya despatched letters to the Aden Protectorate chiefs in which he stressed his ancestral claims to all Southern Arabia and called on those holding documents from his predecessors to renew their allegiance to the central Yemeni authority.[1] In 1914 the Anglo-Turkish Convention delimiting the frontier between Turkish and British Yemen was ratified. From this time is dated the political division of Greater Yemen into 'South' and 'North', which still pertains up to the present.

The final dismemberment of Ottoman power at the end of the First World War enabled North Yemen to become independent and the Anglo-Turkish Convention was rejected by Imam Yahya from the outset. He pursued the traditional Yemeni claim to possession of the whole Yemen, including Aden and the Protectorates, and his forces promptly overran several of the Protectorate states. In 1923 he issued a manifesto to the chiefs and the people of Hadramawt and the Aden Protectorate stressing the unity of Yemen, a territory with one people, one religion and one language, and called on them to return to the fold of their motherland.[2] In the next year he even asked the British government to give general recognition to his claims — to his ancestral land of Aden and the Protectorate. He merely offered certain concessions as regards the way he would administer this southern area and safeguard British interests in Aden over which he, nevertheless, still claimed ultimate sovereignty.[3]

It seemed that the British government itself was contemplating the recognition of some of the Imam's claims. As early as 1919 one of the British alternatives had crystallised in the abandonment of the whole Protectorate to the Imam, apart from Aden's immediate defensive hinterland, notably Lahej. In 1921 the meeting of Middle East experts at the Cairo Conference had proposed offering Yahya a treaty recognising his claims down to that limit.[4] That proposal came forward once more the next year. The aim was to bring the Imam into the British orbit by making Aden his principal outlet. The rationale of this British thinking is well explained by Jacob when he says:

The Genesis of the Call for Yemeni Unity 241

> With the exit of the Turks our borderline goes . . . The *raison d'être* of all these agreements [with the chiefs] no longer holds. An Arab King has come forward and claims these Arabs as his ancestral heritage . . . I believe we cannot be justly charged with a breach of faith if we let these go over and back to the Imam . . . The retention of our Arab stipendiaries . . . is to divide Islam against Islam . . . In the Yemen . . . Aden alone is British soil, and is isolated in one corner, and so the parcelling out of the interior is not our concern . . . A Yemen so unified will look to us in full confidence.[5]

However, this scheme was not carried out because the Resident of Aden, who held divergent views, managed later to fend it off; the result of which was a prolonged confrontation and armed clashes over the hinterland until the signing in 1934 of the San'a' treaty, by which both sides agreed to maintain the *status quo* of the frontier for a period of forty years.

Even this treaty had been drafted in a manner which did not involve a renunciation of the Imam's claims to sovereignty over any part of Greater Yemen. On the insistence of the Iman and his advisers the treaty provides that, should doubt arise on the interpretation, both parties 'shall rely on the Arabic text'. Article III became a source of trouble in later years when the British began to embark on their 'forward policy', in the Western Protectorate. By the *status quo* the British meant that the actual situation on the frontier, roughly established by the Anglo-Turkish Convention separating British Protectorate territory from the Imam's territory north of it, should be established for forty years. 'The Imam meant that the nature of the situation existing in the southern (British) part of the Yemen should be maintained for that period . . .' The valid Arabic meaning of Article III would mean to an Arab, 'The settlement of the question of the southern Yemeni area is deferred . . .'[6] Whatever may be the case, the 1934 *status quo* treaty, like its predecessor, the 1914 Anglo-Turkish Convention, reinforced the process of consolidating the opposition to Imamic claims in the Protectorate area. Professor Gavin concludes: 'given tribal resistance and British dependence on the tribes, a Protectorate antithesis to the Imamic thesis began to emerge and with it a nexus of interests involved in South Arabian or South Yemeni separatism'.[7]

When Britain embarked on her 'forward policy' in the Aden hinterland it naturally angered the Imam who saw in it a flagrant breach of the terms of the San'a' treaty. His claims continued unabated, for example, in a brief prepared for the Minister of State for his conversation with Prince Saif al-Islam Abdullah who was in London about one month before the assassination of Imam Yahya to discuss the issue: the British Under-Secretary told his Minister that the Imam's attitude remained adamant and that he still regarded the whole southern area 'as indivisible from the Yemen'.[8] Throughout the talks the Prince kept labelling the area at issue as 'al-jiha al-janubiya min al-yaman' ('the southern part of the Yemen').[9] In another set of minutes written about one month after the 1948 *coup d'état* to the Secretary of State, who had asked for a full account of the situation in the Yemen, Cable's last paragraph reads: 'The Yemen's importance to us is derived mainly from the nuisance value of Yemeni claims on the Aden Protectorate and on Aden itself.'[10]

When Ahmad succeeded his father he did not hesitate to take up a more active and uncompromising attitude. Near the end of this monarch's life the extent of Yemeni claims, sentimentally at least, had reached unparalleled bounds, corresponding roughly to that area populated by the descendants of Qahtan:

> During the winter of 1959 the Legation of the Mutawakkilite Kingdom of Yemen in Washington startled officers of the State Department concerned with Arab affairs by sending out a handsome and unusual holiday greeting card. On an outline map of the Arabian Peninsula the location of the traditional . . . Yemeni capital, Sanaa, was represented by a small jewel, and a shaded area appeared to define the extent of the kingdom's putative territory. The shading encompassed, in addition to Yemen as delimited on conventional maps of the time, Aden and the entire Aden Protectorate, Dhofar, Muscat and Oman, and the Trucial Coast . . . a generous portion of the Empty Quarter . . . and Nejran and Asir . . .[11]

A British view as sympathetic to the Yemeni claims as Jacob's in the 1920s was expressed by the first Resident and Agent in Hadramawt. When the federal idea was first mooted Ingrams wrote in critical vein. It is difficult, he says, 'to see how a federation organised in this way could ever look anything but a disguised colony in a world which no longer likes colonialism . . . If full federation of Colony and Protectorate were eventually carried into effect, there would be a grave danger of losing Aden itself,' he concludes.[12] When he published his book *The Yemen* in 1963 he used the term al-Yemen for the three territories which were generally referred to as the Yemen, the Western Aden Protectorate and Aden. 'I use it as the Arab geographers and historians used it to designate the province of Arabia known by that name but covering the three political divisions in effect created by the British.'[13] Finally, Ingrams commented in 1966 that the hybrid Federation and the deliberate British policy of imposition of such foreign ideas of government on the people 'had really been reached by a process of unconscious self-deception through the distortion of history'.[14]

A major factor in the awakening of Yemeni consciousness among the Arab people of Aden was the nature of the ethnic composition of the colony's population since its British Indian occupation. British India's most significant legacy was the foreign stamp it had left on the Colony and its hinterland. In the 1920s, for example, an Assistant Resident admitted that Aden was becoming Indianised. Its Post Offices were posted with notices in Hindustani and Gujarati: Arabic appeared to be a foreign language and Arab history was 'not taught in the Government schools. Are we afraid of their studying their national heroes?'[15] In the 1930s a Colony Governor records for us the bitter complaint of a prominent Adeni Arab:

> What has India done for us? Nothing. We are backward . . . and the fault is entirely with India. Education is essential, is essential to all people and to us more than most, for we have none. Where is it? You have seen the schools, you have seen the Indians who teach. Where are the Arab teachers? Oh, I know that you will answer that we must be patient and that we have none in Aden, but they can be brought from other Arab countries, and until we have competent Arabic-speaking teachers of our own language we shall make no progress . . . It is a disgrace, and for that disgrace we have India to thank. We are not part of that country geographically, and we are not the same people and we do not speak the same language.[16]

The picture was not better, if not worse, at the end of the 1940s. When the first British Agent in the Protectorate arrived in the town, he instantly observed that, with the exception of a minority of local Arabs whose only home was Aden, the whole 'polyglot mass' of Indians, Somalis, Europeans and others was 'parasitic'. He found that 'within this curiously mixed and transitory society' the Indians occupied a special position. Aden was, in a sense, 'an Anglo-Indian colony, where it was largely British and Indian hands that made the wheels go round'. The British official concluded, 'I began to understand how deeply and multiply divided society in Aden was, how barely one man in five living there cared a fig for its future . . .'.[17]

In fact the first manifestation of the growing concern for the future of Aden and its Arab Yemeni identity could be traced back to the beginning of the 1930s when brisk movements for the formation of a number of cultural and reform clubs were in full swing. Muhammad Ali Luqman, the then headmaster of Aden's only junior secondary school, was the driving force behind that cultural and reform movement. In his brochure 'Is This A Scrap Of Paper?', Junnis, an anonymous publisher (Luqman himself), wrote, 'No candidate has been sent up for the Matriculation examination of any University in eighty-four years, let alone succeeded.' As a first step, therefore, Luqman and his colleagues took on their shoulders the responsibility of approaching Arab kings and requested them to offer scholarships for some poor Adeni Arabs in the secondary schools of their countries. The first groups of students left Aden in 1936 and 1937 to Baghdad and Cairo respectively. A similar request was made to the Mahdi of the Sudan on 28 Rajab 1356AH (1937). The nationalistic and Yemeni tone in this letter from the Secretary of the Arab Islamic Reform Club is very apparent. The British Colony of Aden is described as 'the eye of Natural Yemen', and Natural Yemen is defined as 'Arabia Felix', extending from the eastern shores of the Red Sea to 'the eastern extremity of Hadramawt'.[18]

The political nature of these clubs is pinpointed by Ladislas Farago, a writer-traveller who visited the Colony in 1937. Farago was taken to many such Arab clubs where he began 'to live the life of an Arab intellectual'. He found more than a dozen, but the most important was the 'Arab Literature Club'. Although 'politics were officially barred from these clubs, and my Arab friends insisted that they were only intended for social purposes', Farago nevertheless had found that in them 'the Aden Arab's awakening political mind was formed'. It seemed to him 'that the British underestimated the importance of these political clubs' and he concludes, 'The walls of those allegedly non-political clubs were covered with highly political slogans, "Arabia for the Arabs," or "People of Arabia, Unite!"'[19]

The growing consciousness of the unity of Yemen among Yemeni intellectuals almost echoed the definition of the great geographer and historian al-Hamdani — written one thousand years previously. When a dispute broke out late in the 1930s between the Imam and the British over Shabwa in the border area, the editor of *Al-Hikma al-Yamaniya* wrote: 'It is stupid and insolent to ask whether Shabwa is part of the Yemen or Hadramawt or to think that Yemen and Hadramawt are two different things' and went on:

> God has ordained that Yemen's natural boundaries should not be obscure and ambiguous. The Yemen is encircled by sea from the west, south and the east. All that is included within these boundaries up to the tip of southern Hejaz is the cradle of Yemen. Hadramawt is not an island in the Indian Ocean so as to consider Shabwa as part of Hadramawt and not of Yemen.[20]

Close contacts and co-ordination between the Yemeni reformers in San'a' and Aden were maintained in the late 1930s. Important Arabic books on political thought used to be smuggled into Yahya's 'closed' kingdom from Aden. In the latest documentary book on the 1948 revolution, one of the participants in the *coup d'état* testified that when he, Zubairi and the Wazirs made their pilgrimage to Mecca in 1357AH (1938) they met there and consulted a number of Adeni reformers among whom was Ahmad al-Asnag, the President of the Arab Islamic Club. The first consignment of smuggled books sent by al-Asnag consisted of seventeen copies of al-Kawakibi's *Tawabi' al-Istibdad (The Nature of Oppression)*.[21] After the development of this rather discreet movement in Imamic Yemen into a political party (Free Yemeni Party) it was not unnatural that its formation should be proclaimed in Aden, in 1944, by its vanguard group which had managed to escape to the Colony.

Luqman's *Fatat al-Jazira* willingly sponsored the exiles' cause. He himself was a founder member and through his newspaper a campaign was vehemently and relentlessly waged by the Free Yemenis against the Imam and his autocratic rule. The Imam protested to the British and both Luqman and the Free Yemenis were warned and ordered to cease their criticism and incitement against the Mutawakkilite Kingdom. To circumvent the prohibition imposed on their political activities, Luqman (who was the first Adeni Arab to study law) advised them to change the party's name to the 'Grand Yemeni Association', and register it as a cultural club. When the Governor approved the licensing of *Sawt al-Yaman*, the Association newspaper, he warned the Free Yemenis that their continued residence in Aden was conditional on their 'good behaviour and on abstention from any incitement of Yemenis to rebel'.[22] The GYA was founded on 4 January 1946. In its constitution the aims were the re-unification of the sons of Yemen, the dissemination of brotherhood and co-operation and guidance in matters of religion, morality and culture.[23]

However, *Fatat* remained the chief campaigner. The most important material was contained in a series of front-and back-page articles by Luqman himself. His recurring theme was the demand for a constitution and a constitutional government. In his highly analytical and critical series on 'the means for the advancement of South Arabia' and the 'future of Yemen', he discusses the problems of the area as a whole. He declares that he was acting out of love and affection for Yemen, 'his and his fore-fathers' country'. To Luqman the two terms 'Yemen' and 'South Arabia' are interchangeable: 'The hearts of the sons of South Arabia are aching, injured and bleeding. The question on everybody's lips in Aden, Lahej, Hadramawt and everywhere in Yemen is what is a constitution?'[24] It is in these articles and others written by leaders of the Free Yemenis and published in *Fatat*, but not in *Sawt al-Yaman*, that one can detect the Free Yemenis' general idea of a united Yemen, and the British apprehension of the idea as expressed by the Colony's Chief Secretary on the eve of the 1948 revolution. On 14 January 1948 Mr A. L. Kirkbride, who was on leave in London, called on the Under-Secretary of State to discuss with him a telegram from the Governor of Aden reporting the imminence of a revolution in San'a'. The Under-Secretary submitted to his Minister minutes on his discussion with Aden's Chief Secretary and ended:

> I asked Mr Kirkbride whether he thought that such a change of regime was desirable. He replied that it might possibly be of some benefit to the inhabitants of Yemen, by introducing a more democratic and progressive Government. In any case a change of regime would be unlikely to benefit British interests since the more progressive Yemenis are also nationalist, with irredentist aspirations. He mentioned that some of the Yemeni exiles in Aden were already talking of a united South-West Arabia which should comprise Yemen, the Aden Protectorate and Aden itself.[25]

A polemic had raged over the concept of 'Natural Yemen'. An anonymous person under the name of Mr Frank addressed the Free

Yemenis: 'What is this Yemenism that you are imposing on others? As you are proud to be Yemenis, so too we are proud to be Hadramis in as much as Egyptians, Syrians and Hijazis are proud of their respective countries.' The writer went so far as to ask the Free Yemenis to go back home if they wanted to continue talking about their Yemenism. One of the Free Yemenis' leaders replied:

> You and I are true Arabs from the Yemen, the cradle of all Arabs. Is there any difference between a San'ani, a Rada'i, an Adeni or a Hadrami with regard to affilation to the homeland? All of them are from Yemen, by which I mean 'Natural Yemen', with its fixed and known boundaries. Politics has nothing to do with this fact because we know that Hadramawt and other parts are now politically separated [from the homeland] but history and geography are different from politics!

Barraq went on to say, 'My dear Mr Frank, you are a Yemeni no matter how much you fled from your greater homeland or how much you disavowed your Yemeni forefathers. I do not think that I offended you or any of my Hadrami brothers when I said that we are brothers in descent, blood and homeland, unless you despise the Yemenis, even though one of them.' However, 'Mr Frank' remained adamant and his last article was entitled 'The Hadramis today have their own nationality.'[26]

After the failure of the 1948 revolution, many of its leaders, including some of the Free Yemenis, lost their heads to the executioner's sword and the majority of the remainder (e.g. Nu'man, Iryani and Sallal) were thrown into the Hajja dungeons. The party regrouped itself in Aden, in 1951, under a new leadership and the new name of the 'Yemeni Union'. Its concept of greater Yemen or the Yemeni homeland was further developed and became more outspoken; for example, al-Hakimi, the party's new leader, wrote, 'The Yemeni Union firmly believes that the cause of Aden, the Sultanates and the Emirates of this South is the party's cause; that Aden and the whole of this South is Al-Yaman; that Yemen, Aden and all these Emirates and Sultanates are the great Yemeni homeland.'[27] Hakimi's ideas are better and clearly embodied in articles (1) and (2) of the National Covenant of 1956 which emphasised the indivisibility of the Yemeni homeland and that no cession or relinquishment of its parts should be permitted.[28] Nevertheless, the Yemeni Union priority was the liquidation of the imamate, as a former Aden

Governor truly remarked, 'They feel that the removal of the Hamid-Ud-din dynasty from the throne of the Yemen and the substitution of a democratic . . . form of Government will remove the principal obstacle to eventual union between the two big South-west Arabian territories.'[29]

With the exception of the cultural and reform clubs of the 1930s there was not much organised political opinion in the Colony — but after the Second World War Arab political consciousness began to be felt. The first political movement to be set up was organised and led by Shaikh Abdullah Muhammad, an able and successful Pakistani lawyer and resident of Aden. Formed in 1947, the 'Muslim Association' was largely supported by Adenese and 'inclined to be Pan-Islamic in outlook'.[30] After Shaikh Abdullah's death the Muslim Association lost most of its drive and had, from a political angle, become merged in Luqman's newly formed 'Aden Association'. As the name implies, this party advocated Adenese independence. The Association was supported by all the leading families and represented merchants and elite opinion. It was willing to co-operate with British authorities for peaceful constitutional advance in the Colony.[31] As a result of its repeated demands the hitherto entirely nominated Legislative Council, introduced in 1947, was in future to include some elected elements. In the first election in 1955 three of the four elected members were candidates of the Association. Similarly, during the second election in 1959, eleven of the twelve elected Legco members were its candidates.

However, up till 1958, when it split into two groups, the Aden Association generally kept an open mind on the question of union with the Colony and the Protectorate, preferring to wait and see how the latter developed politically and economically.[32] The Aden Association was not opposed to unity as Muhammad Luqman's efforts have shown; they were opposed to tribal law replacing the constitutional safeguards of Aden, i.e. they disapproved the terms of the union but not the idea.

It is interesting to note that the initial split within this moderate and liberal organisation which had chosen to participate in the normal evolving political system of the post-war British Colonial Office pattern, eventually leading to an independent state, was over a trivial local issue, namely whether qat should be banned from Aden. Later, however, the determined British policy of imposing the merger between the Colony and the Protectorate played a crucial role in widening the cleavage within the Association, and finally alienated Luqman's faction in favour of Bayoomis' pro-British splinter group the United National Party. Luqman's attitude towards the Yemeni issue in general since the failure of the 1948 *coup d'état* and the formation, first of his Aden Association in 1950, and later its anti-Federation successor the 'People's Constitutional Congress' in 1961, remained consistently sympathetic to the Free Yemenis (later the Yemeni Union). When the British imprisoned the President of the Yemeni Union, al-Hakimi, in 1953, Luqman and his *Fatat* defended their case. As he had previously travelled with the first group of Free Yemeni leaders to San'a' after Yahya's assassination in 1948, so he now revisited the capital immediately after the 1962 September revolution and overthrow of the imamate, but this time on President Sallal's personal invitation in recognition of the old man's services for the Yemeni cause.[33]

The South Arabian League was constituted in 1950, under the leadership of Muhammad al-Jifri as President. The party was set up by the first generation of university graduates who had just returned from Egypt, Iraq and Sudan. The SAL advocated union between the Colony and the Protectorates. However, in 1955 this party platform underwent a fundamental change when some of its members began to advocate union with Imamic Yemen as well as with the Protectorates and then formed their own separate faction.[34] Though based in Aden and concerned with Adeni politics as much as with those in the Protectorate, the SAL in fact had its genesis in Lahej, the largest and most advanced Sultanate in the Protectorate. It reflected the ambition of the young, sophisticated Sultan Ali, a graduate of Victoria College in Egypt, to establish his pre-eminence in an independent South Arabia. When SAL's President, al-Jifri, went to Cairo in August 1956 the Governor of Aden issued an order expelling him from the Colony. On a personal plea from Sultan Ali, al-Jifri was allowed, the next year, to return to Lahej with the proviso that he would not engage in politics. But neither al-Jifri nor his SAL (and behind them Sultan Ali) observed the proviso. Ali had previously succeeded in sabotaging the first British proposals for a Federation of Sultanates and Amirates. When those proposals were put to a meeting of rulers in January 1954 his reaction was recorded, ' "They were like surrender terms dictated to a defeated enemy!" he said in a flurry of passion. "Do you think we want to become a colony of yours?" '[35] He wanted true South Arabian unity and independence.[36] But there are Yemeni intellectuals who genuinely believe that the SAL planted the seeds of division in South Yemen by taking an antagonistic attitude to the inhabitants of Aden, including its doyen politician Luqman. This attitude later infected some of the other political parties.

After the return of al-Jifri to Lahej, SAL's anti-British activities, particularly in the Protectorates, increased dramatically. Pamphlets inciting levies and government guards to desert and to mutiny were distributed about barracks and forts; schoolmasters were encouraged to instruct their pupils in anti-colonialism and many attempts were made to 'convert' officials and clerks. [37] In 1958 armed revolts broke out in the amirates bordering Imamic Yemen. 'Similar acts of harassment also took place elsewhere. Pamphlets were taken from Lahej and scattered about Abyan, inciting the inhabitants to murder the British and their "colonialist stooges".'[38] The anti-British activities of both SAL and Sultan Ali seemed to have brought them closer to Imam Ahmad. Having lost faith in the British, the SAL had turned for help to the Imam and struck a bargain behind their backs. An emissary from Ahmad was sent to the Governor of Aden and indicated to him the Imam's willingness to waive his ancestral claims over the Protectorate if the Federation proposals were to mean granting the Protectorate immediate independence.[39] The British declined the offer.

At the beginning of 1958 Egypt and Syria federated as the UAR, and then united in loose form with Mutawakkilite Yemen as the United Arab States, with the armies of all three countries under a single command. Crown Prince al-Badr stated in Cairo that his country's connection with the UAR 'would lead to the liberation of South Yemen'. The immediate effect of Yemen's association with Nasser, the leader of Arab nationalism, was tremendous in the Arab South. Every dissident prince or shaikh in the Protectorate or in exile in North Yemen was willing to consider union with Yemen if it put them under Nasser's banner. As the exiled rebel Shaikh Muhammad bin Aidrus of Yafa put it:

> It is the wish of the overwhelming majority of the inhabitants of the British-occupied southern parts of Yemen that they, too, be included in the United Arab States Federation, along with the rest of Yemen . . . In their opinion there is no 'South' separate from Yemen, and no federation save that freely entered into by the will of the Yemenite, Egyptian and Syrian people . . . The old arguments against union with the mother country 'until reforms have been achieved in Yemen' were no longer valid.

However, the most profound direct effect of the Yemeni connection with the UAR was on the policy of SAL with regard to the question of unity with North Yemen. SAL, which had always been opposed to union with Yemen, now announced its new policy as 'the liberation of the whole Arab South, natural Yemen, and its inclusion in the UAR'.[40]

In April 1958 the Governor of Aden ordered the arrest of al-Jifri and his two brothers, but al-Jifri and one of them were able to escape to North Yemen. Sultan Ali was soon to follow suit and live in exile in Cairo with the SAL leader. Trevaskis, who had ordered the arrest of the Jifris and neatly driven the Sultan to self-exile, explained his action as follows:

> Lahej had in fact become a Beidha. But this was not all. Following a surprise visit to Lahej by Al-Amri, the Yemeni Minister . . . Jifri left for Cairo . . . it was only on his return, a month later, that the purpose of his mission became common knowledge. Once he had obtained adequate support from other rulers it was, so we understood, Ali's intention to abrogate his treaties, declare Lahej a part of the United Arab States, invite the others to follow his example and so transfer themselves from British to Egyptian protection. With Lahej already a centre of open subversion, and the threat of an Egyptian protectorate on Aden's borders, the time for shrugging shoulders and persuasive argument had come to an end . . . Ali was too proud a person to remain after being humiliated by such a slap in the face. He lodged a formal protest and left almost immediately for London where he remained for some time in an unavailing essay to obtain redress from the British Government. Almost immediately after he had left London . . . the commander of the Lahej Regular Army, and most of his troops defected to the Yemen with the intention, so Cairo informed us, of forming a National Liberation Army . . . The last flimsy thread of gossamer linking us with Ali had broken. The British Government withdrew recognition from him, the Lahej electoral college . . . formally deposed him . . .[41]

However, Ali did not impress the intelligentsia. They saw him as promoting his personal power. Had he succeeded, he would have been only nominally and loosely connected with Egypt.

In 1959 the British set up the Federation of Arab Amirates of the South, comprising only six of the amirates, including Lahej itself under its new pro-British Sultan who had replaced Sultan Ali, but the primary place in this 'minor' federation was taken by the Sherif of Baihan, Britain's staunchest friend and a notorious anti-Yemen-unity figure. The SAL, with a new leader in the person of Sultan Ali, continued to be regarded by Nasser as the most important national party in the South up to 1960, when it was superseded, first by the Aden TUC (a political party in disguise), and then by the People's Socialist Party, the formal political front of the Aden TUC in 1962. After the expulsion of its leaders, and the inauguration of the British-orientated Federation on 11 February 1959, all deposed tribal leaders eventually found their way to the SAL which continued unabated its propoganda and 'little' wars in the Protectorates; the last major tribal armed revolt was that of Ahl Bubakr of upper Aulaqi — al-Jifri's country of origin — in 1960. By that time SAL had reverted to its original aim, namely the establishment of an independent South Arabia comprising Aden and the Protectorates, but not a united Yemen, thereby confirming to intellectuals its separatist sentiments. Nasser was misinformed about the constitutional movement in Aden which was pro-unity but opposed to tribal law. It was, moreover, influenced by Ghandi's example and abhorrence of violence. Would anybody castigate Ghandi as a non-patriot? Nasser later changed drastically his advisers on Yemeni affairs.

The United National Front (UNF) was formed in 1955 under the leadership of Muhammad Abdu Nu'man and a number of his young colleagues including Husain Bawazir, Muhammad Salim Ali, Abdu Khalil Sulaiman and Abdul Aziz Bawazir who would later play prominent roles in the labour movement and its political arm, the PSP. As its name implies the UNF, which initially started as a splinter of SAL, was actually 'an amalgamation of the Nationalists who insist on independence and will be content with nothing less, the left wing of the South Arabian League and a few Free Yemenis'. The Front's stated (but not constituted) policy was the total elimination of British rule and the union of Aden with the Protectorate, North Yemen and Muscat and Oman in a single independent state.[42] It was a Greater Yemen that they aspired to revive and create. The inclusion of Muscat and Oman was later dropped from the programme.

From the beginning, British officials tended to belittle the UNF leadership. They were labelled as a 'vociferous minority' that lacked common sense and were described as 'irresponsible demagogues'.[43] Later, however, when British officals began to realise that such unity programmes as that of the UNF really postulated an ultimate destiny for the Colony, the officials' assessment became more sober. They tried to explain the political and sociological factors that had led to this party's emergence as Trevaskis explained:

> A militant nationalist movement with a Yemeni flavour was clearly taking shape: led by young Adenis, mostly in their twenties . . . This new class of Adeni has tiptoed on to the scene almost unnoticed during the early spring of Nasserism. They . . . had profited by the better schooling available in Aden since the war . . . They were ready-made material for a nationalist movement and it is easy to understand how the revolutionary appeal of Nasserism affected them, as they looked at the small world of Aden with its privileged and comparatively affluent establishment of foreigners and old Adenis. They were mostly young clerks and students and when some of them formed a party called United National Front it was, at first, regarded with avuncular tolerance by their elders and betters . . . They were young and unknown, but had a hidden strength in their strategic deployment across the industrial and commercial face of Aden . . . they quickly set themselves up as champions of the workers' interests in opposition to colonialism which, in the industrial context, they interpreted as exploitation by foreign capitalists . . . By advising workers about their rights, or what rights to demand, and by involving themselves in the increasing number of disputes . . . these young men very soon won the confidence of workers . . . They recited the orthodox Nasserite creed, declaring their belief in Arab unity . . . they declared their determination to destroy colonialism and its agents. And then what? one would ask . . . Was it an independent Aden that they wanted? That would be absurd. South Arabia then? But that was part of the Yemen. Well, a greater Yemen, including Aden and South Arabia? . . . It was, of course, a greater Yemen that they wanted . . . Strip them of their Nasserisms and they were Yemeni nationalists.[44]

To translate its bigger aims into practical politics, the UNF's first action was to demand and agitate for the enfranchisement of Northern and Protectorate Yemenis in the first limited elections of 1955 for the few seats in the Legislative Council. Both categories, who by the definition of the colonial authorities were not 'Adenese', were excluded from participation in the Colony's political system.

Contrary to other minority ethnic foreign groups, they were 'constitutionally' regarded as aliens in Yemenite Aden. The Northern Yemenis were the largest group in the Colony, nearly one and a half times as many as the 'Adenese' (Aden-born Yemenis) and twice as many as the Protectorate citizens. In other words, the two 'non-Adenese' groups who formed about half of the population of the Colony were denied the right to vote or become citizens like their 'Adenese' brethren by accident of birth alone. When the UNF demands were not met the party campaigned for a boycott of the December 1955 Legislative Council elections. It was over this election issue that left-wing members of SAL broke away and joined the UNF. SAL's Adenese candidate for the Legco election, Abdul Rahman Girgirah, failed outright. The boycott in the 1959 election would be more successful; it would keep the poll down to a mere 27 per cent of the limited electorate of 21,500 out of a population of 180,000.

After a sudden visit to Imam Ahmad in Ta'izz to sound out his reaction to the Front's programme for the liberation of the South and then its eventual absorption into greater Yemen, the UNF President, Nu'man, was immediately deported from Aden. Although the Front's programme was not a feasible one for immediate action it was quite at odds with British long-term thinking at that time. As one British official put it: 'To come to terms with Yemeni nationalism we would need to surrender Aden and South Arabia to the Yemen.'[45] From the time of his deportation to North Yemen the former UNF President — who was replaced by Muhammad Salim Ali Abduh — was up to the 1962 revolution active in conducting a propaganda war against the colonial authorities in Aden through a newly opened 'South Yemeni Corner' in the Mutawakkilite Broadcasting Station. He was also active in meeting and organising defecting tribesmen and tribal leaders in Ta'izz as well as vouching for Adeni refugees. Even during the 1958 wave of bomb and grenade explosions in the Colony, one of his juvenile relatives was directly involved in the smuggling of such explosives into Aden. In March of that year a British officer was killed by a grenade thrown on his bed. Explosions continued to occur until July and a State of Emergency had to be declared. Some of those explosions were attributed either to SAL or the Yafa'i rebel chief Muhammad bin Aidrus, who at that time were co-ordinating their efforts in Ta'izz and Cairo and all clamouring loudly for Yemeni unity.

The UNF's wider Yemeni national goals and aspirations were

interlocked with the legal call for the establishment of trade unions, permissible under an ordinance enacted in the 1940s in accordance with the policy inaugurated by Lord Passfield in 1930 for all British colonies. The radical young UNF Adenese leaders were behind the organisation of almost all unions set up in 1955. By March 1956 there were 25 trade unions affiliated to the newly established Aden Trade Union Congress (ATUC). From the formation of this new workers' movement, it was dominated and controlled by the leading members of the UNF in their capacity as leaders of the recently formed trade unions. Members of the ATUC's Executive Committee were therefore office-bearers of the UNF, and the majority of members of the executive committees of individual trade unions were members of that party. The drastic action against the UNF President, Nu'man, in 1956 was thus ineffective because the whole leadership of the UNF had merely abandoned their labels as leaders of the young political party and were effectively absorbed in the newly formed ATUC. Zain Sadiq, a founder member of ther UNF, became the ATUC's first President. It was only later that British officials began to realise that there was something ominous about this relationship and that it was not analogous to the relationship between the Labour Party and the trade union movement in Britain. One had written, speaking of the Passfield policy as favouring the Arab brand of nationalism in Aden, that it 'illustrates the folly of introducing alien institutions to people with different traditions',[46] and another later remarked that the Aden labour movement was nothing like British trade unionism. It was 'an Arab movement through and through'. In Britain the Labour Party 'had been brought into being by the trade union movement as its political complement. In Aden the ATUC had been forged as the industrial weapon of the UNF.' He sarcastically added: 'It was no more British for assuming certain British poses than the young Arabs, who had graduated to its leadership from the ranks of the United National Front, were British for wearing collars and ties and boasting a command of conversational English.'[47]

The ATUC had come into being as an answer to the bad conditions of workers in Aden. Sir Tom Hickinbotham, the Governor of Aden during whose term of office the labour movement was formed, said that when he first came to Aden the general working conditions of the Arab workers

can only be described as disgraceful. There were no superannuation benefits, and as wages left no margin between income and expenditure, nothing could be saved against old age and sickness. There were no holidays with pay, . . . and the vast majority received no medical treatment or benefits through their employers. Labour relations . . . did not exist. There was no form of consultation between master and man and the authority of the master was absolute.[48]

From its inception the ATUC had tried to defend the interests of the workers. After failing to reach agreement with the employers the ATUC had resorted to strikes, but even then several of the leading members of the Congress 'worked indefatigably to end them. Without their help and understanding things would have been worse.'[49] The colonial authorities ordered a commission to be set up to inquire into the causes of the strikes. Its verdict was that the strikes were 'basically industrial in origin'.[50]

The most direct non-material benefit the young Adenese leadership of the ATUC was able to achieve for its comrade workers and brethren, the Northern and Protectorate Yemenis, was an acknowledged labour or professsional status by being registered as trade unionists in the Colony that had previously regarded them as aliens. As for political status, the ATUC leadership continued unabated its struggle for a wider franchise that would include them in Aden's formal political structure in the same way which other heterogeneous Commonwealth minority ethnic groups enjoyed in Yemenite Aden.

By 1958 the ATUC was the strongest nationalist force in Aden: it had virtually taken over the political stage from its moribund partner, the UNF. Its anti-British attitude had been strengthened by the formation of the United Arab States and the ATUC was beginning to use its power for political ends: it now formed the most consistent and formidable opposition to the authorities. During that year it conducted a vigorous campaign including a general strike against immigration from Commonwealth countries and the enfranchisement of non-Arabs in the Colony. The ATUC formed its first political department, under the headship of Muhammad Salim Ali Abdu, in order to 'acquaint workers with sound political doctrines' as its organ *Al-Amil* (*The Worker*) said, on 21 January 1959.

In 1959 there was a second election to the Legislative Council in which the number of elected members increased from four to twelve, but northern Yemenis were not enfranchised. The ATUC called for a boycott of the elections and about 75 per cent of the limited electorate responded to its call. In that year alone there were 84 strikes. A strike of port and refinery workers lasted 34 days and brought most port and bunkering facilities to a stop. In 1960 the Legislative Council passed the Industrial Relations Ordinance which restricted the right to strike and imposed compulsory arbitration. After the introduction of this ordinance a number of union officials were imprisoned on charges of sedition and encouraging strikes contrary to its provisions. However, these measures did not end the increasingly anti-British outlook of the trade union leaders, and in August 1960 the ATUC demanded UN Trusteeship for Aden as a preliminary step to self-determination, on the grounds that Britain had failed to adhere to the UN Charter in the administration of the Colony. The leaders of this most highly developed union movement in the Middle East — as described in 1963 by the ICFTU[51] — made no secret of their Yemeni identity and their ultimate nationalistic aim. One could see this in the address 'Aden (South Yemen)' at the top of the ATUC's official note-paper, one could hear it in the declaration of one leader after another and could read it somewhere in almost every issue of the movement's newspaper, *Al-Amil*. But seldom was its purpose more precisely stated than at a public meeting in 1960 by its Secretary-General Abdullah al-Asnag;

'A nationalist programme will be carried out to strengthen your belief in a United Yemen,' he said. 'One nation, one Yemen and one struggle only. No North, no South, but one Yemen. No Legislative Council. No Federation . . . There is only one Yemen, the occupied part of which must be liberated.'[52]

Following the curtailment of the ATUC use of strikes as a political weapon, the British government decided in 1961 to merge the Colony with the enlarged Federation of Arab Amirates of the South. Sir Charles Johnston (from the Foreign Office) was appointed Governor in order to conduct negotiations between the Sultans and Ministers of the Colony. Both of Luqman's and Bayoomi's factions of the old Aden Association took part in those negotiations. Later, however, when Luqman's PCC found the Federal team was forcing Aden towards a subordinate role in the union it withdrew its negotiator. Minister Saidi was instantly warned by the Governor that under the Secret Ordinance (the equivalent of the British Official Secrets Act) he had to keep silent. He had to comply, but was soon to die of heart failure immediately after the 'shot-gun' marriage was carried through, solely by an act of British will. The PCC wanted a new constitution to enable a democratically elected government in the Colony to negotiate the union. In that party's view Aden should not be committed to the union by a Legislative Council which had come into being in 1959 on a 27 per cent vote without any mandate to make so dramatic a change in its future. Moreover, they contended that, because half of the members in that existing legislative body were either nominated or *ex officio* British members, the terms were of a colonialist nature. Even that moderate and reasonable argument did not appeal to the colonial authorities; they had already put their faith in their friend Bayoomi and his pro-Federal splinter group, the UNP. Negotiations on the 'closer links' between the Colony and the Federation accelerated after the withdrawal of the PCC and by 1 July 1962 the authorities were able to announce the continuation of their final talks in London.

However, the colonial authorities had mistakenly underestimated the ATUC's hidden strength, dormant since the curb on its activities in 1960; they had also not anticipated the potentially dynamic force of its political arm, the People's Socialist Party, which was resolutely determined to scrap the whole edifice of the merger plan. As the future would show, the PSP would be able during the coming crucial period to control the wellspring of national opinion and dramatically influence and mobilise public opinion behind its unity cause.

Notes

1. R. J. Gavin, *Aden under British Rule, 1839-1967* (Hurst, London, 1975), p. 242.
2. Ibid., pp. 265-6.
3. Ibid., pp. 270-1.
4. Ibid., p. 263.
5. H. F. Jacob, *Kings of Arabia* (Mills and Boon, London, 1923), pp. 242-4, 252.
6. W. H. Ingrams, *The Yemen: Imams, Rulers and Revolutions* (John Murray, London, 1963), pp. 69-70.
7. Gavin, *British Rule*, p. 275.
8. J. E. Cable to Minister of State, dated 10 Jan. 1948 (Public Record Office, London, FO. 371/68334).
9. See Abdullah's farewell letter to the Secretary of State dated 17 Shubat 1948

(Public Record Office, London, FO. 371/68335).
10. Cable to Secretary of State, dated 9 Mar. 1948 (Public Record Office, London, FO. 371/68336).
11. R. Stookey, *Yemen: The Politics of the Yemen Arab Republic* (Westview Press, Boulder, Colorado, 1978), p. 1.
12. W. H. Ingrams, *Arabia and the Isles*, 3rd edn (John Murray, London, 1966), pp. 60-1.
13. Ingrams, *The Yemen*, p. ix.
14. Ingrams, *Arabia*, p. 59.
15. Jacob, *Kings*, p. 226.
16. Sir Tom Hickinbotham, *Aden* (Constable, London, 1958), pp. 20-1.
17. Sir Kennedy Trevaskis, *Shades of Amber: A South Arabian Episode* (Hutchinson, London, 1968), pp. 4-6.
18. Sultan Nagi, 'Al-Thaqafa bain al-Taharrur wal-Isti'mar', *al-Mustaqbal al-Arabi*, Beirut, no. 32 (Oct. 1981), pp. 96-107. (Text of letter to the Mahdi, p. 102).
19. Ladislas Farago, *The Riddle of Arabia* (Robert Hale, London, 1939), pp. 74-5.
20. A. al-Warith, *Al-Hikma al-Yamaniya*, no. 8 (July-Aug. 1940).
21. *Thawrat al-Yaman 1948* (Markaz al-Dirasat wal-Buhuth al-Yamani, San'a', 1982) pp. 353-4.
22. See Cable's brief for Minister of State dated 10 Jan. 1948 (Public Record Office, London, FO. 371/68334).
23. *Thawrat al-Yaman*, p. 542.
24. Sultan Nagi, 'Dawr Jaridat Fatat al-Jazira fi Ahadith 1948 bi San'a' ', *Majallat Dirasat al-Khalij wal-Jazira al-Arabiya*, no. 5 (Kuwait University, 1980), pp. 37-9, 45-51, 54-62.
25. Cable to Minister of State, dated 14 Jan. 1948 (Public Record Office, London, FO. 371/68334).
26. See text in Nagi, 'Dawr', pp. 40-1.
27. Al-Hakimi's article was originally published in *Manbar al-Sharq*, 1 Jan. 1954, and was reproduced in *Majallat al-Hikma*, Aden, no. 96 (Sept. 1981).
28. Ahmed Afif, *Al-Haraka al-Wataniya fil-Yaman* (n.p., 1982), p. 335.
29. Hickinbotham, *Aden*, p. 197.
30. Ibid., p. 195.
31. Tom Little, *South Arabia: Arena of Conflict* (Pall Mall, London, 1968), p. 32.
32. Hickinbotham, *Aden*, pp. 195-6.
33. As a result of this visit, Luqman and his son Farooq wrote *Qissat al-Thawra al-Yamaniya* (Aden, n.d.). He also wrote a series of his memoirs in *Fatat* before his death in 1966, which covered the period 1948-62.
34. Hickinbotham, *Aden*, p. 196.
35. Trevaskis, *Shades of Amber*, p. 45.
36. Ibid., p. 38.
37. Ibid., p. 112.
38. Ibid., p. 136.
39. Ibid., p. 103.
40. Little, *South Arabia*, p. 55.
41. Trevaskis, *Shades of Amber*, p. 137.
42. Hickinbotham, *Aden*, pp. 196-7.
43. Ibid., p. 198; Little, *South Arabia*, p. 32.
44. Trevaskis, *Shades of Amber*, pp. 96-8.
45. Ibid., p. 99.
46. Ingrams, *The Yemen*, p. 98.
47. Trevaskis, *Shades of Amber*, pp. 98-155.
48. Hickinbotham, *Aden*, p. 183.

49. Ibid., p. 190.
50. Ibid., p. 191.
51. Gillian King, *Imperial Outpost — Aden* (Oxford University Press for Royal Institute of International Affairs, London, 1964), p. 53.
52. Trevaskis, *Shades of Amber*, p. 157.

17 PROSPECTS FOR YEMENI UNITY

Ursula Braun

It cannot be the purpose of this short chapter to present a full account of the relations between the two Yemens since the early 1960s. Its intention is rather, after a brief historical overview, to focus on events and developments which are of importance in the context of unity and which will finally allow an assessment of the chances of Yemeni unification.

The Two Yemens in History

The history of Yemen, documented over three millennia, gave the population of the present two parts of the country a sense of a common cultural heritage and is the basis of their 'dream of unity', as it is frequently called. Yet it was not always a history of unity, of a single political entity. Developments were determined by rivalries and power struggles between different states and within varying boundaries, as well as by the fragmentation of society along tribal and kinship lines, by widely differing geographical conditions and by religious cleavages. In the recent past, the Imam who dominated the northern part of the country extended his reign over great parts of southern Yemen. Since the beginning of the eighteenth century smaller amirates in the South had become independent and since 1839 Britain had occupied the port of Aden and influenced developments in that area.

Present North Yemen was twice occupied by the Turks (1539–1630 and again from 1849 until the end of the Ottoman Empire in 1918). At the beginning of this century they agreed with the British on the present delimitation of the border between North and South Yemen. The government of North Yemen never recognised this frontier but in 1934 the imbalance of power forced it to agree to respect it for forty years.[1]

Republican Yemen: Division; Fighting; Negotiations

A Chance for Unity in 1967

The fall of the Imam and the installation of the Republic in the northern part (1962) encouraged the struggle for independence in the South. Both developments were closely interlinked: Yemenis from the South fought with the republicans in the North against the royalists whereas North Yemen offered sanctuaries and logistical support for the liberation movements in the South. The sense of Yemeni solidarity grew accordingly, all the more so as the wish to create a new social order united the republicans in the North and the freedom-fighters in the South. Consequently, November 1967, when the British left and South Yemen became independent, should have been the historic moment for unity. A couple of weeks before, the Egyptians had left North Yemen. They had supported the republicans with a strong contingent of troops — a support which after seven years was resented by a great part of the North Yemeni population as an occupation.

Both countries were finally free in their decision and there was a unique constellation for unification, but the historic chance at that juncture was missed. Looking more closely at those events, one discovers all the elements which were to determine developments during the years to come: internal rivalry, different ideological orientations and outside influence.

In Aden the movement for independence had split into two rival groups which had started fighting each other without mercy. The more moderate one, the Front for the Liberation of Occupied South Yemen (FLOSY) was closer to San'a' than the National Liberation Front (NLF). This is not the place to elaborate on ideological cleavages between, and different affiliations of, these Fronts but it may suffice to say that the struggle for liberation and the moment of independence were over-shadowed by their rivalry which plunged South Yemen into a virtual civil war. At the time of the British departure the NLF had gained the upper hand and took over power. The leading FLOSY members went into exile, a great number of them to North Yemen — one factor to determine future developments.

When the Egyptians left North Yemen a change of government was the immediate consequence. The Egyptian protégé, President Sallal, was deposed. At the same time the royalists mounted a new military offensive which led to the siege of San'a'. For months the town could survive only with the aid of a Soviet air-bridge. Aden set out to help the republicans by sending troops to San'a' and by launching a relief attack in the Baihan area. In the course of 1968, talks on unity started and delegations from Aden visited San'a'. Yet mistrust dominated relations from the outset. North Yemen resented the elimination of FLOSY and South Yemen suspected the new government in San'a' of trying to compromise with the royalists. While developments in Aden went in the direction of militant socialism, North Yemen pursued a more conservative course; Islamic traditions as well as traditional social values prevailed. In addition, refugees from the South organised attempts to overthrow the regime in Aden with support from Saudi Arabia and North Yemen. In such an atmosphere unity talks could not be fruitful.

Diverging Trends in Both Yemens since 1970

By 1970 events in both states had highlighted the stark divergences. While high-level meetings continued and declarations in favour of Yemeni unity were issued, political separation took its course. In South Yemen the more radical wing of the NLF prevailed and a new wave of refugees arrived in the North. The 'People's Republic of South Yemen' changed its name into 'People's Democratic Republic of Yemen' (November 1970) — an open claim to the whole of Yemen under the banner of socialism. Although the new constitutions of both countries expressed the will to strive for unity, from 1970 onwards events went in diametrically opposed directions.

In the northern part 'national reconciliation' — achieved with the aid of Saudi Arabia — brought royalists back into the government and strengthened conservative forces, while in Aden Marxist forces fought their way to the top. Unity would have signified that one or the other side was prepared to sacrifice its political value-system for the sake of a higher goal. In this phase and in the course of a continuing government-to-government dialogue committees were set up to pave the way but they never started working. Instead, armed clashes occurred between the government in Aden and opposition forces in the former amirates in Aden's hinterland; the latter were joined by South Yemeni exiles from the territory of North Yemen and from Saudi Arabia, with the support of both countries. By 1972 these incidents had developed into open war between both Yemens.

The Arab League succeeded in achieving a ceasefire agreement linked to an obligation on both Yemens to prepare for a union. The Arab League was evidently convinced that a union would once and for ever end hostilities and lead to stability in this corner of the Arab world. Both governments, however, tried to steer negotiations according to their own political concept: South Yemen put the accent on socialism, North Yemen stressed Islamic and traditional social values.[2] Such different interpretations made the discussions in the preparatory committees for a union meaningless. Aden made it clear that union could take place only according to the precepts of Marxism and this provoked sincere opposition in North Yemen.

Intermittent Wars and Unity Agreements

Against this background the pattern of relations in the 1970s became quite clear: for the government in Aden Marxist ideology had priority. Whenever rigid ideologists dominated there, this led to phases of confrontation; in periods of greater pragmatism the dialogue continued. The latter condition particularly prevailed in the mid-seventies when in both parts of Yemen the Heads of State were, above all, nationalists; they focused on Yemeni interests and hoped by better inter-Yemeni relations to achieve more independence in their foreign policies.

Both countries are economically weak and need foreign assistance. This made San'a' dependent on Saudi aid while it tried — with a certain success — to gain some independence through more international aid. Aden realised that the socialist countries were not able or not prepared to give the necessary assistance for economic development and started looking for aid in the Western world; this necessarily meant less ideological rigidity. Such periods of 'pragmatism' on both sides, however, alarmed those opposition groups in both states who watched with suspicion closer contacts between Aden and San'a' which could, in their view, only progress at the expense of each one's system of values. Consequently, such a policy was not without risks for both governments.

In 1979 new military clashes occurred in the frontier area between the two Yemen states. This time the fighting started in North Yemen between armed opposition groups and the regular army. Various 'progressive' groups had united in March 1976 in the 'National Democratic Front' (NDF). The Front gets financial and military support from 'radical' Arab states, but above all from South Yemen. Aden finds in it an instrument for influencing North Yemeni affairs, all the more so as the NDF has strong socialist leanings. For a background to the 1979 clashes one has to take account of some developments in the socio-political sphere.

Forces of Change and of Continuity

In South Yemen the government has succeeded during the past ten years in eliminating internal opposition and in creating a relatively coherent and centralised state with a powerful party apparatus and party organisations which reach all groups of the population. North Yemen, on the other hand, is a country with much more complex social structures, where ancient traditions have survived and are resilient enough to resist centralisation. A great variety of loyalty-structures exist which are an impediment to the creation of a modern functional state. Young people tend to get impatient with the pace of development in this traditional society; among them the NDF finds an echo. It is difficult to assess how far loyalty to the NDF goes and whether it is solidly rooted and overrides other, traditional, loyalties.

The question whether old loyalty-structures in North Yemen are disintegrating is not a subject of this chapter. Here it is only of interest to note that, with modernisation, new organisational patterns are developing, with the possible effects that conservative forces might lose ground and influence, and that newly evolving social structures might lead to a degree of convergence between both Yemens. The division of North Yemen into Zaidi and Shafi'i areas has in the last decade lost most of its relevance since the government in San'a' is no longer purely Zaidi as it had been during the reign of the Imam. Opposition to unity in North Yemen comes partly from the Zaidi tribes who fear becoming a minority in a united Yemen dominated by Shafi'is.[3] On the other hand religious bonds between the Shafi'is in North Yemen and their brethren in the South are certainly still of importance but might have been superseded, among younger people, by ideological affiliations. One criterion could be to what extent the NDF is a Shafi'i movement.

Steps towards a Distant Goal

In the confrontation in early spring 1979 the NDF played an important role, siding with South Yemeni forces. Again the hostilities ended after mediation by the Arab League with an armistice, coupled with a joint agreement to revive the work of the preparatory committees for the union which were agreed upon in 1972. In addition to seven other committees, one had been charged to work out a constitution for a united state and it started only now with its activities. The work of all committees was intensified; concrete steps were taken for closer co-operation in the cultural field, tourism, infrastructural projects, co-ordination of development planning, exploration of resources and commercial exchanges. North Yemen accepted a demand from the South to dismiss two Ministers, former refugees from Aden and critical of the government there. In accordance with the armistice agreement, each side promised no longer to support opposition forces in the other state. This clause was of particular interest for San'a', as the NDF vitally depends on support from Aden. In reality, however, the promise was of very limited effect as the leaders of the NDF continue to have their base in Aden.

Certain changes are evident in both parts of Yemen which might inspire some hope of closer co-operation. In the South a more pragmatic course seemed to prevail after government changes in April 1980 which brought less ideological rigidity and an opening-up in foreign relations and external trade. Inter-Yemeni talks were also facilitated by a *rapprochement* between Aden and Riyadh which seemed to lessen Saudi suspicions of closer contacts between North and South Yemen.

A more pragmatic policy in the South partly offset mistrust on the part of conservative forces in the North. On the other hand the government in San'a' decided to try to integrate the NDF into North Yemen's political system by starting a 'National Dialogue' with the opposition. The NDF demanded participation in the government but the posts offered to it were apparently not attractive enough, so the dialogue in early 1980 ended without any result. It was resumed in 1981, but again brought no progress. At the same time as those talks, military clashes took place once more between the NDF and the regular North Yemeni Army close to the South Yemeni border. They have since flared up repeatedly.

The NDF evidently wanted to put pressure on the government in San'a' which, for its part, tried to crush this militant opposition. A number of ceasefire agreeements were signed between Aden and San'a' (always under the auspices of the Arab League) in which the NDF was included. It should, however, be expected that hostilities will not come to an end in the near future. The pattern of dialogue and confrontation will, according to all experience, persist. Too many power factions and too many differing interests are involved on both sides, and Aden's support for the NDF is part of the ideological confrontation between North and South Yemen.

Despite continuing military clashes, practical co-operation has nevertheless improved during the last three years. In December 1981 the Presidents of both Yemens at a meeting in Aden signed an agreement to 'develop cooperation and coordination between the two parts of Yemen', aimed at 'achieving the supreme interest of the Yemeni people in reunifying Yemen — land and people . . .' A council of the two leaders was to be formed, the 'Yemen Council'. It was supposed to meet every six months and whenever the need arises. A joint Ministerial Committee was formed at the same time, consisting of the two Prime Ministers, the Foreign Ministers, the Interior Ministers, the Ministers of Supply and Planning, the Ministers of Education, and the two Chiefs of the General Staff of the armed forces. (A joint Military Committee had already been established.) The joint Ministerial Committee was supposed to meet every three months or whenever need arose. During the meeting of the Heads of State in Aden a special effort was made to co-ordinate foreign policy 'with the aim of unifying political positions in Arab and international conferences and forums'.[4]

In January 1982 the constitutional committee finalised a draft constitution for a united Yemen.[5] This draft was to be submitted to the legislative and executive bodies in both states before being submitted to the people of both states for a referendum. According to available information the draft provides for a united Yemen being a parliamentary democracy, Islam the state religion and San'a' the capital. Legislative power will be held by an elected parliament; the judicial system will be headed by an elected Attorney-General, although the shari'a is considered to be the main source of legislation; executive power will rest in a Council of Ministers; the economy will be a mixed one; a transitional period will precede the complete merger of both states. After the draft constitution was submitted no spectacular progress was made to implement it. From declarations by members of both governments it can be concluded that time is not a factor. 'We have a very flexible time-table for achieving unity,' said the North Yemeni Prime Minister.[6] 'Every great objective needs a lot of hard work,' the South Yemeni President explained.[7] The experience of the last decades has had its effect and cannot be forgotten overnight.

Meetings of the Heads of State continue, however, as do those of the Ministerial Committee. Commercial exchanges are expanding and co-operation in the fields mentioned above increases. A new field of co-ordination has developed — diplomacy. Both states try to co-ordinate their attitudes in the framework of the Arab League; both governments also launched a common initiative for a

Pan-Arab summit after the Israeli invasion of Lebanon in summer 1982.

Outlook: Union by Convergence or Persisting Divergences?

It would probably be wise not to press for an immediate merger as proposed in the draft constitution: a formula for federation or confederation might be a better solution because social structures and political orientations are too diverse for a truly unified state. What was achieved in South Yemen at the price of sacrifices by large parts of the population cannot be imposed on the northern part. Traditional structures in North Yemen might change, as mentioned above; a considerable part of the population would, however, not be prepared to abandon its way of life or its values for the sake of unity. A long process of convergence could be conceivable if, at the same time, the ruling elites in the South were prepared to change their priorities, for instance their present conviction that international proletarianism ranges above Yemeni or Arab interests. This, however, is difficult to imagine in a short- or middle-range perspective. To conclude from all experience, pragmatism seems to prevail only temporarily.

Continuing divergences in foreign policy are evident. While in the Arab context Aden is part of the 'Rejectionist Front', San'a' follows the course of the so-called moderate Arab states. Differences exist over the Iran-Iraq war: Aden has particularly close relations with Tehran (and Damascus) while San'a' supports Baghdad's standpoint and has even sent soldiers to support the Iraqi Army against Iran. South Yemen's alliance with Ethiopia and Libya is considered a threat to North Yemen, as members of the government in San'a' have repeatedly told their counterparts in Aden. All these positions might be subject to change, yet two essential differences remain: North Yemen's economic development depends on good relations with Saudi Arabia and the Western world, whence it gets considerable aid. At the same time it buys the bulk of its armaments in the Soviet Union, so a policy of neutrality and real non-alignment is vital for San'a'. On the other hand the government in Aden has established good relations with the conservative countries of the Arabian Peninsula in the last three years, although it has never renounced its declared priority, i.e. international socialist solidarity. Both Yemens declare themselves non-aligned although, in the West, Aden is considered to be squarely in the socialist camp; witness the military use of facilities on its territory by the Soviet Union. Both Yemens cannot escape their geo-strategic location and for this reason alone cannot isolate themselves from regional and global developments. It might not be possible for them to ignore these realities which have a momentum of their own.

In conclusion, it is likely that any precipitate merger would create instability, provoke unrest or even lead to civil war. The present formula of co-operation and co-ordination in various fields and of frequent meetings and talks at all levels will, we may hope, lead to peaceful coexistence. In the long run, and after substantial changes in the distribution of power, both within Yemen and outside, a union by convergence could become a reality.

Notes

1. Imam Yahya claimed authority over the Aden Protectorates, considering at the same time Asir and Najran in the north as part of Yemeni territory. In the south Britain disputed these claims; in the north the Imam met with Saudi Arabian opposition. As Britain was the more powerful adversary, Imam Yahya decided to accommodate London by signing a treaty of friendship and co-operation which included a clause referring to a settlement of the border question.

2. For more detailed information on the negotiations in Cairo and Tripoli see U. Braun, *Nord- und Südjemen im Spannungsfeld Interner, Regionaler und Globaler Gegensätze* (Forschungsinstitut der Deutschen Gesellschaft für Auswärtige Politik e. V., Bonn, 1981), pp. 69–70.

3. Some Yemenis, however, contend that the difference between Zaidis and Shafi'is has no impact on political life. 'Islam is one,' they argue.

4. YAR-PDRY Agreement; BBC, *Summary of World Broadcasts*, ME/6898/A/1, 5 Dec. 1981.

5. It was not possible for the author to get the text of the draft constitution.

6. Interview in *The Middle East*, London (Mar. 1983), p. 30.

7. Ibid. (July 1982), p. 28.

GLOSSARY OF ARABIC AND TURKISH WORDS NOT EXPLAINED ON FIRST APPEARANCE

ahl al-bait	descendants of the Prophet Muhammad's family.
Alid	descendant or follower of Ali, cousin and son-in-law of the Prophet (see *shi'a*)
'asabiya	sense of group solidarity.
ayyam	epic tales of pre-Islamic fighting in the Arabian Peninsula, preserved in prose and poetry.
awqaf	(singular *waqf*) in Islam, a pious and inalienable endowment for charitable purposes.
badu	nomads of the desert and its fringes.
bait al-mal	the central treasury of early Islamic states.
baraka	a state of grace, believed to exist in certain individuals and to be capable of transmitting good fortune.
da'wa	propagandising mission on behalf of a *shi'i* sect, e.g. Zaidis or Isma'ilis.
faqih	a legal scholar.
fida'i	(plural *fida'iyin*) a fighter prepared to sacrifice his life.
fiqh	Islamic jurisprudence.
futuhat	the early Islamic conquests.
hadd	punishment determined by Islamic law.
hadith	Prophetic tradition.
hakim	secular ruler or administrator.
hijra	(1) the Prophet's migration from Mecca to Medina in AD 662, from which the Muslim era dates.
	(2) a tribal institution whereby protection is given to non-members of the tribe in return for certain services; see Gochenour.
imam	a religious leader — in *shi'i* contexts usually credited with divine powers and authority.
kaza	Turkish administrative district.
madrasa	a school, in this case a religious boarding school attached to a mosque.
mamluk	a slave, particularly one trained as a soldier.

Glossary of Arabic and Turkish Words 271

qadi	a judge, operating in the field of the *shari'a* (*q.v.*).
qanun	the secular law.
qat	Catha edulis — a shrub whose leaves are mildly stimulant when chewed.
qudat	plural of *qadi* (*q.v.*).
sada	plural of *sayyid* (*q.v.*).
sayyid	see Gochenour, note 9.
Shafi'i	one of the four rites or schools of 'orthodox' or *sunni* Islam.
shari'a	Islamic law, deriving especially from the Quran and *sunna* (*q.v.*).
shi'a	(adjective *shi'i*) originally the party supporting Ali's (see Alid) claim to succeed as Caliph; later becoming a religious sect owing allegiance to Ali and his descendants and typically attributing to their *imams* (*q.v.*) greater authority than do other Muslims.
sira	biography.
sunna	the customary words and actions of the Prophet, used as a guide and legal yardstick.
sunni	a follower of the *sunna*, conventionally applied to an 'orthodox' Muslim as opposed to a *shi'i*.
suq	market.
tanzimat	lit. 'reforms'; a long period of modernising reforms in the nineteenth-century Ottoman Empire.
'ulama'	(plural of *'alim*) those learned in the Islamic sciences, including religion.
Zaidi	belonging to a moderate division of the *shi'a*, long-established and dominant in North Yemen.
zakat	the Islamic alms-tax or tithe.

INDEX

Aden and Protectorate
    and British rule 77, 88-90, 126-9, 145n5, 241-3
    administration 246, 250-8
    armed struggle against British rule 254
    Legislative Council 248, 254, 256, 258
    strategic importance of 125-6
    work-force 255-6
    see also Federation of South Arabia
Aden Association 248, 249, 257
Aden Trade Union Congress 49, 65, 252, 255-8
al-Aini, Muhsin, YAR Prime Minister 65, 165, 199
Ali, Abdul Karim, Sultan of Lahej 46, 52, 249, 250, 251, 252
Ali, Salim Rubai'a, PDRY President 48, 58, 94-5, 130, 131, 132, 219-20
al-Ansi, Muhi al-Din 35, 36
Arab League 230n2, 263, 264, 265
Arab Nationalists' Movement 47-9, 52, 58, 65, 69
al-Asnag, Abdullah 52, 57, 69, 72, 257
Aziz Bey, deputy governor of Hodaida 27-30

Ba Dhib family 233, 234, 235, 237
Bab al-Mandab, Strait of 126, 140, 204
Bakil, tribal confederation 14, 80, 154, 156, 166, 167, 170

China 130, 219
customary law 159-64, 178, 192

economy
    of Ottoman Yemen 23-4, 29
    PDRY 129, 131, 134, 222-4
    YAR 80-2, 196, 198-9, 200, 220
education
    in Aden and Protectorate 102-4, 108, 114-15, 244

Ottoman Yemen 24-5, 30, 36, 78
PDRY 104-23; objectives 104-9; policy 110-3; structure 115-23
YAR 78, 82-3
Egypt
    and National Liberation Front 46, 50-1, 57-8, 73
    relations with PDRY 116, 200, 204, 227-8, 238; Yemen (Imamate) 43, 78, 250; YAR 71, 79, 148, 166, 167, 168, 204

Fatat al-Fulaihi 35-6
Fatat al-Jazira 245, 246, 249
Federation of Arab Amirates of the South 251, 257
Federation of South Arabia 106
    and British policy 69-70, 90-1
    insurrection against British rule 51-2, 59-60, 65-9
    see also Aden and Protectorate
Free Yemeni movement 34-43
Free Yemeni Party (Hizb al-Ahrar al-Yamaniyin) 38, 245-7
Front for the Liberation of Occupied South Yemen (FLOSY) 46, 58-61, 217-18, 262, 263

geographical regions 2-3, 5-8, 156
al-Ghashmi, Ahmad, YAR President 93, 95, 132
Grand Yemeni Association (al-Jam'iya al-Yamaniya al-Kubra) 39-42, 245-7
Great Britain
    and Yemeni civil war 50-1, 66
    relations with Yemen (Imamate) 42, 77, 240-3, 246, 261
Gulf States 63, 71, 203-4, 207n25

Hadramawt 47, 59, 178
Hamdi, Ibrahim, YAR President 92-3, 98, 131, 199

274

Index 275

Hamid al-Din, Ahmad, Imam of Yemen 38, 41, 87, 88, 166, 242, 250
Hamid al-Din, Ibrahim 40
Hamid al-Din, Muhammad al-Badr, Imam of Yemen 43, 67, 250
Hamid al-Din, Yahya, Imam of Yemen 35, 37, 39, 41, 87, 88, 157, 269n1
Hashid, tribal confederation 14, 80, 154, 156, 166, 167, 170

Ibn Hawshab, Abu al-Qasim Hasan 11-12
al-Iryani, Abd al-Rahman, YAR President 35, 39, 41, 92, 97, 197, 199
Islam 1, 8-19
  shi'ism 8-15
  sunnism 15-17
Isma'il, Abdul Fattah, PDRY President
  and NLF 48, 58, 130, 131, 219, 228, 234
  as head of state 95, 132, 220, 221
Isma'ilis 11-12

Jam'iyat al-Islah 38-9
al-Jifri, Muhammad 249, 250, 251

al-Katiba al-Ula 36-7

land tenure 156-7
legal profession
  in PDRY 178, 189-90, 191-2
legal system
  in Aden and Protectorate 176-8, 185
  Ottoman Yemen 25-6
  PDRY 178-94; courts 176-8, 180-2; criminal procedure law 186-9; legal aid 190-1; prosecution process 179, 182-4; trials 184-5
Libya 95, 200, 205, 238
Luqman, Muhammad Ali 244, 245, 246, 248-9, 250

Memduh Commission, 1904 22-7
al-Mu'allimi, Ahmad 39, 42, 65
Muhammad, Ali Nasir, PDRY President 95-6, 133-5, 220, 221, 234-5, 238
Muqbil, Taha 48, 53, 58

National Democratic Front (NDF) 170, 205, 227, 265, 266
and 1979 war 132, 199, 200, 264
National Front *see* National Liberation Front
National Institute of Public Administration (NIPA) 147, 150-1, 152
National Liberation Front
  armed struggle against British rule 51-2, 59-60, 65-9
  development of 1963-7 period 46-51, 58, 65, 68, 71-2, 217, 262; 1967-78 period 94, 130-2, 218-9, 233, 263; 1978-80 period 95, 132-3, 219, 220; 1980 – period 95-6, 133-5
National Charter 53-7, 73-4
Nu'man, Ahmad Muhammad, YAR Prime Minister 65, 174n29
  and Free Yemeni movement 36, 37, 38, 40, 41, 43
Nu'man, Muhammad Ahmad 43, 65, 72

Oman 131, 197, 226, 227, 237
Organisation for the Liberation of South Yemen (OLSY) 71-2
Organisation for the Liberation of the Occupied South (OLOS) 52-3, 57, 58
Ottomans in Yemen 20-33
  administration 26, 28-31
  reform programmes 20-7

People's Democratic Union 219, 232-9
People's Democratic Republic of Yemen 175-6
  armed forces 224
  compared with Cuba 208-10, 219
  Constitution 107, 176, 179, 191, 193n12
  domestic policy 131, 132, 134, 141, 218-220
  foreign policy 95, 129-32, 134-5, 224-5, 228, 237-8, 267-9
  foreign relations of *see* under individual country
  relations with YAR 131, 132, 196-7, 200, 262-7
People's Socialist Party 49, 52, 71, 90, 252, 258
People's Supreme Council 176, 219, 232, 233, 235
political opposition
  to British rule 48-50, 58-61, 64-5, 71-2, 236, 244-5, 250-7
  to the Imamate 36-43, 48-9, 245-8
public administration 147-53

276   *Index*

Radfan uprising 51, 66, 67, 128

Salih, Ali Abdullah, YAR President 93, 196, 199, 200, 202, 204, 205
al-Sallal, Abdullah, YAR President 42, 50, 167, 168
Saudi Arabia
  and Yemeni civil war 50, 71, 80
  opposes Yemeni unification 197, 199
  relations with PDRY 143, 196-7, 198, 219-20, 225, 263
  relations with YAR 131, 132-3, 195-203
Sawt al-Yaman 39, 43, 245
sayyids 9, 18n9, 159-60
al-Sha'bi, Faisal Abdul-Latif, PDRY Prime Minister 48, 53, 58, 69, 130
al-Sha'bi, Qahtan, PDRY President 48, 52, 58, 65, 130
Shafi'is 15-16, 17
social change 80, 82, 83, 192
society, tribal
  islamisation of 1-2, 8-17
  structure of 2-8, 9, 10
South Arabian League 46, 71, 90, 249-50, 251, 252, 254
Soviet Union
  policy in Middle East & Africa 137-144n1, 201, 210-15, 225-9, 238
  relations with PDRY 95, 208-10, 216, 218-25, 227-9, 234, 238-9
  relations with YAR 200-3, 210, 226
Sulaihid dynasty 12-15, 16

tribes
  in Upper Yemen 5-14, 154-174
  customary law 159-64
  organisation 158-64, 168, 169-71
  role in national politics 158, 165-72, 198-9

unification of Yemen
  pre-1962 period 240-3, 246-8, 249, 252-4, 257, 269n1; 1962-7 period 54, 262; 1967 – period 131, 197, 200, 205, 227, 237, 263-9
United National Front 64, 252-5
United National Party 249, 258
United Political Organisation of the National Front (UPONF) 219, 233, 234
  see also Yemeni Socialist Party
United States
  policy in Middle East & Africa 133, 143, 145n9, 201-2, 216
  relations with PDRY 129, 143, 137-8, 225
  relations with YAR 201-3, 226-7

Vanguard Party (al-Tali'a) 219, 233

al-Wartalani, Fudail 37, 41
al-Wazir, Abdullah Ahmad 41, 165, 245

Yemen (Imamate) 76-8, 86-8, 147
  relations with tribes 157-8, 160, 161, 163-4, 166
  see also Hamid al-Din
Yemen Arab Republic
  civil war 48-9, 79-80, 166-7, 168, 262-3
  domestic policy 200, 262, 263, 264, 266, 268
  foreign policy 199-200, 204, 205, 267, 268
  foreign relations of *see* under individual country
  government institutions 147-53
  relations with PDRY 262-7
Yemeni Socialist Party 98, 107, 219-21, 232-4, 235, 236
  see also National Liberation Front
Yemeni Union (al-Ittihad al-Yamani) 42-3, 247, 249

Zaidi-Shafi'i relations 16, 17, 86, 265
Zaidism 8-10, 11, 12, 16, 17, 77, 86
al-Zubairi, Muhammad Mahmud 65, 165, 167, 245
  and Free Yemeni movement 36, 37, 38, 39, 40, 42, 43

For Product Safety Concerns and Information please contact our EU
representative GPSR@taylorandfrancis.com
Taylor & Francis Verlag GmbH, Kaufingerstraße 24, 80331 München, Germany

www.ingramcontent.com/pod-product-compliance
Lightning Source LLC
Chambersburg PA
CBHW070555300426
44113CB00010B/1261